CANADIAN HOCKEY LITERATURE:
A THEMATIC STUDY

Hockey occupies a prominent place in the cultural lexicon of Canada, as evidenced by the wealth of hockey-centred stories and novels published within its borders. In this exciting new work, Jason Blake examines five recurring themes in Canadian hockey literature: nationhood, the hockey dream, violence, national identity, and family.

Blake analyses the work of authors such as Mordecai Richler, David Adams Richards, Paul Quarrington, and Richard B. Wright, arguing that a study of contemporary hockey fiction exposes a troubled relationship with the national sport. Rather than the storybook happy ending common in the sports literature of previous generations, Blake finds that today's fiction portrays hockey as an often glorified sport that in fact leads to broken lives and ironic outlooks. The first book to focus exclusively on hockey in print, *Canadian Hockey Literature* is an accessible work that challenges popular perceptions of a much-beloved national pastime.

JASON BLAKE is a professor in the Department of English at the University of Ljubljana.

Canadian Hockey Literature

A Thematic Study

JASON BLAKE

UNIVERSITY OF TORONTO PRESS
Toronto Buffalo London

© University of Toronto Press Incorporated 2010
Toronto Buffalo London
www.utppublishing.com
Printed in Canada

ISBN 978-0-8020-9984-6 (cloth)
ISBN 978-0-8020-9713-2 (paper)

Printed on acid-free and 100% post-consumer recycled paper
with vegetable-based inks.

Library and Archives Canada Cataloguing in Publication

Blake, Jason, 1972–
Canadian hockey literature / Jason Blake.

Includes bibliographical references and index.
ISBN 978-0-8020-9984-6 (bound)   ISBN 978-0-8020-9713-2 (pbk.)

1. Hockey – Canada.   2. Hockey – Social aspects – Canada.
3. Hockey in literature.   I. Title.

GV848.4.C3B53   2010   796.9620971   C2009-906666-1

University of Toronto Press acknowledges the financial assistance
to its publishing program of the Canada Council for the Arts
and the Ontario Arts Council.

 Canada Council Conseil des Arts    ONTARIO ARTS COUNCIL
for the Arts du Canada   CONSEIL DES ARTS DE L'ONTARIO

This book has been published with the help of a grant from the Canadian
Federation for the Humanities and Social Sciences, through the Aid to
Scholarly Publications Programme, using funds provided by the Social
Sciences and Humanities Research Council of Canada.

University of Toronto Press acknowledges the financial support for its
publishing activities of the Government of Canada through the Book
Publishing Industry Development Program (BPIDP).

For Wolfgang

Contents

Acknowledgments

This book was written in an unlikely place, and I could not have completed it without support from an international team: Andy Holman was eager and enthusiastic from the start, answering historical questions and sending information my way. Olaf Hahn and Sébastien Socqué made sure the latest hockey literature arrived at my door, and Michael Devine, Jernej Možic, and Eugen Baunach each helped out with last-minute requests for secondary literature from faraway libraries.

Sympathetic academic strangers, or then-strangers, pitched in with enthusiasm. Michael Robidoux and Benoît Melançon kindly forwarded some of their work, and the publisher Fides generously sent me a copy of Melançon's book on Maurice Richard. Ages ago, Jamie Dopp, Michael Kennedy, and Don Morrow examined my list of hockey fiction and pointed out omissions, while hockey aficionado Brian Kennedy answered some tricky theoretical questions on his other area of specialization. Anthony Rezek, Mirko Jurak, and David Staines all encouraged me to think about publishing this study, and steered me in the right direction. My patient and very bright students at the English Department here in Ljubljana kept me focused on what really matters in academia; my hockey team kept me feeling honest by letting me play with them as I worked on this book.

I thank those who read the manuscript in its earliest stages, including Meta Grosman, Igor Maver, and Werner Delanoy. Each went beyond the advisor's traditional call of duty, and never did I have to wait more than a week for written feedback.

Most of all, I am grateful to Michelle Gadpaille, whose guidance in everything from argument, to style, to the avoidance of awful puns was as invaluable as it was unobtrusive. Showing her true cultural range, she also set me straight on the press's reaction to 1976 Philadelphia Flyers – Central Red Army hockey game.

University of Toronto Press, especially Siobhan McMenemy and Ryan Van Huijstee, whisked me through the publishing process, and came up with two peerless anonymous reviewers who provided excellent and detailed advice. I am also thankful to Ken Lewis for his exquisite copy-editing.

My mom and dad deserve special thanks for generally helping me and loading themselves down with materials whenever they visited. My sister Liz sacrificed her pride by picking up the odd racy title for me. Alenka was wonderful throughout, and when the dissertation became more serious, we decided to acquire some backup named Nina.

The faults are mine.

CANADIAN HOCKEY LITERATURE:
A THEMATIC STUDY

Introduction

In Scott Young and George Robertson's 1971 novel *Face-Off,* a sports reporter hands in a sordid story about a hockey player's personal life. His editor-in-chief is delighted with this bit of muckraking and decides to lead with it. 'We'll use your column head in the usual place on sports,' he says, 'with a note directing people to look at the front.'[1] The insult to sports fans is obvious, but there is also self-irony here. The chief newspaperman is well aware that he has given his stamp of approval to gossip just because it is hockey gossip. This invented, fictional example is entirely realistic. Canadian newspapers regularly lead with hockey stories, and banal breaking news items such as 'New Uniforms for Team Canada' or 'Wayne Gretzky's Wife Gambles' are often on the first page.

Ice hockey is omnipresent in Canadian society, and it exists in many varieties: most obviously, it is an actual, physically played sport; then there is the sometimes fervent, sometimes detached, but always ritualistic watching of the game in person or on television; and if one misses that all-important playoff game, there are endless newspaper, Internet, and television reports on which to rely. Hockey so dominates Canadian conversation that we regularly drop the qualifier. Only foreigners refer to 'ice hockey.' Canadian hockey talk ranges from empty banter about rooting for the home team, to a means of avoiding more serious or uncomfortable topics, to involved discussion of strategy or the cultural significance of the game. Unlike baseball or cricket, hockey is a simple 'ball' game, and the first-time watcher can immediately understand what is going on at a hockey game. Since everyone from the rookie spectator to the seasoned couch potato can comment in some way on the game, the hockey chorus contains many voices. These voices range from top-level professional players to recreational weekend warriors, from insightful strategists to shameless bluffers, from fanatical diehards to more casual observers. Social pressures aside, playing or watching hockey is theoretically a matter of choice – one tunes in to the game instead of a movie on television. If the conversation turns to hockey in the boardroom or the bar, though there might be pressure to contribute, there is no need to add one's two cents.

Other instances of hockey are unavoidable. Hockey saturates Canadian life to an absurd extent. We use it to sell everything from beer to banking services, since in the Canadian advertiser's bag of tricks hockey ranks just behind sex for peddling products. If in the past sales-hungry magazine publishers would eagerly place hockey or the Queen on the cover, today few weeklies would lead with royalty. Hockey in the news and in advertising differs from actively played and watched hockey because it is no longer a matter of preference or choice, and commercials, newspaper headlines, and passing images or comments enter our consciousness before we can reject them. Come playoff time, people in search of 'hard news' on television will have to suffer through several minutes of hockey highlights. At such times hockey envelops us like second-hand smoke, and, some would argue, it is just as dangerous because it beclouds other cultural options or more serious issues. Hockey culture surrounds Canadians to the extent that even those who do not like the sport will recognize many of the allusions to great players or events such as Maurice Richard, Paul Henderson's 1972 goal, Bobby Orr in general, or Don Cherry and his suits, to mention the four most frequent references in hockey fiction.

In addition to an enjoyable game and a ready source of cultural references, hockey is an easy marker for, or symbol of, Canada. It is therefore a useful point of entry to Canadian culture. While it is wrong to claim that hockey is the essence of Canada, Canadians and foreigners alike closely associate the game with the country. Even such a thinker as Roland Barthes, who spent much time *questioning* symbols and mythologies, has wildly exaggerated the hockey-Canada connection. In Hubert Aquin's 1959 film *Le Sport et les hommes / Of Sport and Men*, for which Barthes wrote the text, the French philosopher considers hockey the classic example of a national sport. Barthes knew nothing about hockey, and Hubert Aquin allegedly had to provide him with a crash course by planting him in front of the television. Perhaps this lack of knowledge led to Barthes's enjoyably reductive rumination:

Qu'est-ce qu'un sport national? C'est un sport qui surgit de la matière même d'une nation, c'est-à-dire de son sol et de son climat. Jouer au hockey, c'est chaque fois redire que les hommes ont transformé l'hiver immobile, la terre durcie, la vie suspendue et que précisément de tout cela, ils ont fait un sport allègre, vigoureux, passionné.[2]

Barthes's script also examines soccer in England, bullfighting in Spain, car racing in the United States, and the Tour de France, but he favours hockey as the quintessential national sport because of its link to the land and its ability to transform winter.

That Canada should play hockey might seem as natural as the game's symbolism is convenient. The sport requires a communion of two fundamental Canadian realities: water and the cold. The many lakes and rivers were the original passageways into Canada, winter the original nemesis, and hockey is thus often naturalized in Canadian thought as if it grew magically from the soil or ice. Long before academic discussion of the game and demythologizing began, novelist and short story writer Hugh Hood questioned this idea of hockey's naturalness:

> If hockey did not exist, and somebody dreamed it up, then told his psychiatrist that he'd dreamed of a sport played by men with knives on their feet and clubs in their hands, on ICE, what would the psychiatrist think?[3]

By relating hockey to the pathological, Hood reminds us of what we all know: hockey is not a natural phenomenon but an imaginative, cultural activity.

The belief that sport and culture are antipodes is clearly dated, and it is now equally clear that studying hockey can reveal much about broader Canadian culture. There are reasons why so many Canadians feel passionately about hockey, and a logic or causality exists behind its having been adopted as a national game. Yet in spite of potential cultural revelations, sports in general and hockey in particular were long neglected as subjects for serious academics. Although hockey writing has always been immensely popular in Canada, until the 1990s fairly little scholarly attention was paid to the role of sports in culture. Richard Gruneau and David Whitson's seminal *Hockey Night in Canada* – 'written partly out of frustration with the ambivalence of Canadian academics towards hockey'[4] – was published in 1993, over a century after hockey was popularly adopted as a Canadian sport and crux of Canadian identity. Today, professing any sort of academic 'ambivalence' rings false. Especially in fields such as cultural studies and sociology, there has been an explosion of specialized writing over the past two decades or so. The advancement of academic hockey research is reflected in the types of studies that are now being published. Contemporary authors have shown that, since hockey does not exist in a cultural vacuum, the game can reveal much about both labour relations and Canadian history, along with popular culture.

In a 1925 review of Ring Lardner's fiction, including his baseball novel *You Know Me Al*, Virginia Woolf focuses on the importance of sports to American society and to interpreting or understanding the United States:

> It is no coincidence that the best of Mr. Lardner's stories are about games, for one may guess that Mr. Lardner's interest in games has solved one of the most difficult problems of the American writer; it has given him a clue, a centre, a meeting place for the divers activities of a people whom a vast continent isolates, whom no tradition controls.

Eighty years later, something similar could be said about hockey's role as a binding force in Canada. Yet in spite of a constant longing throughout the twentieth century for a distinctive Canadian literature, only recently have writers begun to create fiction in which hockey plays a prominent role. In 1987 Doug Beardsley argued in *Country on Ice* that it 'is not possible to imagine what Canadian life would be like without hockey,' while scratching his head at the fact that only one 'novel of note on the subject' has had been published (Roy MacGregor's 1983 *The Last Season*). Things have changed for the better. The majority of the fiction examined in this study was published after 1990, and many books appeared after 2000.[5]

Most overviews of hockey fiction express surprise that there is not more of it. This is especially odd given our proximity to the United States, which leads the sports literature world with its copious baseball writing, and which is so often accused of invading Canada's cultural space. As George Bowering wrote in 1979 in his introduction to *Great Canadian Sports Stories*, 'If the dreaded American influence is real, why is it that so many of our writers, myself included, have never written novels or stories about sports?' Those writers who grew up playing hockey forgot the standard advice to write about what one knows best. In Brian Fawcett's short story 'My Career with the Leafs,' a poet unexpectedly finds himself starring for the Toronto Maple Leafs. He excels on the ice, but hockey culture ostracizes him for giving an overly articulate interview. Having seen what the players read, he provides a kiss-and-tell story of their erudition. Although 'everyone knew [one star] was a big Henry

James fan' and highbrow books litter the locker-room, hockey players have to hide their true selves from the public eye. They have to act dumb if they want to succeed, just as past writers were expected to shun childish games. Fawcett's story ends with a facetious mini-manifesto: 'If more poets were to play pro hockey instead of pretending flowers or vacant lots are really interesting things might get better.' Theme and subject, of course, are no guarantee of great writing, but the argument that writers could vivify their work by including more sticks and pucks is surely compelling – at least to publishers and educators who have noted a decline in literacy and love of reading. Hockey sells, and the otherwise reluctant reader might be tempted to pick up a book about Canada's game.[6]

The core of this study is hockey literature in English, almost all of which has been published by Canadian authors. Such fiction draws on a common cultural tradition, on modern folklore so to speak, to create an artistic object in the traditional sense. Those few works written by non-Canadians, such as Peter LaSalle's 1996 New England–based short story collection *Hockey sur Glace*, Jack Falla's 2008 *Saved*, set in Boston, and Australian Ray Rains's 1991 *Hockey Night Down Under!*, refer constantly to the homeland of hockey in the way much postcolonial literature refers to the 'mother' country. Although this study includes some non-fiction, as well as a few plays and hockey poetry, prose fiction remains the focus. In order to maintain this focus, and in hopes of keeping the primary literature in the spotlight, I have relegated most academics' observations to the endnotes. This is aimed to be primarily a literary rather than a more general study of hockey.

Most of the works chosen fit Michael Oriard's claim that sports fiction is writing 'in which sport plays a dominant role or in which the sport milieu is the dominant setting.' As circular as this definition may seem, it is useful in limiting the genre. One swallow does not make a summer, and one puck does not make a hockey story. It would, for example, be a disingenuous reading strategy to look at Hugh MacLennan's *Two Solitudes* or Robert Kroetsch's *Gone Indian* (both of which contain hockey player protagonists or characters) solely in terms of hockey. However, some knowledge of hockey culture will inform and enlighten our reading of parts of those novels in the same way that an appreciation of Beethoven's Sonata in A Major will shine a light on Tolstoy's 'The Kreutzer Sonata' – even though there is relatively little music in that tale of uxoricide. Oriard clarifies his definition by adding that 'a sports novel is not a novel that happens to be about an athlete' but one that 'finds its vision of the individual and his condition in the basic meaning of the sport he plays, formerly played, or watches.' Hockey's meaning is rarely basic, and it will always be coloured by the narrator's or speaker's subjective attitude towards the game. Even if similarity exists between the reader's views on hockey and the narrator's, there will be a kaleido-scopic effect as views collide, are adjusted and infused with new mean-ings. In contrast to televised hockey, with commentators who deliver an often streamlined hockey gospel from above, literary hockey promotes active co-creation and consideration of the game's importance and sig-nificance.

Each work of fiction looked at in this study contains a considerable amount of hockey or commentary on the game, has no claim to factual, verifiable truth, and lends itself to contemplation of the game's mean-ings. Most importantly, and in line with traditional views of literature, we can return to these works for strictly aesthetic purposes. Though Morley Callaghan's *The Loved and the Lost* is included here, its short chapter that takes place at the Montreal Forum hardly qualifies it as hockey fiction in the sense of Roch Carrier's 'The Hockey Sweater,' Clark Blaise's 'I'm Dreaming of Rocket Richard,' or other stories marked for inclusion and re-inclusion in hockey anthologies. Neverthe-less, Callaghan's short novel does tell us something about significances attributed to hockey, as does Richard Wagamese's 1994 novel *Keeper 'n Me* – a story about a young man's return to an Ojibway reserve that includes an illuminative hockey scene.[7] The relatively minor hockey tableaux in these two novels are considerable not in the sense of pages devoted to the game but in that they urge consideration. Why, the reader must ask, did Callaghan or Wagamese decide hockey was a needed ingredient in his novel? What point did it make? What did it add to the novel?

In the past, Canadian sports fiction was rather simplistic, predictable, and aimed at a young audience. Radical individualism was the straight-forward path to winning, and plots were easy to follow (especially after one had read a few, because they were basically all the same). The pattern, as laid out in a 1972 article by Walter Evans, is this: the protag-onist is introduced, a bully attacks, the protagonist proves his mettle, the bully is regenerated, and then there is a gloriously upbeat 'apotheosis.' Evans's decision to call the happy ending an 'apotheosis' intimates the way we often revere athletes as godly figures. Sports fiction took its basis from unlikely upsets and miraculous outcomes on the sporting field, reg-ularizing the life out of them and pressing them into a template.[8]

In Richard Ford's novel *The Sportswriter* (1986), narrator Frank Bascombe equates the life of a sportswriter with literary failure precisely because it means churning out story after story based on the same pattern. In the narrator's gloomy view, a typical sports story is this:

> ... an American hockey player who becomes a skid-row drunk, rehabilitates himself at AA, scores forty goals and wins the Stanley Cup as the captain and conscience of the Quebec Nordiques.[9]

Hockey followers know that such Hollywood endings do not normally occur. In fact, in quality sportswriting, they are also rare. Contrary to the reputation of sportswriting – whether fictional or non-fictional – as a genre, some years the annual non-fictional *Best American Sports Writing* is obsessed with death, drug abuse, violence, criminal prosecution, and other seedy sides of the sporting life. In contemporary sports fiction and non-fiction there are few happy endings.

Yet even without literary happy endings, the hockey dream maintains a firm grip on the Canadian imagination. Contemporary hockey fiction constantly examines hockey culture in light of this dream, of this plot pattern. For example, in Mark Anthony Jarman's 1997 novel *Salvage King, Ya!* a hockey player reflects on the gap between childhood dreams and the current reality of adult players:

> When I was young I had an iron bed and a bedspread with tiny hockey players on it, all of them skating upright, smiling pleasantly. Now, when the shinpads come off, your eye sees the zippers on the knees around the room: let us compare scars.

The surgery-scarred knees do not accord with the warm images of smiling children at play, who will presumably grow up to star in the perfect hockey success story (or at least become model citizens through their involvement in the national sport). In another departure from traditional sports fiction, Jarman sprinkles literary allusions throughout his novel, and here there are clear echoes of Leonard Cohen's 'Let Us Compare Mythologies.' The Canadian mythology of hockey, like the war-based lore of many other nations, is also a matter of bloodshed at times. Hockey is a magnificent, but not always pleasant, story that leads Neil Earle to ask, 'If there is no Canadian Stalingrad or Marathon, might not the Stanley Cup playoffs and the international Canada Cup competitions form an imaginative substitute?' As Stalingrad claimed well over a million lives and happened only once, this comparison is grotesque.[10] Still, the very asking of the question speaks volumes about Canada's emotional attachment to hockey and the events that we have often seen mythologized in print.

Hockey fiction exists at the crossroads of an often conservative, nostalgia-driven culture and the traditional path of high art as a way towards change. Especially when there are references to real games and players, it is sometimes difficult to determine precisely where hockey fiction begins. Newer works of fiction regularly make such references; consequently, they are generally realistic and formally conventional (though rarely formulaic in the style of pulp fiction). Hanford Woods's short story 'The Drubbing of Nesterenko' revolves around specific and real games and players; Roy MacGregor's *The Last Season* adds a fictional player to the 1970s Philadelphia Flyers roster, while pointing to hockey events and incidents many Canadians will remember; Paul Quarrington's novel *King Leary* all but assumes a familiarity with Senators/Leafs legend King Clancy. The 1996 anthology *Original Six: True Stories from Hockey's Classic Era*, which Quarrington edited, has an overt truth claim, even though the tales consist of internal monologues and other clearly creative acts. One story 'was supposed to be about the Chicago Blackhawks but is really about heaven.'[11] Novels such as Eric Zweig's *Hockey Night in the Dominion of Canada* adhere to the historical fiction genre, thus more directly raising the age-old question of 'truth-or-fiction?' Further complicating the decision of what to include in this study is that many authors wear two hats: Bill Gaston, Mark Anthony Jarman, Dave Bidini, Paul Quarrington, Michael McKinley, Scott Young, and Mordecai Richler have all published both fiction and non-fiction about hockey. In such cases, their writings in both genres are included. Not included are the many hockey biographies and popular histories whose sole purpose – there are exceptions – is to glorify the game. Even the most romanticized hockey fiction tends to be more critical than the flashy picture books that sell hockey dreams.

In 1988, Robert G. Hollands wrote that 'the major point of view taken in the Canadian sports novel is that of … a third-person narrative limited to a single character (i.e. the main hero) in a kind of "over-the-shoulder," personal, account.'[12] This has changed. Though most of the novels and stories examined here focus on a single protagonist, the 'standard' is now a first-person narrator. Since we can only see so much with our own eyes, first-person narration entails a limited perspective. Hockey players in fiction are especially limited or naive in outlook. As well, the typical protagonist in a hockey story or novel is no Gretzky, and very few works published within the past two decades focus on a star player. Fred Stenson's short story 'Teeth' does, but since the goal-scorer does not really want to be a hockey player, there is no generic dream fulfilment. Intellectually, morally, and physically, the characters in hockey stories are often damaged goods. Having spent their lives in hockey surroundings, for the most part in a time before professional hockey players had a chance to educate themselves, they have renounced opportunities and eliminated off-ice possibilities. The result is often a structural irony: the reader knows more than the 'hero' of the story. But the main protagonists are never buffoons, never caricatures of the proverbial dim-witted hockey player, and there is thus a sadness to watching them stumble through life as men who are old in hockey terms but still youngish in real terms. Because we have made hockey so important to life in Canada, there is always an overriding irony to seeing people brought down by a wonderful game. Unlike Stalingrad, hockey is not a life-and-death matter, or even sacrifice for a greater cause. Hockey is not important; but neither is it *not* not important. Fiction always invites us to look carefully at the choppy cultural waters of hockey, to re-examine the game's role in our lives. This, at least in terms of cultural studies and considerations of Canada, is its greatest virtue.

This book examines regularly discussed hockey themes as they appear in fiction, and it is this focus on fiction that differentiates it from the many previous popular and academic examinations of hockey culture in Canada. In addition to providing a synthesis of the spattering of literary studies that consider hockey for the brief length of an article or essay, this study is entirely up-to-date, and strives to include all relevant works published to 2008. This topicality should prove particularly useful because, as indicated above, the nature of sports fiction has changed greatly with its progression from the trivial or predictable to the tragic and ironical. Previous studies of sports literature in Canada were looking at a greatly different body of literature, at a corpus that was more geared to the generic and the adolescent. Obviously that led to different conclusions about how Canada's national sport is reflected in fiction. As well, only now do we have enough fictional literature to warrant book-length examination – in other words, even ten years ago there was far less published hockey fiction. This study also considers views on hockey from outside the anglophone Canadian world; no literary examinations of hockey to date have included academic works published in French, which means that half of the hockey story was missing. Lastly, especially in the Conclusion, I take hockey literature in English beyond the Canadian and North American context, and look at what happens when readers without a hockey past pick up a hockey story.

This study is not entirely about hockey as part of Canadian identity because, as I point out in the chapter 'National Identity and Hockey,' contemporary hockey fiction never produces the hockey-equals-Canada equation in earnest. Fiction therefore differs greatly from the many popular histories and biographies that are uncritically and jingoistically in favour of hockey. At the same time, most academic studies demythologize the game's status by shedding light on such topics as sexual abuse in hockey, homophobic tendencies in hockey culture, and the blithe acceptance of violence on the ice. What makes hockey fiction different from non-fiction is that it offers a nuanced, literary view of the game. There is no either/or thinking in fiction, and readers take the good with the bad. In Canada, one cannot approach hockey fiction naively – that is, without any awareness of the game's importance as a playing-out of Canadianness in symbolic terms, or without knowledge of hockey's singular history of violence. It will surely come as a surprise to many that no scholarly or popular book exclusively on hockey in fiction has ever been published. Like sports, fiction is a key moulder of identity and community. It is for this reason that, in English Canada, finding or creating a literature that would differentiate us from American or British works was a decades-long obsession. This obsession is analogous to the over-valuing of hockey, including the widespread belief that hockey stops at the Canadian border and that other popular sports (like baseball and football), though followed fervently in Canada, do not count as part of our identity.

Any hockey lover (or hater) will be familiar with the themes examined in this study, though perhaps not as they are acted out on fiction's stages. The first chapter, 'Hockey as a Symbol of Nationhood,' outlines the cultural background of hockey symbolism in Canada. Chapters 2 through 5 look at common and crucial links in the hockey chain, namely: (2) 'The Hockey Dream: Hockey as Escape, Freedom, Utopia'; (3) 'Representations of Hockey Violence'; (4) 'National Identity and Hockey'; and (5) 'The Family Game.' Each of these themes appears and reappears in both fiction and non-fiction, and I have provided examples from a wide range of works (while never claiming that hockey novels are *only* about these particular themes). The thematic approach did mean, however, the exclusion of certain fine short stories, such as Hugh

Hood's 'The Sportive Centre of Saint Vincent de Paul' from his 1967 story cycle *Around the Mountain: Scenes from Montreal Life*, or many of those in Peter LaSalle's *Hockey sur Glace*. In addition, quality novels like Richard B. Wright's 1995 *The Age of Longing* receive short shrift because the chosen themes, though present, are not dominant.

Some themes, such as hockey as art, appear regularly but too fleetingly to justify extended examination. Though sexual abuse in hockey culture is well covered in both journalism and non-fiction books, even fiction that paints a grim picture of life in hockey virtually ignores the topic. Unlike sports journalists, whose guild 'was often little more than a promotional appendage of the NHL,' writers of fiction have little to lose by tarnishing the game's image; novelists do not have to fear the revoking of locker-room privileges. Because much fiction looks so honestly at the game and its culture, and so much was written after serial sexual abuse at hockey shrines like Maple Leaf Gardens came to light in the 1990s, this avoidance does not appear to be due to a conspiracy of silence. Although one would expect such dark secrets to be grist for the novelist's mill, up to now this has not been the case.[13]

The most surprising lack in English-language hockey fiction is Quebec, more specifically, Quebec's role within Canada. Anglophone Canada has adopted Roch Carrier's 'The Hockey Sweater' and clearly recognized the difficulties with *les anglais* in that story. The importance of hockey to a sense of identity in Quebec is widely known, and Quebec has been officially recognized as a nation in Parliament. Yet literary examinations of Quebec as a society with a perceived or real distinct status are absent. This suggests unfamiliarity with the francophone element in Canada, even though, as Graham Fraser writes in a *Globe and Mail* article of 2 May 2008, 'there are few activities that provoke similar levels of passion among English-speaking and French-speaking Canadians.' In a throwback to a less secular age, the Toronto-Montreal NHL rivalry, for example, is more often examined as a battle between Protestants and Catholics than between anglophone and francophone Canada.

Chapter 1, 'Hockey as a Symbol of Nationhood,' sets the foundations for the book by explaining the cultural background for how and why hockey became such a prominent symbol of Canadianness. It also considers the qualities of symbols in general, as well as the historical rise of hockey in Canada as a 'naturalized' marker of what it means to be Canadian. Many Canadians identify keenly with hockey as a national symbol, and many non-Canadians view us a nation of hockey players. Chapter 1 comes closest to cultural studies by looking at hockey culture in the broadest, rather than exclusively literary, context, and it contains the fewest examples from hockey fiction. This is because hockey fiction depends on an understanding of what came before.

One of the reasons hockey has been so enthusiastically accepted as a national symbol is that, for many, it evokes emotions and rosy memories. Chapter 2, 'The Hockey Dream: Hockey as Escape, Freedom, Utopia,' examines this link. Beginning with a discussion of play theories by Johan Huizinga, Roger Caillois, and others, it investigates the idealistic hidden assumptions of hockey. The belief that hockey should be enjoyable arises from an almost Edenic conception of play, as well as a confusing of the terms 'play' and 'sport.' It is possible to argue that play, or the play spirit, is necessarily a good thing; not so, sport. There are too many negative aspects – ranging from greed, to drug abuse, to horrendous injuries. Nevertheless, this utopian assumption is a paragon for most hockey fiction, meaning that something is wrong when players are not having fun on the ice. The chapter then examines instances of a corrupted play spirit, which most often occurs when players adopt a professional attitude towards the game. Positive literary portrayals of hockey are the focus of the chapter's final portion. The rosiest depictions of hockey in literature occur when people play shinny instead of regulation hockey. As we so often hear, hockey is best enjoyed outside, beyond the indoor arena's confining walls.

One of the roadblocks to sporting utopia is violence, the focus of chapter 3. 'Representations of Hockey Violence' investigates at length the spectre of violence in the national game, in particular, the apparent contradiction between a nation that prides itself on being peaceful and a game that many consider to be a modern-day bloodsport. Catharsis theory is briefly examined with regard to sport, as well as concepts such as controlled or simulated violence. Other focal points in this chapter include violence's effects on fans, the unwritten rules that govern violence on the ice, the theatrical aspect of hockey fights, violence as an arbiter of justice that supplants rule-book equality, violence as another corruption of the play spirit, violence as an indication of failure, instrumental violence – violence that is not 'value added' but put to the service of sporting victory – and, finally, violence as an imperative in certain hockey surroundings.

The fourth chapter, 'National Identity and Hockey,' follows the themes of utopia and violence to help illustrate the discrepancies in hockey culture. Being a player or a fan means taking the good with the bad. It is for this reason that chapter 4 does not immediately follow 'Hockey as a Symbol of Nationhood.' Despite the similarity of theme, there is a difference in mode. Whereas the imagining of community or the proposing of hockey as an official national sport is entirely celebratory, fiction's regard of hockey is more ambivalent. Chapter 4 also reveals a surprising feature: most hockey fiction does not dwell directly on the Canadianness of hockey. Rather, hockey in Canadian fiction is taken for granted – it is a point of departure for writing in fiction about the game. The Canadianness of the game is often more questioned than affirmed, and hockey literature thus shakes the conversational common ground. As so often in Canadian life and letters, irony is the predominant mode here. Chapter 4 looks at symbolic representations of hockey's relation to Canada, as a simplistic, essentialist vision of the nation, as a metaphorical and real indicator of immigrants' integration into Canadian society, and, lastly, as a feared grounds of losing Canada through the loss of hockey.

Chapter 5, 'The Family Game,' looks at hockey's movement from the national to the family level. After explaining why hockey is a particularly familial sport – primarily because of the tremendous investments required just to play organized hockey – the chapter investigates the parentless star who seemingly springs from the frozen land, the role of hockey in (primarily) father-son relationships, hockey as a bonding factor between family members, as well as hockey as a cause of familial division. The chapter ends with a search for the 'missing daughters' in hockey fiction.

If the decline in reading is real, perhaps hockey can do its part to attract readers. Yet regardless of the quality of the writing, hockey prose is bound to polarize. A work like Brian Kennedy's 2007 memoir *Growing Up Hockey: The Life and Times of Everyone Who Ever Loved the Game* is written for a specific audience, and the very title will repel readers who do not like the game. In the Conclusion, I consider not so much those readers who do not like hockey as those who may never have seen a puck or been exposed to a television commercial featuring hockey. Outside Canada and the northern United States, passing references to hockey can forestall aesthetic pleasure or prove a barrier to basic comprehension. After considering the provincialism of hockey fiction, I offer three examples of brief allusions in three unlikely candidates: Leonard Cohen's *Beautiful Losers*, Alistair MacLeod's *No Great Mischief,* and Alice Munro's 'The Bear Came over the Mountain.' Just a few words in length, each of these references deftly adds social context or humour to the work. It is this expansive use of hockey, rather than waving a flag at a hockey game, that demonstrates its cultural value and importance to Canadian literature.

Chapter One

Hockey as a Symbol of Nationhood

You cannot live in Canada without being touched somehow by hockey.
Andrew Podnieks, *A Canadian Saturday Night*, p. 5

Canadians associate themselves with hockey primarily because its modern roots are Canadian and because we excel at it. But there are other reasons for its fecundity as a national symbol, and Canada's geographical, linguistic, and multicultural complexity has helped anchor the game's status. Over time, the game has evolved into a self-understood indicator of Canadianness, both for Canadians and for the rest of the world. Hockey is an effective unifying symbol for a vast and heterogeneous country. The geographical surroundings may differ from East to West, from North to South, but the rink's dimensions and the game's rules remain the same. A matter of choice, hockey is a fitting New World sport because a new Canadian can easily latch on to the game and participate in 'playing' Canada. All of these aspects have aided the rise of hockey, and all have been examined to some degree in hockey literature. In examining the national game, though, hockey literature assumes a common ground without specifically stating the mutual or widely held beliefs. When two Canadians talk about hockey, even if they have never met before, the game is already in conversational play.

Non-fictional hockey writing tries to explain the attraction, importance, or, especially in academic writing, the baneful qualities of the national game. Fiction is more laconic, and Canadian fiction that spent too much time explaining *why* hockey is important would seem artificial. Hockey talk, whether in spoken or in written form, often serves phatic or emotional, rather than informational, purposes. Individual scores, statistics, and analysis are mere footnotes to the larger hockey story that is assumed to be all-inclusive for (especially male) Canadians. The purpose of this chapter is to survey the ground on which the house of hockey fiction is built.

Symbols, Literary and National

The joy and wealth of a literary symbol often rests with its ambiguity and complexity, with the fact that a single image can whisper various meanings. A rose in a poem can trigger a number of associations and feelings in any reader, not all of which were planted or intended by the author. Even if two readers recognize the obvious importance of that poeticized rose, unless its significance is made explicit in the manner of simple allegory (where the rose stands exclusively for 'love' or only for 'a maiden'), the readers will differ in their understanding of its symbolism. Of course, not all symbols have inexpressibly aesthetic aims. In a more general sense, a symbol is a sign, and we encounter more mundane types of symbols every day. The language of a traffic light is far less thorny than William Blake's symbolic idiom in his poem 'The Sick Rose.' Once we have learned that red means stop, green go, there is no more ambiguity.

If literary symbols are often a winding, labyrinthine path, national or state symbols[1] are a narrow one-way street. They are more like a stop sign in that the aim is immediate recognition and identification of what the symbol stands for: the nation. When a flag is raised on a national holiday, or burnt in protest, we do not have to puzzle out what that particular flag represents or the basic sense of the message being conveyed. Recognition seems automatic, inevitable – as though the inanimate flag had an inherent meaning. National symbols are reductive and exclusive. They are reductive because they imply that the essence of a nation can be distilled into a single image; they are exclusive because choosing one image for a nation means not choosing another one. Favouring the maple leaf for Canada, or the shamrock for Ireland, is an arbitrary choice. Through time and tradition, national symbols – from the national flower to the national flag – become naturalized. As the symbol is accepted, a choice that was once arbitrary comes to seem necessary or inevitable. Our recognition of the Union Jack or the Stars and Stripes as suitable emblems of Great Britain and the United States is made automatic by our having seen these flags – supported by political authority – over and over again.

Even before we can link the flag to a nation or a state, a simplification has to take place. A national symbol must be broad enough that the entire nation can identify with it, and a unifying oversimplification is a required first step. A choice among many potential symbols, the sanctified or chosen symbols are squeezed into the space of a shield or flag. In turn, that flag and those symbols supposedly define a people as members of a national or regional political community. This can only happen in a reductive, usually abstract, manner, as the specificity and concreteness of symbols are bound to alienate by evoking a particular region, ethnicity, or language.

Like the first white settlers, Canada's first flags came from somewhere else. The Red Ensign, with its bold Union Jack in the corner, advertised Canada as British property. When Canada moved towards replacing the Red Ensign in 1964, the parliamentary squabbling (complete with a special flag committee composed of representatives from all three main political parties) went on for months. There was even an indirect hockey aspect to the Great Flag Debate. Conn Smythe, a staunch monarchist and then-owner of the Toronto Maple Leafs hockey team, recalls,

> I and millions of other Canadians were quite happy with the flag we had –
> the Red Ensign. We had fought under it in Europe during the two wars.
> The Union Jack up in one corner signified the British connection, which
> in my opinion was the most important single fact of life in Canada.[2]

Since the red maple leaf flag is now happily accepted and proudly waved by Canadians – and never more proudly and vigorously than at hockey games – past disputes seem petty. Yet despite the current consensus, the Canadian flag remains a surprising national symbol because the maple does not grow in all provinces and territories. In its very inappropriateness, the Maple Leaf is a reminder of the difficulty of national symbols, in general, and for large countries, in particular. National symbols cause problems because they always arise from the forceful folding together of groups and regions.

The goal here is not to reopen flag debates but to show how hockey profited from the sticky issue of Canadian symbols. For a population divided by vast distances, six time zones, two federally recognized official languages, two island provinces, and seven climatic zones, finding an acceptable common symbol is difficult. Prime Minister Joe Clark stated in 1979 that Canada is 'too big for simple symbols' and that this 'preoccupation with the symbol of a single national identity'[3] ignores the reality of Canada's diversity. Nevertheless, Canadians search for simple symbols with the grail-seeker's fervour, and Clark, with his honest admission of Canada's complexity, was not long in office.

Winter, though difficult to depict on a flag and hardly indigenous to Canada, is a popular topic for conversation and art. Margaret Atwood writes that winter is 'the "real" season. You can use winter themes and images as a kind of touchstone.' But it is a variegated touchstone, since winter in the abstract means nothing when it comes to symbols. In the Canadian mindset and mythology, winter needs a place to whiten, people to freeze. It needs snow (though we begrudgingly make exceptions for those in the balmier parts of British Columbia). This is why Canadians routinely and absurdly assert that warmer climates are excluded from the natural seasonal cycle because they do not 'have winter.' Once the question of place arises, the familiar problem of regionalism follows. In geographical terms, one would have to ask, Which Canada? Which *part* of Canada? or – to repeat Northrop Frye's famous question – 'Where is here?' A Prairie farmer or a Newfoundland outport resident will recognize the snow on the Rocky Mountains, but the peaks will not be an experienced reality; neither will a francophone Québécoise always be able to complain about the cold in a common tongue with an anglophone Albertan. They will all, however, be familiar with hockey. In Birk Sproxton's prose poem 'A Sunny Day in May – Newfoundland Time,' the Albertan records the different accents in the island province, feels entirely out of place, but is comforted by homely 'Signs of hockey everywhere.'[4]

The boards enclosing a hockey rink, as well as the rules and tools needed to play, are the same from coast to coast. Even when we substitute a river and a chunk of ice (or an asphalt road and a tennis ball) for the standardized rink and puck, the sporting form is easily recognized. As author Michael McKinley writes with telling hyperbole, hockey was a means of adapting to the land:

> Hockey was encoded in the genes of those who had survived a couple of centuries' worth of insanely cold winters north of the 49th Parallel and had learned how to play in them. Hockey was our game.

In the popular view, hockey links Canadians more than the maple leaf flag. Canadian Broadcasting Corporation radio host Tom Allen recalls enduring the cold with fellow Torontonians while their children, for a change, played outdoors:

> We would console ourselves with the knowledge that there, in the midst of the largest urban sprawl in the country, we were giving our children what we'd all been told was the true Canadian hockey experience.

In Toronto, most children play hockey indoors, and the 'we'd all been told' suggests that the parents do not know outdoor hockey either. Yet, in Canadian hockey mythology, the sanitized game in heated indoor arenas does not count as the true hockey experience. For reasons of history, popularity, and recognition, the game is ours – especially outdoors, where urban sprawl can be forgotten as we play at being true Canadians.[5]

Hockey is not universally adored in Canada, but it is universally recognized. When former professional player Ken Dryden published his fine study of hockey some twenty-five years ago, he chose a simple title: *The Game.* For the Canadian audience, he did not have to specify which one. Hockey's omnipresence in Canada goes beyond active participation, and there is no segment of society shielded from the national affinity and addiction. The dominant hockey reference is *Hockey Night in Canada*, the wildly successful CBC show that began as a radio broadcast in 1931 and moved to television in 1952. Much hockey literature adopts or puns on the show's name, including Diane Schoemperlen's 'Hockey Night in Canada,' Edo van Belkom's 'Hockey's Night in Canada,' Don Bell's 'Hockey Night in Métabetchouan,' and even Australian Ray Rains's *Hockey Night Down Under!* Writers allude to the show the way wordsmiths of past generations alluded to the King James Bible.

Like the beaver that is the official symbol of Canada's sovereignty, hockey is on our money. Roch Carrier's words from his short story 'The Hockey Sweater' grace the Canadian $5 bill: 'our real life was on the ice' – 'la vraie vie était sur la patinoire.' The story takes place during the 1950s, but was first published in 1979. Carrier's story, originally penned in French, is the only Canadian story with which anglophones and francophones identify equally. In the cultural sphere, only a hockey tale could cross the linguistic divide with such ease – even one originally titled 'Une abominable feuille d'érable sur la glace.' This is particularly ironic given that much of Quebec adopted Maurice Richard as a hero of the people, an athletic freedom fighter *against* the rest of Canada. Thus, anglophone Canada has appropriated, or at least adopted, a story highlighting a certain animosity. Carrier's claim that 'our real life was on the ice' suggests that hockey is a deeper reality, the essence of a Canadian existence. We spend the rest of the time, the rest of the year, waiting for the game to start, for the real season to begin. Atwood stated that 'winter themes and images' work wonderfully as a touchstone, but the specific theme that works best is hockey. The game has a mythic presence in Canada, surrounding us with a hazy system of binding cultural symbols. There is a play aspect to watching hockey, to watching French and English come together on the ice. The majority of hockey fiction in English ignores hockey's symbolic ability to split identity within Canada.

For Canadians and non-Canadians alike, hockey's overwhelming status often spills over into essentialism. The claim is made – not always in jest – that a true Canadian has an ingrained, cradle-to-grave attachment to hockey and accompanying comprehension of the game. It is assumed that all Canadians play hockey. Levi Dronyk, in a short story called 'The Puck Artist,' gently satirizes this supposed link between nation and game. 'Any kid without an instinctive understanding of the game,' claims his hero, Billy the Kid Semeniuk, 'is genetically un-Canadian.' The Canadian Billy the Kid is a gifted athlete, great orator, and schoolyard philosopher who, unlike his more violent American namesake, shoots with a stick not a gun. This is the commonly heard phrase that hockey courses through the blood of all Canadians, that hockey is a matter of genes rather than weaning, while the name Billy the Kid is a nod to hockey's violence. The speech's plumpness, meanwhile, reminds us how far removed hockey is from any blood-and-soil nationalism (and Billy himself is a second-generation Ukrainian Canadian). When one listener challenges him with 'So how come all of us ain't in the NHL?' a clarification follows: 'What I said, butternuts, is that we all have an understanding. Not everyone has the skills.'[6] Excelling at the game or physically playing the game is not required. Semeniuk's literary version of the common argument is this: hockey is a part of the cultural air Canadians breathe, and we understand it in the way that people who grow up singing folk songs comprehend (and often tire of) those melodies.

In 1994, Senator Alisdair Graham used his day at the office to propose parliamentary acceptance of hockey and lacrosse as Canada's national sports. The Senate debate must have been tame. Hockey is the only thing about which political adversaries in Canada agree, and publicly admitting a dislike for the game would be politically foolish.

Graham's soupy eloquence could have escaped from any throat in the Senate or the House of Commons:

> The sound of the first slapshot, the first puck hitting the boards, was and is the first shock of psychic electricity that unites hearts and minds in this country. All that irrespective of regions, time zones or ethnic backgrounds, because if there ever was a visible, passionate and inspirational spirit of our magnificent multiculturalism it was, and is, hockey.[7]

Less lightheartedly than Dronyk, and with a stronger emphasis on multiculturalism, Graham praises hockey as a catalyst for unity even while the vocabulary emphasizes difference: 'hearts and minds' are individual, and regionalism and varied ethnic backgrounds are often highlighted as challenges to nationhood. Perhaps even more revealingly, Graham did not mention class or social lines. Unlike their European counterparts, North American spectator sports like hockey, baseball, and football have long appealed to all tax brackets. 'I like hockey' is not a statement of income level.

Hockey's rise has been helped by a Canadian cultural insecurity, the widespread belief that we have an impoverished cultural tradition. Lacking a claim to the roots of a jazz or a polka, for years Canadians have been trumpeting ice hockey as both Canada's cultural heart and our one contribution to world culture. It has the crucial function of putting Canada on the map. Mordecai Richler comments,

> If, in larger terms, our indigenous culture had always been suspect, most of it not for export ..., we were at least armed with one certitude, and it was that when it came to playing the magnificent game of ice hockey we were, indeed, a people unsurpassed.

Hockey belongs to low or popular culture, and for much of the twentieth century it was kept away from serious fiction. George Woodcock's observation that 'literatures are defined as much by their lacks as by their abundances' says much about perceptions of proper cultural topics. Even while the literati chased distinctively Canadian themes to validate a new literature, they ignored hockey. They ignored the body in favour of the strictly cerebral.[8]

F.R. Scott lampoons this searching in 'The Canadian Authors Meet,' his caustic poem describing a dilettantish group that puts the emphasis on *Canadian* in Canadian poetry. 'The air is heavy with Canadian topics,' he writes, before asking, 'O Canada, O Canada, Oh can / A day go by without new authors springing / To paint the native maple ...?' The suggestion is that third-rate verse about a tree is always ripe for publication in Canada. Canadian literature has affirmed itself since Scott first published this poem in 1927, and it would be outdated to suggest hockey is a literary quick-fix for the nation's psyche. Nevertheless, and in spite of highbrow aspirations, it is ironic that the sport was ignored in the thick patriotic air smothering Scott. Most hockey fiction has appeared in the past twenty-five years. Before that, hockey was relegated to the realm of trivial and children's literature – and even today the best-known hockey novels are undoubtedly Scott Young's trilogy for young readers, *Scrubs on Skates* (1952), *Boy on Defence* (1953), and *A Boy at the Leafs' Camp* (1963).

Hockey fiction for adults may have come of age in terms of both quality and quantity, but hurdles remain as far as literary acceptance goes. Roy MacGregor writes that hockey is 'still considered a rather unworthy and silly topic,' and even works with a literary bent 'are usually classified by CanLit commentators and even bookstores as genre' fiction. Yet Canada was not alone in keeping the worlds of sport and literature apart. Except for in its older, bloodier, and more gentlemanly sense of hunting and fishing, the modern-day cultural behemoth of sport was all but absent from literature well into the twentieth century. England may be the cradle of both modern sport and literature in English, but rarely do they come together as they did in Thomas Hughes's 1857 adolescent fiction classic *Tom Brown's School Days*. That novel, with its rugby and cricket and gentlemanly ethos of fighting fair even in schoolyard brawls, set the standard for school fiction, but there was little sports fiction for adults emerging from colonial headquarters. Even in the United States, the exception that proves the rule with its happy glut of baseball literature, sports fiction was a latecomer. Though baseball was proclaimed 'the national game' as early as 1866, and regardless of Virginia Woolf's praise for Ring Lardner's work cited in the Introduction, the game that defined America did not appear outside of the trivial until Bernard Malamud's 1952 novel *The Natural*.[9]

Don Gillmor's 2005 *Walrus* magazine review of four hockey books points out an incongruity: 'Hockey is our mythic game, as almost every hockey book states somewhere. It sings in our blood. Yet, unlike boxing or baseball, it has not produced a mythic literature.' Gillmor passes over some excellent hockey fiction in his article (most notably Mark Anthony Jarman's *Salvage King, Ya!* and Paul Quarrington's *King Leary*), but his point is valid. In accounting for hockey's failure to produce larger-than-life literature, he does not repeat the uppity, facile answer that hockey and fiction do not belong together, or that any real hockey game will inevitably be more exciting than a print version. Gillmor notes that the problem is one of reception, not production:

> There are hundreds of books, many of them good, but only a few have entered the public imagination, have translated the game – its grandeur and meanness and poetry – into something lasting.[10]

Though Canadians have enthusiastically accepted hockey as a national cultural symbol, literary representations of this symbol seem to have left the reading public cold. There may be candidates out there for the Great Hockey Novel, but no single novel has been critically or popularly accepted as the literary essence of the game.

Novelist Robertson Davies once remarked that Canadians felt too insecure in their literature to produce comedy; the same could be said for hockey fiction. The unwritten rule was that hockey was too frivolous to be included in a literature and high culture just becoming established. Poet and hockey cognoscente Doug Beardsley states, 'We in Canada suffer from an intellectual snobbery where hockey is concerned.' In the postmodern age, with the marrying of high and low culture, Canadians are adding more and more value to hockey, and no longer are concert stages, operas, and national theatres the only legitimate forms of culture. David Gowdey claims in his 1989 hockey anthology *Riding on the Roar of the Crowd* that it is 'the one truly Canadian art form.' This global change in cultural attitudes helps account for the extensive body of hockey fiction now emerging. Rick Salutin, in the Foreword to his play *Les Canadiens*, says hockey is 'probably our only universal cultural symbol [and] even those who haven't played ... nevertheless *relate* to the game.' Hockey-themed literature thus has a wide potential audience in Canada; even though Salutin's play focuses on the cultural identity of Quebec (a topic not widely examined in English-language literature), hockey helps bring this message across the divide.[11]

Don Bell's hilarious essay 'Hockey Night in Métabetchouan' revels self-consciously in purple prose and wistful reminiscing about real hockey and the essence of Canada. Bell's essay uses a hockey lens to provide insight into a small Quebec town – that is, a part of Canada not commonly seen by anglophone eyes. He describes a semi-talented hometown team and declaims:

> Here is boondocks hockey in its rawest form, hockey as the fundamental
> Canadian experience. Here, the very soul of hockey can be tapped. In
> Métabetchouan, as in many similar-sized communities across the land,
> hockey isn't just a game, but a way of life, a philosophy, a religion.

Bell's essay is effective because it trails saccharine commentaries on
hockey that see only the good in the game, including its cultural value.
It also travesties those previous accounts. Hockey may be a way of life
and guiding light in the Quebec town's life, but only because there is a
dearth of other cultural and entertainment options:

> There isn't a Museum of Fine Arts, there's no Chinatown, no bookstores
> … You can book a room in the Motel Terrasso and have an affair, but it's a
> small town: sooner or later you'll get caught.

Bell argues that hockey is popular in this typical town because there is
nothing else to do, and the alternative seems to be emptiness or
boredom. This devalues the game considerably.[12]

A common argument is that Canada's real language is hockey rather
than French or English. Talk of hockey as a language becomes more
than tired metaphor when we recall that, while anglophone Canadians
are generally unaware of even popular Franco-Canadian films, hockey
players such as Mario Lemieux and Patrick Roy are household names.
In *Blood and Belonging: Journeys into the New Nationalism,* Michael Ignatieff draws a disturbing conclusion about Canada as he watches a hockey
game with a friend from Quebec:

> We cannot share a nation – we cannot share it, since I am English-speak-
> ing and he is French-speaking, and he was born in Quebec and I was not.
> Because we do not share the same nation, we cannot love the same state.

This seems simplistic, and it is surely coloured by his examinations of far
bloodier and fiercer manifestations of nationalism in Northern Ireland
and the former Yugoslavia. Although this is an intimate image of two
friends watching a hockey game, the text bypasses the fact that hockey
itself is a crucial vehicle of identity. Far from being exclusively pleasant
entertainment, the ice rink can also be a place for contesting and assert-
ing a group's sense of self, sometimes in antagonistic and often in
aggressive ways. But Ignatieff tempers his absolutist claim that two
nations cannot love a single state with a second, benign conclusion:

Perhaps the gentleness, tolerance, and good-naturedness of so much of Canadian life depends, in fact, on that absence of a fiercely shared love. Yet one can sit in a hockey arena in Trois-Rivières on a Tuesday night, watching a young man skating his heart out, with a wild grin on his face, and wish, suddenly, that we did actually love the same nation and not merely cohabit the same state.

No other cultural activity moves as freely across the nation, traversing the linguistic divide, as hockey. Peter Gzowski, twenty years before our $5 'hockey bill' came into circulation, wrote that hockey 'was the common Canadian coin.' Relating the language of hockey with a common currency implies a Canada made slightly smaller, slightly more intimate, through the common recognition and love of the game. In this sense, hockey clearly and neatly fulfils the role of a national symbol. Most Canadians do not wake up thinking about hockey, but the sport remains a comfortable confirmation of the nation's existence.[13]

Populist identity discourse often assumes there should be homogeneity along linguistic, ideological, or ethnic lines. But even when a nation has a common language that more or less coincides with its borders (such as Denmark, Norway, or Slovenia), there is no guaranteed intimacy and uniformity of population. As Benedict Anderson has famously written, a 'nation is an imagined political community ... because the members of even the smallest nation will never know most of their fellow-members, ... yet in the minds of each lives the image of their communion.'[14] Conceptualizing a nation as a community means constructing a streamlined, simplified version of a nation's complexity; it is the mental, philosophical equivalent of finding a specific national symbol. That said, Anderson's thesis is intuitively understood by most Canadians because of the vastness of the country and because the concept of an 'ordinary' or 'typical' Canadian is not a given in Canada. You do not spend any time convincing Canadians that the land is big and varied.

If all nations are complex and therefore require imagination to create their community, some nations require more imagination than others. John Ralston Saul writes that Canada's very 'strength – you might even say what makes it interesting – is its complexity; its refusal of the conforming, monolithic nineteenth-century nation-state model.' Whereas the nation-state model promotes cutting out what does not easily fit a core myth, Canadians can only speak of an onion core. Canada's basis of development was triangular, made up 'three deeply rooted pillars, three experiences – the aboriginal, the francophone and the anglophone.'[15] Add to this wave after wave of immigration and the original mixture of two dominant languages and religions and a few skin colours becomes far more flavoured. Thus, a Canada based on language and ethnicity would not be a realistic option – which partly explains why so much hockey literature focuses on the coming-together of various ethnic groups in hockey.

The American sports historian Allen Guttmann argues that 'from the remnants of wickets and bats, future archaeologists of material culture will be able to reconstruct the boundaries of the British Empire.' Canadians are fairly docile colonialists, and jettisoning the Monarchy has never been seriously considered as an option in English Canada. Nevertheless, in contrast to former British colonies like Trinidad and Tobago, Australia, and India, after the 1860s Canada all but rejected cricket. Hockey played a key role in this rejection. Sociologist Michael Robidoux pits hockey against the literal and figurative colonizers, calling it a 'vehicle of resistance against British and American hegemony.' Unlike India and Pakistan, we opted against resistance on the pitch (though hockey has fulfilled this function in Quebec). As well, though we play baseball and (Canadian) football, hockey is the only sport that symbolizes a form of sporting resistance. This was convenient because until the rest of the world caught up there was little danger of losing.[16]

Steve Lundin's hockey novel *When She's Gone* highlights a common cultural juxtaposition: the massive portraits of the Queen that keep watch over many hockey arenas throughout Canada. The narrator notes that the depicted Queen looks 'a little confused' about what she is watching.[17] She casts an anachronistic gaze over a late twentieth-century hockey game, and Lundin concisely shows how hockey accompanied an awakening of national identity and a moving away from colonial status. Our games are not those of the mother country, and gone are the days when a band could allegedly stop a hockey brawl by playing 'God Save the King.' The predominant sense in Lundin's novelistic aside is one of slight loss of control. No longer can one tell what is happening out there in the (former) colonies. These days, Canadians' identity barometers are concerned with American air pressure.

Despite the surface similarities between Canada and the United States (including vast distances and immigrant cultures), American tradition has gone further in cultivating a spirit of uniformity. The Latin mottoes of the two countries reflect a key difference. Against the American '*e pluribus unum*,' our motto is a far more open '*a mare usque ad mare.*' 'Out of many, one' postulates a centrality to which the many new-comers are both attracted and adhere. 'From sea to sea' is merely a statement of geography, with no sense of imperative values or a simpli-fied centre. Even today, Canada 'lacks a genuine sense of authoritarian culture' because no single 'set of ideas has won over all the other com-peting ideas.' This reality in Canada is often apprehended as fear, namely, that once the ethnic, linguistic, and regional skins are shed, no Canadian culture will remain. In the past twenty-five years, two refer-enda on Quebec sovereignty have contributed to the fear of the country splitting politically. And this fear has been incorporated into national conceptions of the self. Leonard Cohen, in his pre-referenda novel *Beautiful Losers*, refers to our cursed 'nightmares of identity,' and thirty years later, Linda Hutcheon wonders how it is that 'Canadians still feel the need to publish books with titles like *A Passion for Identity*?'[18] The source of both the nightmares in *Beautiful Losers* and Hutcheon's frus-tration is the recognition that there is no uniform identity – even as the Canadian search for an identity bonanza or Shangri-La continues.

If the unifying pot of gold will not be found, neither will the melting-pot. At least not officially. Margaret Atwood, in *Survival: A Thematic Guide to Canadian Literature*, postulates the new arrival in Canada, eager to adapt to a new nation:

> ... if he does wipe away his ethnic origin, there is no new 'Canadian' iden-tity ready for him to step into: he is confronted only by a nebulosity, a blank; no ready-made ideology is provided for him.[19]

The ideological Other looming behind this quotation is clearly the United States, with its 'Pursuit of Happiness' creed. In most countries, mixing national identity and words like 'nebulosity' and 'blank' would be frowned upon; in Canada, Atwood's book and its insights were almost universally praised, especially for its promotion of the fact that Canadian literature exists.

For a country that often feels fragmented, the hockey arena is a con-venient gathering place and focal point. Like any activity, hockey has its expert fans, but the minimum comprehension required to watch and derive *something* from the game is much less than for other cultural forms such as opera and modern dance. Thus, it is easier for Canadians to latch en masse onto hockey as a marker of nationhood. This is not to argue that we are alone in this sporting nationalism. As Allen Guttmann writes,

If nations are what Benedict Anderson's influential theory claims them to be, imagined communities, then modern sports are an important and popularly accessible aid to this politically indispensable form of imagining.

Whether it is by cheering for a particular player, wearing a Calgary Flames cap, or sporting a hockey-themed tattoo, sports are a convenient and often public means of classifying oneself and constructing identity. This sporting identity also occurs at group and national levels. The common European examples are Gaelic football, Welsh rugby, and the Scottish highland games, but there are many other examples (including the *Sokol* mass gymnastics movement in Czechoslovakia, which was suppressed behind the Iron Curtain precisely because it was felt to promote nationalism). Moving to North America, Canada 'has' hockey, while the United States 'has' baseball – even though both games are widely played in both countries. It is because of these conceived spheres of sporting influence that losing to the United States in baseball is acceptable; losing to them in hockey is regarded as shameful. Or, to provide a more lighthearted example of hockey as a surrogate form of war or struggle, the usual assertion of nationhood, Mordecai Richler wrote: 'So far as red-blooded Canadians are concerned, the real Russian menace to our manhood comes on ice.' Linking a sporting event to national shame in such an exaggerated manner has been called the 'athletic fallacy,' and Canadians often profess it with less humour than Richler.[20]

Marking the Other, Marking Canada

The different-coloured uniforms we see on the playing field exemplify how we differentiate ourselves from the Other. When Canada and the United States play, for once the anglophone Canadian can see exactly where difference begins, ignore the often very similar accents, and look at international relations in black-and-white terms. This sporting identification process goes beyond donning team jerseys. Sports sociologists refer to the '90–minute nationalism' of the stadium in which spectators cheer the representatives of a cacophonous nation made up of many ethnic, linguistic, and religious strains. Like all nationalism, this is simplistic, at least if it means that the essence of a nation is distilled into a sports team.[21]

Morley Callaghan wrote of a multicultural hockey dream decades before 'multiculturalism' entered the lexicon. In a poignant essay first published during the Second World War, Callaghan emphasizes the inclusiveness of hockey. Using hockey as a metonym for Canada, Callaghan produces a clever diatribe against blood-based nationalism; the essay is a fine, and early, example of how Canadians use hockey to enlighten more important topics. He lists professional players such as 'Orlando, Benoit, O'Connor, Grabowski, Pratt, Schmidt, Apps, Stewart, Shewchuck, Bouchard' and says this ethnic cornucopia will surely frustrate those who propagate a Canada that is a mere extension of England; 'you might begin to think,' he states, 'that there were a lot of people in Canada who didn't come from your favourite neighbourhood in Toronto or even the older settlements in Ontario.' The references to 'favourite neighbourhood' and 'older settlements' are Callaghan's euphemisms for a particular type of anglophile, colonial White Anglo-Saxon Protestant mentality. By including the typically Irish and francophone names, he slyly alludes to the prejudices and shortcomings of a Canada built solely as an extension of England. Hockey contradicts such a mentality as it creates the nation imaginatively – and the title of the essay is 'The Game That Makes a Nation.'[22]

Callaghan notes that the nation is *made* up of the various individual ethnic groups that form the multicultural mosaic. The story has not changed much in fifty years. Some thirty years after multiculturalism became official policy in Canada, writers continue to focus on ethnic heritage. For example, Ken Dryden and Roy MacGregor write of fans that 'come to cheer for prairie kids with distinctly Canadian names, like Katelnoff and Kocur, Snesar, Kuntz, Holoien, Lelacheur, Bauer, Yellowaga, Smart, and Sutton.'[23] Cynics may point out that this name game is antiquated in a vibrantly multicultural society, or that the sentence's arc leads from foreign-sounding names to typically English ones. The more subtle point, however, is this: these names may evoke Old World countries, but in contemporary Canada it is not possible to predict how long someone has been in the country judging by their name.

In spite of such views of hockey as the raw material of Canada, Team Canada does not offer an accurate miniature of Canadian life. Nonetheless, it *is* a representation. What the maple leaf–clad national team does offer is visibility, a concrete symbol of the abstract imagined community. A national sports team, put together to win medals, is symbolic in the sense that it is a place-marker of the nation. Or, to quote Eric Hobsbawm, an 'imagined community of millions seems more real as a team of eleven named people.'[24] There are two reasons why the team seems more real. First, nations are so vast and abstract that they, like all abstractions, can be best comprehended through symbols or concrete images, even if those symbols are active, sentient beings. It is easier to grasp the flow and patterns of a game with relatively few players than the limitless comings and goings in a country. But the imagined community is also more real in the way that the undiluted grief of a Tosca or the impossible, staged love of a Romeo or a Juliet can seem more authentic than our own cluttered emotions.

To link this sporting nationalism to another aspect of national symbols, hockey is not just what Canadians rally around, relate to, or understand. It is also an outward marker, a means of representing the nation on the world stage. Bruce Dowbiggin describes the search for a suitable beacon to the Canada Pavilion at the 1986 World Exposition in Vancouver:

> Your assignment is to create the definitive symbol of Canada. To sum up, in a single image, the passions and predilections of a people drawn from over 130 years of history. Which symbol would you choose? A sheaf of wheat? A Canada goose in flight? An Inuit carving? The maple leaf? The fleur-de-lys? If you were the executive in charge of iconography at Expo 86, you manufactured the biggest damn hockey stick you could.

The massive phallic sporting utensil that stood outside the Canada Pavilion was 60 metres tall and as gaudy as the 1980s. Yet 'there wasn't a peep of complaint about the stick as a symbol of nationhood'[25] – even though no normal mind would agree that the stick sums up the myriad 'passions and predilections' of the country as a whole. At Expo 86 the hockey stick literally loomed over visitors regardless of passport, and it was therefore a fitting symbol of how hockey dominates other cultural areas in Canada. This massive stick at Expo 86 was an all-too concrete example of how hockey is put on display, how it is used to perform Canada.

The problem with the other potential symbols listed by Dowbiggin is that they are either too limited or politically weighted, sometimes both. The Inuit carving and the sheaf of wheat are clearly relevant only to particular areas of the country; the fleur-de-lys is indelibly linked to Quebec and therefore unsuitable as a representation of Canada as a whole. (When the Quebec Nordiques, with their fleur-de-lys crests, became that province's second National Hockey League team, they were widely believed to be more representative of Quebec than Montreal.) The reason why complaints were limited – aside from our having been worn down through repetition into accepting hockey symbolism – is hockey's almost universal appeal in Canada. Hockey is played in every province and territory in this country ... And though its symmetry is far from perfect, hockey does far better than most in cutting across social division – young and old, rich and poor, urban and rural, French and English, East and West, able and disabled.[26]

The need to bridge distance, particularly from East to West, has been a common concern in Canada since Confederation. Even today, the vast majority of Canadians huddle within a few hours' drive of the American border. Indeed, when British Columbia joined the Canadian confederation, it did so because a railway link within ten years had been promised. It took a line of communication to make Canada what it is, a nation that stretches *a mare usque ad mare*.

The common mythology is that if the railway brought British Columbia and the other ocean to Canada, the nation is held together by a second line of communication, the weekly hockey broadcast *Hockey Night in Canada*. For decades, every Saturday night – the prime social night of the week – Canadians nestled around the radio in the kitchen, and later in front of the television, to hear Foster Hewitt's play-by-play. As Bruce Kidd writes in *The Struggle for Canadian Sport*:

> Millions tuned into it avidly at some point of their lives, and ... it gave many people their strongest sense of pan-Canadian identity [and] helped the anonymous individual feel more like a person and the mass more like a community.

In a word, *Hockey Night in Canada* brought the country together, if only for the length of the game, by eradicating isolation through technology. In the novel *Bus-Ride,* Don Gutteridge describes the sensation of community and imagination in more personal terms as a family listens to hockey on the radio:

> They, like a million others on this night in March of 1939, would be content to listen, to focus all senses on a single voice riding outward to the far stretches of the land, carrying in its rhythms and intonations the legends of its generation. On such poetry the mind builds its own arenas.

Even though clock time varies by four and a half hours from Newfoundland to British Columbia, Canadians celebrate and despair over Stanley Cup and Olympic hockey goals at the exactly same time.[27]

Hockey as Artistic Representation of Canada

Hugh MacLennan's *Two Solitudes* contains the comment that Howie Morenz, Aurel Joliat, and their peers 'are about the best artists this country ever turned out.' They just needed a Virgil to versify their combative exploits. If hockey was a latecomer on the Canadian cultural scene, things have changed. Gary Genosko points out that artists have recently discovered hockey as a source of material: 'From the mainstream to the avant-garde, hockey has served as an all-terrain vehicle for the aesthetic explorations of English and French Canadians.' There has been relatively little truly experimental hockey art, but there have been movies about hockey, art installations about the game, even a display of perfectly useful goalie masks at the McMichael Art Gallery's 1981 exhibition 'Soultenders.' The theme of coast-to-coast uniformity in hockey is most commonly felt in the Canadian publishing industry, as dozens of glossy hockey books appear each season.[28]

These books may chronicle and celebrate hockey, but many have in common dissatisfaction with the spectacle of professional hockey, with its million-dollar contracts, strikes, lockouts, and all the offshoots of mammon. Ken Dryden, reflecting on being a professional player, writes in *The Game*:

> It is a different game from the one I played on a driveway twenty-five years ago, grown cluttered and complicated by the life around it, but guileless at its core and still recoverable from time to time.[29]

Dryden's 'still recoverable from time to time' echoes the nostalgia in much hockey fiction. Other writers are less confident that any guileless core can be recovered in NHL hockey. The general feeling is that the playful soul of the game has been lost, with the repercussion that an important part of Canada has also been lost. In a few cases, this has spurred creative acts. Paul Quarrington pessimistically states it was a sense of nostalgia that led him to collect stories for *Original Six: True Stories from Hockey's Classic Era*. 'I'm not mourning the passing of the good old days,' he writes, 'I'm lamenting the lack of good days, period.' Similarly, it was bad NHL hockey that sent Rheostatics rhythm guitarist Dave Bidini into temporary exile and writerdom. His book *Tropic of Hockey: My Search for the Game in Unlikely Places* is a travelogue of his hockey-fuelled journeys to China, the United Arab Emirates, and the Transylvania region of Romania. Disdain for what he viewed as a corrupted form of the professional game led Bidini to wonder, 'What would the game be like so far from its home?' and, more importantly:

> If I were to travel to look for the game in distant lands, would I glimpse our game being born? Would I see it as it had existed at the dawn of the last century? See hockey as it was before it became complicated by economics, corporate lust, the ravages of progress ...?

According to Bidini's and others' books, this soul of Canada's game and, metaphorically, of Canada is to be found away from the madding crowd. The love of hockey perhaps too often means cheering for professionals rather than playing the game ourselves. As will be seen in the next chapter (on escape, freedom, and utopia), hockey fiction longingly seeks out the original, untangled roots of the game.[30]

Eric Zweig's historical novel *Hockey Night in the Dominion of Canada*, about a group of pre-NHL professional hockey players who manage to save Canada by saving the prime minister's life, carefully points out that hockey is both an invented sport, like basketball, and one with hazier folk roots, like soccer:

> ... hockey had been practically born in Montreal. Though the real history of the sport was unclear, the game that fans had come to know traced its roots to Montreal in the mid-1870s.[31]

The first modern game, a well-documented social event with clearly stated rules controlling the action, took place at the Victoria Skating Rink in Montreal on 3 March 1875. We do not know much, however, about what sorts of hockey were played before that match. Though the Montreal game is more or less accepted as the beginning of modern hockey, debate still rages about whether the game as we know it began in Nova Scotia, Quebec, or Ontario (three of the four provinces that formed Canada in 1867). The first puck was used in 1860 in Kingston; the first organized indoor game took place in 1875 in Montreal. In 1867, between these two seminal events, Canada found time for Confederation. The modern form of the game and the nation itself came of age about the same time. In other words, virtually from the start of the game and of Canada, hockey was a national as well as a local pastime. Hockey's universality for Canadians is the main thrust of non-fictional writing on the game. We are generally tuned into hockey as an entire nation, in the manner that Bruce Kidd described tuning into *Hockey*

Night in Canada on television – not everyone in every town will be watching, of course, but every place in Canada will have its hockey-watching contingent.

Long before that Montreal game, and not so long before the *Terror* and the *Erebus* became stuck in the ice on Sir John Franklin's ill-fated search for the Northwest Passage, Franklin mentions the game. In an 1823 letter that reads like fiction, he tempts fate by writing:

> We have, as yet, had no severe weather. We endeavour to keep ourselves in
> good humour, health, and spirits by an agreeable variety of useful occupa-
> tion and amusement. Till the snow fell the game of hockey played on the
> ice was the morning's sport.[32]

Though there are many other reports of hockey being played in the early nineteenth century, Franklin's is apparently the first written instance of the term 'hockey.' Surely no figure as iconic as Franklin referred to the game even later in the century. Though he calls it 'hockey,' this would have been a very rudimentary form of the game, probably more similar to games played in England at the time than the current Canadian obsession. But that English part of the game is conveniently forgotten in the wild fictional and non-fictional search for hockey's genesis.

Hockey is not the only winter sport in Canada. The landscape and climate invite a variety of winter sports, from snowshoeing to Nordic skiing. 'Compared to hockey, writes Laura Robinson, 'these winter sports are intimate acts that connect individuals to the snow and ice.' But unlike hockey, 'they are not seen as being distinctly Canadian, as a way in which this country is defined, both at home and abroad.' In the sporting symbolism typical of national identity – where only one sport 'counts' – enjoying a day on the ski trails is mere recreation; playing (or even watching) hockey is a symbolic affirmation of being Canadian. Though the freezing of water and cow dung is a natural process, playing hockey on ice or using that dung as a puck is not. When hockey is played inside, with refreshments available to all, there is none of the man-versus-nature survival element inherent in sports like mountain-climbing or hiking. But these facts are forgotten in the widespread 'myth of hockey as a "natural" adaptation to ice, snow, and open space.'[33]

Hockey in Canada may be unnatural, but its relative inclusiveness is laudable. If hockey can be linked to nationalism in Canada, it is at least a nationalism based on choice rather than blood, or language (which, though a choice, is difficult to master). One can usually refuse to play this game. This aspect of hockey has been noted to the point of romanticizing by many Canadian writers and intellectuals. To return to Callaghan's essay 'The Game That Makes a Nation,' the writer recalls strolling through his neighbourhood and stopping to watch some children playing street hockey:

> They were all neighbourhood kids, and when a wet shiny face was lifted to the light, it was apt to be round or high cheekboned, or lean and blue-eyed: they were Anglo-Saxon faces and Scandinavian faces and Italian and Slavic faces. On the street that night, though, they were all one, they were just a collection of Canadian kids playing shinny. The game held them all together.

In this passage, the focus shifts from names to physical features, just as it does in Scott Young's adolescent novel *Scrubs on Skates*. A sportswriter observes a team practising and reflects:

> He didn't know how many races there were represented there, but now they were all on one team ... and forever after this season these boys like Wong and Krsyschuk and Big Canoe and Martin would remember the names on this team and know that people of all races could get along when they had something in common, a puck or a ball.

The language in these passages, with the focus on specific and clearly discernible racial features and the stereotypical names like 'Wong' and 'Big Canoe,' is dated. Nevertheless, the superficial message of multi-ethnic harmony remains positive.[34]

Frank Orr's 1982 potboiler *Puck Is a Four-Letter Word* is a comic novel about a ragtag team of semi-talented professionals; it is also probably a more realistic example of past attitudes about 'non-Canadians' (i.e., those who are not from Quebec, or are not Anglo-Saxon) in hockey. As in Scott Young's *Scrubs on Skates*, minorities function as shorthand for the ineptitude of a ragtag hockey team. The father of an Italian player is 'a mobster,' the Czechoslovakian player defected merely 'to get away from his old lady and six kids,' while the black player is 'tougher than pig shit and slower than molasses in January, was married when he was seventeen and has seven kids.'[35] The novel is a humorous critique of professional hockey culture that jokingly subverts hockey's holy aura,

but it is unsettling that Orr uses racial stereotypes to build his case. At
the same time, the novel's vulgar tone is perhaps a better reflection of
hockey culture than messages of harmony are.

Michael Robidoux argues that hockey became Canada's game partly
due to late nineteenth-century prejudice. The early athletic clubs in
Montreal, the hub of mainstream Canadian sports culture at that time,
were too economically and ethnically exclusive. Gentlemen who did not
grow up speaking English, or listening to sermons in English, were not
welcome on the lacrosse team. In contrast, 'hockey was accessible to
men of various ethnic and class backgrounds, and thus, to a greater
degree than lacrosse, it became a game of the people.'[36] It has subsequently been embraced as a symbol of the nation – sometimes
lamented, often applauded, but always acknowledged as a ready indicator of Canadianness.

Chapter Two

The Hockey Dream:
Hockey as Escape, Freedom, Utopia

Backyards are for fantasy and play; rinks are for aspirations and making it.
Ken Dryden and Roy MacGregor, *Home Game*, p. 71

Canadian culture idealizes hockey as a play space that is always and necessarily fun. This chapter examines depictions of hockey as an escape from daily life that takes us into the free, limitless world of dreams. It also considers the opposite: literary examples of when hockey ceases to be fun and when happy dreams turn into nightmares. Beginning with an explanation of the standard Canadian hockey dream, this chapter looks at utopian philosophical conceptions of play by theorists such as Johan Huizinga, Roger Caillois, and Bernard Suits, as well as at how adopting a professional, or overly serious, attitude corrupts these ideals. I then provide definitions of shinny while considering this more chaotic game's importance to the Canadian imagination, before examining other sorts of dream-like hockey themes. These are: the joy of escaping the confines of organized, over-regulated play; the pleasure of becoming something else while playing hockey; searching for hockey's playful essence; defying gravity on the ice; and, finally, the liberating effects of taking the game from the confining arena back outside.

For many parents and children in Canada, fulfilling the hockey dream is understood as making the National Hockey League, the world's premier professional league. This is by far the preferred brand of hockey in North America, and even Europe's top leagues recognize the NHL's prowess. If a player makes it to the NHL for even a single game, he has made it, in the same way that a hometown cyclist achieves lifelong fame by completing the Tour de France. In addition to the

celebrity status bestowed on a professional player, there is the widespread belief that playing professionally means never having to toil at an
unpleasant job. NHLers receive a paycheque for doing something the
rest of us do for free, or pay to do. 'We were all going to make the NHL
when I was ten or eleven,' writes David Adams Richards in his non-
fictional *Hockey Dreams: Memories of a Man Who Couldn't Play.*[1] The dream
is individual yet typical and axiomatic. Each child playing alongside
Richards on New Brunswick's frozen Miramichi River had similar aspirations about a career in hockey, and the ambitions were no different
for young players across the country. This specific concept of what it
means to make it in hockey is a constant in the male Canadian imagination, where the NHL represents hockey salvation.

   In contrast to widespread Canadian views of hockey glory, recent
hockey fiction rarely depicts professional leagues as a utopia. A financial
windfall, yes; heaven, no. The idealized play spirit does not make its
home in the upper echelons of the sport. Conceptualizations of play are
tightly connected to freedom, a freedom which is lost when a professional attitude towards the game enters. When the focus of play is on
wages or other rewards extrinsic to the game, the rink is transformed
from a place of enjoyment into one of strictures and control. The
hockey novel that most clearly exhibits an immoderately professional
attitude towards play and games is Roy MacGregor's *The Last Season.*
Felix Batterinski ('The Happy Batterer') makes his living as an on-ice
fighter who thrives for the Philadelphia Flyers in the fight-happy NHL
of the 1970s. MacGregor's novel, first published in 1983, represented a
watershed in Canadian sports fiction because it was a literary effort that
neither followed the traditional plot nor tried to perpetuate an entirely
rosy hockey mythology; it is for this reason that I devote a fair amount
of space to it. As shall be seen, Batterinski blatantly contradicts more
pleasant and Edenic views of the relation between play and games,
between enjoyment and the hockey rink, because he does not know
how to play in the traditional sense.

   While most reflections on hockey, fictional or not, are happy ones, it
is less-structured versions of the game that offer the most alluring
descriptions. Whereas 'organized hockey is about following instruc-
tions,' more relaxed hockey can be 'a game of endless variety, spontaneity, adaptation, and unspoken rituals ... [that] lends itself to an
often beautiful creativity.'[2] As hockey moves from overly organized
teams towards the near-chaos of shinny or pond hockey, the enjoyment
level rises exponentially. Everyone can play, risky rushes or save attempts

that would be punished in other hockey environments are encouraged, and what Johan Huizinga called the 'magic circle' of play, with its utopian characteristics of timelessness and freedom, is more likely to appear. All games and sports require rules, but the abundance of rules and stifling strategies (such as the neutral zone trap or playing dump-and-chase) in organized hockey can easily crush spontaneity and any sense of freedom or escape. Shinny is a foil to professional or high-level hockey, and the hockey fiction interpreted in this chapter consistently shows that the real fun begins in less-regulated varieties of hockey.

As its title indicates, Lawrence Scanlan's study *Grace under Fire: The State of Our Sweet and Savage Game* condemns aspects of hockey culture. Recalling his own playing experience, however, Scanlan writes, 'The rink is all about freedom; I do not remember cold.' Remembered enjoyment has overwhelmed and erased the unsavoury from Scanlan's boyhood memories. This sort of nostalgia reigns throughout hockey writing, and not only because lovers of the game are the only ones who write books about it. (Hockey writing is thus less balanced than political commentaries or studies of history. Anti-hockey bias results in literary silence, not skewering words on the page.) Such reminiscing highlights the positive, while playing down or simply ignoring the negative – whether that negative is something as bothersome as the cold or as gratuitous as on-ice violence. When Scanlan evokes 'freedom,' he is recalling the hockey he actually played, but this same mode of remembering exists for fans that never played the game on ice.[3]

This nostalgic belief that things were better in the old days is the same whether one was playing or watching. Dave Bidini's non-fiction *Tropic of Hockey* provides a prime example of how freedom has left the ice. He recalls a playoff game in which neither team took risks, wryly recording what happens when teams flee defeat instead of playing to win:

> The play volleyed from blue line to blue line. Both the Red Wings and Capitals were employing the Trap, a form of hockey which is the athletic equivalent of playing [the simplistic video game] Pong.

Perhaps a younger person watching the same game would look back on it years later and remember it more favourably. After all, as Ken Dryden writes in *The Game*, 'the "golden age of sports," the golden age of anything, is the age of everyone's childhood.' This is partly an echo of the conservative belief that childhood is a romantic, magical period in one's life, but there is also a more mundane reason: never having seen the great players of the past, young fans have no yardstick for comparison. They lack experienced hockey history and have only statistics – and handed-down tales – to help them compare today's heroes with those of the past. As the ancient King Leary in Paul Quarrington's novel of the same name states, with the wisdom of a fool, 'Numbers and mathematics got no place in the game of hockey.' Leary steadfastly refuses to acknowledge a new star, ridiculing him because he is 'out to smash all the numbers in the record book, as if numbers could defend themselves.' In our mind's eye, hockey players of all generations compete against each other, thus adding a subjective, aesthetic angle to the hockey story.[4]

A favourite Canadian moan is that the NHL has declined, and nobody moans more convincingly than Mordecai Richler. In 'The Fall of the Montreal Canadiens,' he recites the common refrain that hockey was better in the past. Nowadays,

> the players ... are fat, indolent, and overpaid. Frenetic expansion, obviously fed by avarice rather than regard for tradition, has all but ruined a fine institution. The season is horrendously long and the present playoff system an unacceptable joke.

Claiming that players are less fit now than in the past is simply not true, and this passage is typical Richleresque tongue-in-cheek criticism. After furnishing an epic list of hockey's malaises, Richler continues: 'And yet – and yet – Saturday night is still *Hockey Night in Canada*. Diminished or not ... my eyes [are] fixed on the television set.' For hockey-mad Richler, tuning out is not an option, even if more edifying cultural options are available on other channels, and even if his team has seemingly decayed beyond redemption. The curmudgeonly narrator in Richler's novel *Barney's Version* laments a similar decline. When he watches 'the new, improved, no-talent, chickenshit Canadiens ..., each one a multimillionaire,' he longs for the days of

> fire-wagon hockey. Soft but accurate passes. Fast-as-lightning wrist shots. Defencemen who could hit. And no ear-piercing rock music played at 10,000 decibels while a face-off was held up for a TV commercial.

Barney longs for a time when commercial interests did not dominate the game, when the live game did not have to be stopped for the sake of television, and when there was no sense that fans had to be stimulated constantly by extraneous entertainment. In spite of this, Barney still attends the games in person. Though they are of different generations, Scanlan, Bidini, Richler, and his literary alter-ego Barney all sun themselves in the same rays of nostalgia.[5]

Eric Zweig's novel *Hockey Night in the Dominion of Canada* takes place before the First World War, before the NHL and Barney's beloved Canadiens. Yet the novel ends with a similar sort of sorrow. Anticipating the hockey economics that forced NHL teams to move away from smaller television markets in the 1990s, the narrator sighs, 'Gone forever were the carefree days ... when small towns like Renfrew [Ontario] could capture the hearts of a nation in their quest for ... the Stanley Cup.' Here, as so often in later accounts of professional sport, Zweig's narrator bewails big money's effects on hockey.[6] The difference, however, is that this novel predates any personally remembered experience of hockey, and it is thus a purely literary or textual nostalgia. More importantly in light of Canada's reverence for the National Hockey League, there is a suggestion that the loss of hockey with which fans can truly and intimately connect coincides with the birth of the NHL – rather than expansion from the Original Six teams.

Nostalgia is probably the strongest tendency in hockey culture, and it exists for the most part outside of what the television commentators tell us about the game. *Hockey Night in Canada* may deal in tradition and legacies, but, for obvious marketing reasons, it rarely argues that hockey was better in the old days; instead, it inserts modern hockey into a glorious tradition. In a throwback to the days before radio and television, it is primarily print culture and conversation that produces this popular nostalgia. As anthropologist Philip Moore argues, such discourse 'finds value in the remembered or imagined past. Nostalgia is a way of giving meaning to the past, of attributing a personal significance to historical narratives.' When these feelings are harnessed for hegemonic or commercial purposes, nostalgia's appeal wanes. It is, however, usually harmless to produce nostalgic hockey memories by suppressing details such as the cold or the odd painful puck in the knee, or by claiming that the players were better, the game more free in the old days. Moore continues,

> When Canadians write about hockey they write more about themselves than about the game. It is about identities constructed through the game, the sentimental memories of growing up and learning about life and what it is to be Canadian.

Moore emphasizes that most hockey writing intersects the individual with the national by celebrating personal hockey memories within the wider metaphorical framework of hockey as an emblem of Canadianness. No matter who is writing, the hockey story is really about the individual holding the pen.[7]

Brian Kennedy writes in *Growing Up Hockey*, his memoirs about his career as a mediocre child hockey player before he moved to the United States, 'What makes these stories interesting is that my stories are also your stories, tales that have been tucked away in your memory...' The tone here is precisely that of the first story in Stephen Leacock's 1912 *Sunshine Sketches of a Little Town*: 'I don't know if you know Mariposa. If not, it is of no consequence, for if you know Canada at all, you are probably well acquainted with a dozen towns just like it.' The days of *Sunshine Sketches*, with its steam trains and sinking pleasure boats and small-town Canada, are past, and much of urbanized Canada can better identify with hockey.[8]

Sports are widely believed to reveal character because reactions and retaliations on the playing field are immediate. They also develop character in ways that might not be positive, and Peter Gzowski wonders whether paternalistic and often sexist 'attitudes, formed on the rinks and rivers and sloughs, have not stayed with us into our marriages and our boardrooms.' Hockey culture clearly moulds the individual in some way, yet writers of hockey memoirs and sketches rarely show exactly how the self develops through hockey (hockey novels, on the whole, depict characters damaged through their affiliation with hockey). If, as Moore claims, 'Canadians write more about themselves' than the game, it is always with an eye to collective identity. In this sense, hockey writing is more a matter of memoirs than autobiography – with hockey's constancy, rather than fleeting events, as the focus. The self exists solely as a function of the game and, as Gzwoski's inclusive 'rinks and rivers and sloughs' states, where and when that game was played is secondary. There is nothing specific about the backyard hockey described in Ken Dryden's *The Game* ('we could move across the asphalt quickly and with great agility in rubber "billy" boots'), the outdoor hockey on the Miramichi River depicted in David Adams Richards's *Hockey Dreams* (where, come April, one 'might suddenly spy fifteen kids wandering about on the Miramichi River, on ice floes, with hockey sticks, looking like trapped penguins'), the slough in Robert Harlow's novel *The Saxophone Winter* ('a stinking mess' until winter, when 'it was solid black ice under a fresh covering of snow'), or the outdoor rinks in Frank Paci's novel *Icelands* ('As soon as they started playing they forgot their real names [and] it became fun and silly at the same time'). What these varieties of recreational hockey do have in common is a form of play in which the individual self is subsumed into the playful collective.[9]

Utopian Ideals and Conceptions of Play

In addition to the myth of hockey's intrinsic Canadianness, wistful remembering depends on idealistic views of games, play, and sport. Play and play spaces are Edenic or utopian because they are commonly (and erroneously) thought to be absolutely and happily separated from the workaday world of daily life. Entering a hockey arena means passing into another realm of existence in which the usual societal rules do not apply. Though not always enclosed, the baseball diamond and the football field exist as a virtual other space, not unlike a church or amusement park. When players take over a frozen pond to start a game of hockey, they temporarily colonize it for the sake of fun, enjoyment, and a slice of paradise. It is a stepping-back into a mythical time, or at least an attempt at escapism. In fact, Neil Earle argues that hockey is analogous to religion insofar as a 'prerequisite to understanding hockey in Canada is the Paradisiacal Myth.'[10]

In Steve Lundin's *When She's Gone*, a rollicking hockey novel about two brothers who travel through Great Britain by canoe in order to attend a hockey try-out in Wales, the narrator presents the delight of escaping problems by going to the hockey arena. He describes how everyone comes together as a community as they watch a professional game in 1970s Winnipeg. All spectators at the arena are both 'in and out of the real world,' away from 'the kitchen arguments, dying parents, dying children, alcohol haze, fists in the face, midnight tears …'[11] This is a uniquely double-existence because the fans temporarily forget one type of reality and replace it with another. Since the deceiver hockey is an authentic rather than simulated entertainment option, they are not denying reality in the manner of a video game or narcotic stupor. Lundin's extreme examples are a grim reminder that this escape is temporary: sickness, domestic violence, and anguish will still be there when the game ends. Sports are a distraction, a respite from the real world that is a secluded area in which the player (and even spectator) is not subject to the vicissitudes of real life. The rules are clear, understood, and accepted even by the penalty-takers. This means that spectators and players think they can better comprehend the importance of and motives for victory and defeat on the ice than the murky motives behind the 'midnight tears' and 'dying.' Lundin's list of serious problems makes fans' desire to forget entirely understandable; hiding from our existential shadows for a brief spell is comforting.

Don Gutteridge's *Bus-Ride*, which takes place just before the Second World War and focuses on a rising young hockey star, includes a very similar passage of small-town jubilation after a hockey game. The difference in Gutteridge is that there is a greater focus on togetherness and community, precisely because the townspeople all know each other and the players on the ice:

> So the victory was to be shared, the triumph communal. And in the sharing
> and the spontaneous approbation of their applause, all the petty human
> divisiveness, the pain of ordinary days, the long dream-distorted nights, the
> memories of Wars on far-away ground, the half-healed scars – all that
> divides us from each other and ourselves faded with the blending voice,
> the harmony of the universal cheer.

Although the examples are as extreme as in Lundin, there is an aesthetic quality attributed to the game, which augments the sense of healing. The hockey arena becomes a choir loft as 'harmony' emerges from the chaos of individual pain and pettiness. The experience is all the more magical because it is 'spontaneous.'[12]

Of course, hockey is not just a means of escaping daily life. The memory of the hockey one played or watched in youth is supported by particular concepts of play as an essentially good feeling or experience. But what is play? And how is it related to games and sports? Is the child forced onto the ice by dad really playing? In addressing questions like these, Brian Sutton-Smith's *The Ambiguity of Play* begins with the simple observation that though 'we all know what playing feels likes ..., when it comes to making theoretical statements about what play is, we fall into silliness.' We may as well ask the lion to tell us what prey is. Philosopher Eugen Fink avoids silliness by arguing that 'play is an essential element of man's ontological makeup' and 'a basic existential phenomenon, just as primordial and autonomous as death, love, work and struggle for power.' Play is thus an essential part of all of us, which is why someone who does not know how to play is less than human. The view that play is part of our 'ontological makeup' is in direct contradiction to the idea of play as escape.[13]

In English the terms 'play,' 'game,' and 'sport' are often used synonymously. Whereas games and sports have strictly determined rules, it is perhaps most useful to think of play as an often dormant mood that activates us from time to time. It is, after all, possible to feel playful even when doing the dishes or shovelling snow. While definitions exist that clearly delineate what constitutes a sport or game, the semantic field of play is less charted. Formal definitions of hockey entail that even if all players are having a terrible time and therefore not playing per se, one cannot deny that a game is taking place. In contrast, if we regard play as an attitude or a mood, the playing stops when the good mood ends. We may continue to participate in the sport or game, but the removal of all enjoyment means that we are playing in the transitive sense, like a child forced to play the piano. If 'for "play" we can substitute the expression "doing things we value for their own sake,"'[14] then it makes little sense to claim that sport is exactly the same thing as play. Play is autotelic because, unlike sport, it has its purpose (or *telos*) within itself. While humans have always played, the games and sports dreamed up for the sake of fun change continuously. A child playfully and repeatedly throwing a teddy from crib does not belong in the same categorical box as games or sports. The urge to play is much broader than any game or sport. The attraction of hockey is that it encourages play moods, not that it is always play.

The goal here is not to label play definitively or provide an extensive overview of the various philosophical positions on play, but to articulate the silenced background of the nostalgia and utopian images in hockey writing. Many contemporary and popular beliefs about play are in line with Johan Huizinga's 1938 *Homo Ludens*, the first important modern examination of play. His main argument is that competitive play is a significant cultural catalyst, and that, as a result of the competitive nature of play, 'civilization arises and unfolds in and as play.' Huizinga defines play as a voluntary activity or occupation executed within certain fixed limits of time and place, according to rules freely accepted but absolutely binding, having its aim in itself and accompanied by a feeling of tension, joy, and the consciousness that it differs from everyday, ordinary life. This dovetails with popular views on play as something we do after the work is done. By describing play as being 'distinct from "ordinary" life both as to locality and duration,' Huizinga establishes a binary. Play exists only in opposition to work or separate from the rest of life. There are problems with this theory, and Huizinga has come under attack for a variety of reasons. For example, play theorist Jacques

Ehrmann says Huizinga 'delimit[ed] too categorically the sphere of play by opposing it to the real, to work, and so forth.' Wrong or not, this is the escapism so common in hockey literature and sporting culture in general.[15] Outside of this idealistic mental framework, hockey nostalgia would be difficult to produce.

The French thinker Roger Caillois wrote the other grand book of play theory most relevant to this study. Though heavily indebted to Huizinga, Caillois begins with a critique of his forerunner. He says Huizinga's definition of play focuses too much on competition and rules and is therefore simultaneously too broad and too narrow. It is, for example, difficult to accept Huizinga's contention that both law and war are forms of play just because they are governed by competition and rules. The sport-war parallel is made by lovers and haters of hockey alike, but this parallel is symbolic because hockey is at best a playful imitation of war – as the journalists who write headlines like 'War on Ice' are hopefully aware. For Caillois, play is no junk-room for anything that happens to have rules. Caillois divided games into four categories:

1) *agon*: competitive games won through skill and strength (e.g., hockey, wrestling)
2) *alea*: games of chance (e.g., gambling, tossing a coin), in which fate, luck, or fortune determines the winner
3) *mimicry*: simulacrum or make-believe (e.g., theatrical games, children playing 'house')
4) *ilinx*: games of vertigo that upset our usual physical stability through bewilderment (e.g., alpinism, hang-gliding).

Though hockey most obviously belongs to the category of *agon* and the ruling principle of the sport is always 'may the best team win,' Caillois's other three categories are also present. There is an omnipresent element of chance in sport: hitting three goalposts and losing by a goal is decidedly unlucky. Designed to slide easily along the ice, the flat, cylindrical hockey puck simultaneously encourages whimsical hops and unpredictable bounces (*alea*) when it careens off boards and skates. Tom McSorley argues this randomness makes hockey all the more attractive to Canadians: 'Hockey is full of accidents, random physical possibilities occurring at blinding speed; it lacks the more predictable tensions and premeditations of American sports like football and baseball.' Dressing or suiting up to play hockey also adds a touch of Halloween as individual identity is relegated to team identity, and grown men are temporarily transformed into Panthers or Mighty Ducks (this *mimicry*, or make-believe, becomes even more obvious when amateurs don uniforms with names of professionals emblazoned across the back). Finally, there is a whisper of *ilinx* akin to mountain-climbing when players sprint about the ice on thin skate-blades. Part of the exhilaration for less able skaters – especially adults – is giving up stability.[16]

Caillois's and Huizinga's theories have their shortcomings, especially as regards the idealization of play as a special world separated from everyday life, but they cannot be dismissed outright. These theories feed sports discourse, including Canadian beliefs about hockey that are as tenacious as myths. That a myth may not be true is less important than the effects that myth has, and in this case the myth is that hockey is pure, uncorrupted, and therefore perfect play. Michael Oriard writes that mythical thinking in much American sports literature 'celebrates the ideal of sport without acknowledging at all the intrusion of a less-than-ideal real world.'[17] There are, of course, exceptions south of the border, but contemporary Canadian hockey fiction rejects such celebration.

In his seminal work *The Grasshopper: Games, Life, and Utopia*, philosopher Bernard Suits sets out to determine theoretically what games are all about. The hero in this series of philosophical dialogues is the Grasshopper, 'the same Grasshopper whom Aesop made everlastingly famous as the model of improvidence' because he did not prepare for winter. The playful Grasshopper would surely be more pleasant company than the fable's diligent, moralistic Ant; Suits makes the Grasshopper the hero because that insect martyrs himself to play. This is entirely in line with Friedrich Schiller's observation that we are most fully human when at play because only then are we freed from the constraints that control so much of our lives. Suits argues that, for the Grasshopper, 'Utopian existence is fundamentally concerned with game-playing,' and games provide him with a space to be entirely himself.[18] To twist the quotation: 'utopian Canadian existence is fundamentally concerned with hockey-playing.' Hockey as a higher, *better* reality is a red thread in hockey writing, and even when the words on the page contradict this myth, it lingers in the background.

The Taint of Professionalism

Hockey fiction often focuses on high-level players whose entire identity is determined by the game. These are players like Drinkwater in Mark

Anthony Jarman's 1997 novel *Salvage King, Ya!* and the long-retired Leary in Paul Quarrington's *King Leary*, or even many of the young stars in Frank Paci's *Icelands* (1999), who play(ed) amateur hockey in hopes that they will one day turn their skills into concrete gains. In each case, the attitude is professional because the game is, or can become, a career. The 'professional player' is a seemingly paradoxical term because one suspects that remuneration is the *primary* aim. Marshall McLuhan (echoing the utopian Canadian assumptions about hockey) claims that there is a 'contradiction in "professional" sport. When the games door opening into the free life leads into a merely specialist job, everybody senses an incongruity.' The feeling that something is not quite right arises because traditional play theory dictates that any bene- fits be secondary. Improved physical fitness, or even finding friendship on the ice, are incidental to hockey and therefore acceptable within an idealized concept of play. However, if the game serves 'some ulterior purpose,' it represents a 'degradation' or 'corruption of sport,' as Christopher Lasch writes. In other words, it is not seriousness that damages the play spirit but a concern for perks beyond the playing field. Both Lasch's and McLuhan's criticisms of professional sport more or less assume that play and sport are the same thing: at the same time, they imply that professionals play *only* for money. The school game 'dodge ball,' also revealingly called 'murder ball,' may qualify as a sport, but when the class systematically targets one child, he or she knows it is not play. As a character in Zweig's *Hockey Night in the Dominion of Canada* declares after some shoddy results on the ice: 'From now on ... there will be less emphasis on fun and games and more on hockey.'[19]

Mark Anthony Jarman's short story 'Righteous Speedboat' portrays the world of professional hockey as a joyless dystopia, at least for those beyond the NHL pale. It takes place in a 'loser bar,' where a would-be professional player watches the NHL draft in the company of others who are down on their luck. But even here, the talented player is nothing special: the bartender had also been an NHL prospect, until injury ruined his career. Every bar in Canada can produce patrons who claim, sometimes legitimately, to have almost made the big leagues. Jarman takes the reader into the border area between skilled amateurs and professional players as the bar and the television set assume their rightful places as focal points of Canadian hockey culture. The narrator / potential draft pick gazes longingly at the Gorgon television as (in his view) less talented players are selected:

Even now the vibrating screen maims the very molecules of my eyes but
how I have to gaze. How many beserkers, how many peckerwood imposters
will they call to the silver microphone before they call to me ...?

The narrator will not be drafted because he once punched a former
coach and has therefore been blackballed by the hockey world.[20] By
focusing on professional hockey as a tight circle of comrades, the story
provides a biting commentary on the milieu of professional sports. It
also shows the downside of what happens when money and sport
collide, not least the effects this has on the also-rans who do not make
the NHL after sacrificing their youth to the dream.

In addition to the tragic sense of unfulfilled destiny, there is also the
minor tragedy of a character who clearly feels his life is already over at
an age when his peers would just be entering the work world, or starting university. The bartender with injured knees is now an alcoholic:
'Wheelbarrows of cash will alter anyone, but he's been changed by the
cash he never got, by what could have been that draft year.' In an atmosphere that should be pure competition based on skill and talent – the
various NHL teams pick the best players available in the draft – Jarman
highlights the aspect of chance, of the near-miss. This is a far cry from
Caillois's contained and limited *alea* of the game world because there
are drastic consequences for the rest of the players' lives. If not for his
serious injury, the bartender 'could have been the one under the blinding television lights, the one getting offered a million seven.' No longer
in control of his hockey destiny, the narrator, meanwhile, is an anxious
gambler in this 'hexed process, this amateur hour crapshoot.'[21]

But chance plays an even larger role in 'Righteous Speedboat.' The
narrator has recently survived a car crash that killed his friend Ryan. If
appellation confirms existence, Ryan comes back from the dead as his
name is called (those calling the shots obviously do not yet know that
Ryan has died). In the system of professional hockey, there is no room
for those who break unwritten rules on authority: 'I knew I would not
be drafted, as I knew they would take a dead man before they would
take a player who clocked a coach.'[22] The figurative expression about
preferring 'a dead man' becomes literal when Ryan is drafted, and with
that the story moves from a tragic background to a grotesque present.
Punching the coach precluded any NHL hockey career, and in his
mind, one instant of hot-headedness ruined the narrator's life. Even the
law tends to look more generously or compassionately when it comes to

teenagers who have committed a minor transgression. Professional hockey circles are less forgiving and more prone to damning.

Jarman's story is enriched by references to real NHL players, teams, and historical events. Most Canadian readers will recognize the infamous case of Quebec Nordiques draftee Eric Lindros, who refused to play in *la belle province*. The reason, most outside of Quebec felt, was the simple fact that Lindros wanted more money than the Nordiques could offer. Jarman incorporates this into the story but comments also on less visible instances of greed:

> Everyone thinks Lindros is a greedy arrogant asshole but meanwhile the team's owner is mulling over juicy offers of seventy-five million U.S. dollars for the franchise ... The owner will cry all the way to the bank. Who's the greedy asshole then?

In the ongoing battle between allegedly overpaid players and owners who make money off the backs of those players, the narrator clearly sides with the players. He cites another real-life example, asking rhetorically, 'What did our pal [Edmonton Oilers owner] Peter Pocklington get for selling Gretzky to Los Angeles, for selling a person, a *human being*?' Only now does it apparently dawn on the narrator that professional hockey is a world of human commodities. Overt self-pity clashes with overt self-praise and bravado when this realization occurs: 'They don't care about my plus-minus, they don't care about my Grade Eight blues records or sensitive feelings or that I move like silt and stick like glue.' Focusing on the records he had in the eighth grade, as opposed to the hockey records which interest team management, suggests arrested development. Those who plan on playing for a living do not have, or are ultimately unable, to grow up. Aiming at a professional hockey career is a dangerous career game: developing hockey skills can leave one incapable of doing much else.[23] Not exactly dream material.

Fred Stenson's short story 'Teeth' also examines the incongruity of sport and professionalism. The title refers to the narrator's full set of teeth, to his lack of a 'hockey smile.' The hero, Burns, is a talented but cautious player. He explains how he has managed to preserve his lovely smile:

> My secret is regular brushing, flossing and a total avoidance of anything resembling a fight, an elbow or a high stick. It was once said of me by a smart-ass reporter that I could go into the corners with fresh eggs in my hockey pants and never break one. So what? It's true.[24]

The reporter's insult is a cliché indicating a lack of aggression (often euphemistically called 'heart,' 'spirit,' or willingness to 'take one for the team'). By refusing to play the game like the rest of his teammates, Burns is a hockey misfit in these professional surroundings.

Burns has no illusions about his professional career and is oblivious to salubrious play myths. Not concerned about play ideals, dreams of hockey glory, and the quest to make the NHL, Burns is a hero in search of a narrative. A romantic narrative of hockey success cannot exist if the star player refuses to acknowledge the importance of his professional surroundings and lot in life:

> They say that some people play this game for fun. I personally can't imagine it and suspect this of being something cooked up by the owners and the press. I do have a foggy recollection of thirteen-year-old kids flailing away on corner lots in the freezing cold for reasons other than money or coercion, but I also know that I was never one of them.

His motivation for playing professionally is money, and he started playing for an equally clear reason: his parent made him play. During a melee, Burns absent-mindedly 'skate[s] around the perimeter of the six fights now in progress, trying to look as unmenacing as possible.' He begins to drift mentally as well, thinking about a girl he knew when he was thirteen – an obvious symbol of the childhood he missed through his forced devotion to hockey, and another hint at stunted development. An opposing player is 'frustrated to total insanity by the faraway, seraphic smile' on this spoilsport's face and 'drives the top of his helmet into [his] mouth.' Both break unwritten hockey rules: one by refusing aggression, the other by being improperly aggressive. Burns loses a tooth and immediately begins to reconsider his career options, looking to life after hockey, to the future instead of to the past. In hockey circles, a lost tooth is a minor injury, and giving up the NHL for the sake of a smile is a type of vanity:

> Somehow, every time I lick up under my swollen lip, I am reminded of this near future and the many sources from which money can come. Money, unlike teeth, can be replenished. A missing tooth is a hole in the head for life.

The deadpan conclusion to this comic story rings proverbial, almost like a warning to younger players, and 'Teeth' thus ends with a coming-to-clarity. By turning away from hockey, the narrator repairs the intellectual shortcoming, that other 'hole in the head,' that kept him playing a game he did not like.[25] After all, mandated play is not play proper, and even as he, externally, lives out the Canadian dream – and in contrast to Suits's frolicking Grasshopper – he is untrue to himself. In this story, professional hockey means literally and figuratively giving up one's smile.

Using hockey to gain rewards beyond the ice negates the ideal of play as a 'magic circle' we inhabit just for the fun of it, with no extrinsic motivation and no consequences after the game ends. While professional players may have fun while playing, they are always aware of the score, the need to perform for spectators, the scrutinizing talent scouts and coaches who watch and ultimately allow them to play. This means that their play is never entirely carefree and that they are less likely to be taken over by, or to lose themselves in, the game. Their hockey is usually controlled or constrained by the need to perform, both in the sense of playing to the best of their abilities and in putting on a show for others (excitement that may well provide ample compensation). This is arguably already a corruption of the play attitude that emphasizes freedom, spontaneity, and, above all, enjoyment.

The most corrupted play attitude is Felix Batterinski's in Roy MacGregor's *The Last Season*. Batterinski is so far removed from playing for the fun of it, playing for 'nothing' or without purpose, that he is unable to differentiate between exhibition games and league games. Having worn out his welcome in the NHL, battling Batterinski, a fighter or 'goon,' ends up in Finland as player/coach of the dismal Tapiola Hauki. There he offers his players monetary bonuses for aggressive play: 'twenty-five Finnmarks for solid body contact, double for a hit where the opponent ends up on his butt.'[26] He had wanted to reward those who fought, but the league's strict anti-fighting rules made this impractical because any benefits would be undercut by harsh penalties. Since the Finnish team was aware of Batterinski's reputation and penalty-filled NHL history when they hired him, they carry some of the blame. They had no illusions about Batterinski. The problem lies in this fighting machine's inability to temper or adjust his way of playing in any way. When the team travels to Sweden for a goodwill exhibition game, an official reminds Batterinski that the game has no effect on the team's standing in the Finnish league and that the bonus for aggressive play is therefore not needed. More significantly, the on-ice benefits of intimidating the Swedish team would be negated by the embarrassment of having played dirty. The game's purpose is neither to win nor to have fun but to represent Finland in a way that pleases the diplomats (proof that the world of games is rarely divorced from the world of politics).

Bernard Suits has written that, although 'game-playing very often *is* playing,' 'there is no logical relationship whatever between playing and playing games.' Batterinski is beyond the danger of confusing the two. 'As far as I'm concerned, this is a game,' says Batterinski to the team official before the Sweden game, meaning the monetary bonus for aggressive play will remain, even at the expense of the team's reputation in international, friendly play. For Batterinski there is only one type of game, and there are no varying levels of frivolity, or occasions when aggressive play and playing to win should be secondary goals. When a Finnish official gently reminds him that this game is 'not one that counts,' the underlying plea for non-violence is lost on the Canadian. 'I have him now,' thinks Batterinski, before asking, 'Then why are we playing it?' This rhetorical question shows Batterinski's greenness in political matters and simultaneously exposes the hypocrisy – at least in terms of idealizations of play – of playing for political gain.[27]

Batterinski perceives playing a game as trying to win at all costs, with no regard for limits. Having played aggressively and usually violently all his life, and having been rewarded constantly for this, he cannot suddenly begin playing differently. Nor can he conceive of the political gesture of goodwill between Finland and Sweden and the potential political fallout of an on-ice fiasco. Batterinski's political naïveté is an understandable corollary of his sense that real life is on the ice, in the supposedly apolitical game world. Through Batterinski, who is often confused and bewildered when not on the ice, MacGregor shows the contrast between the ordered world of hockey and the relative disorder of the rest of life. If the spoilsport ruins the magic of play by refusing to respect the constitutive rules,[28] Batterinski kills it through an utter lack of levity. Unable to understand intrinsic play, Batterinski is devoid of the play-mood and therefore less than human.

Batterinski's attitude towards play, sports, and games is illuminating in its extremeness, and it is hard to see anything utopian about Batterinski's world. Having formally fulfilled the conditions of the Canadian dream, his behaviour and way of thinking subvert that dream. Games are the axle of his life, yet his violent manner of play and the absence of fun in his games are clearly not the stuff of dreams or myth. Batterinski is close to being a caricature, but he effectively portrays the intemperance that certain professional or highly organized hockey nurtures. In literary representations, professional hockey is rarely a glorious play realm.

Shinny: Playing beyond the Rules

Happy hockey memories in print seem to require physical participation as well as an absence of professionalism. Much hockey writing expresses a longing to escape the restrictions of organized hockey by playing a different variety of the game. The game exists in what Michael Robidoux calls 'vernacular forms,' and we play it on backyard rinks, or ponds, or sloughs, or even asphalt. This less-regulated sort of hockey, commonly called 'shinny,' is the participatory form with which Canadians most intimately connect. As Daniel Sanger writes,

> In the unwritten code of pickup hockey, democracy is primordial: anyone
> who shows up gets to play. If a player isn't very good, the game might whir
> around them at a dizzying speed. But once they pick up a loose puck or are
> fed a pass, the game will decelerate abruptly. They'll be allowed to skate a
> little, take a shot, or make a pass themselves.

Shinny nourishes the most nostalgic descriptions of the national game. It is looked upon with utopian eyes as a space of pure bliss.[29]

Doug Beardsley writes in 'The Sheer Joy of Shinny,' a chapter of his 1987 book *Country on Ice*, 'Everyone who ever played hockey has memories of shinny called pond hockey, street hockey, or boot hockey, depending on what part of the country you grew up in.' The Canadian identification with shinny is more comprehensive than with organized hockey because games like 'street hockey' or 'boot hockey' are open to all and do not cut off those who cannot afford team registration. In literature, those who play organized hockey often play shinny on their days off. (In Eric Zweig's *Hockey Night in the Dominion of Canada*, Fred 'Cyclone' Taylor joins in a shinny game on the Rideau Canal – temporarily forgetting his date to join in the fun with the little boys whom he has heard crowing, 'I'm Fred Taylor!')[30] Canadian boardroom and barroom culture is rife with anecdotes of professional hockey stars brightening local shinny games among the plebs. Shinny provides a forum in which fun, enjoyment, and the spirit of play are promoted by inclusion, lack of pressure, and spontaneity.

Merriam-Webster's Collegiate Dictionary defines 'shinny' as 'a variation of hockey played by children with a curved stick and a ball or block of wood.' In Canadian English this definition is delightfully inaccurate – yet even its inaccuracies hint at the attraction of the game. Whereas hockey is played with a round puck made of vulcanized rubber of a specific size (2.5 cm high, 7.6 cm in diameter), this definition of shinny asserts it can be played with either 'a ball or block of wood.' In fact, anything that is handy can substitute for a puck. Tennis balls are highly recommended, but everything from lumps of coal to small rocks to temperature-sensitive 'road apples' will do. Roy MacGregor recalls a group of NHL players who 'would even play hockey using a dead rat as a puck.' Roch Carrier's short 1968 novel *La Guerre, Yes Sir!* includes a scene in which village boys play shinny with the severed hand of a villager who had mutilated himself in an effort to avoid Second World War conscription.[31] The second edition of the *Canadian Oxford Dictionary*, meanwhile, defines 'shinny' as a game requiring 'a ball or puck or an object serving as a puck'; the *ITP Nelson Canadian Dictionary of the English Language* elliptically suggests 'a ball, can, or similar object.' Though *ITP Nelson* makes no reference to a puck, it is assumed that readers of this Canadian dictionary will understand what is meant.

The second inaccuracy in the definition in *Merriam-Webster* is that this type of hockey is limited to 'children.' This implies that adult hockey exists primarily in an organized or professional form, as if, come adulthood, one stops playing for fun. One of the greatest aspects of shinny is that it is not played only by specific age groups. Whereas young players are divided into teams and leagues according to age and even skill level, people of all ages and abilities can mingle sportingly on the ice and give themselves over to the childlike, unstructured, and unregulated play of shinny. Brothers and friends who are even a few months apart in age might never meet in league hockey. Because of the strict gender separation in hockey, there are few instances of girls playing organized hockey with the boys, which has sometimes resulted in legal battles over the right to play with the other sex. Opposite-sex siblings will be limited to playing shinny with and against each other. As well, several generations can play shinny together (though this is often overstated – as chapter 5 shows, girls and women are rarely invited to play).[32]

According to the reams of memoirs, shinny is best played in public arenas or naturally frozen bodies of water that are free or inexpensive, where there are no strict time slots allowing or denying access to the ice. Whereas the games for twelve-year-old girls at the local indoor arena might end on Saturdays at twelve sharp, shinny games end with darkness, boredom, or, parent-depending, the flexibility of the dinner bell.

Teams change quickly as new players arrive and depart, and they are often not even in number. Ten skilled players may play against a dozen less able bodies to produce a 'balance of ability' – in place of the strictly mathematical equality that sports demand.[33] Equality in sport is important not just for reasons of fairness, but also to add excitement: if the game is too one-sided, it will be boring to play or watch. A level playing field and an equal number of players, however, does not necessarily help if one team is far superior to the other. Shinny takes athletic mediocrity into account. As well, the constitutive rules of the game are far more lax than in organized hockey, and play will rarely cease because someone was offside by a few centimetres.

Played by many at the same time on a surface that may be as irregular as the local pond, shinny flies in the face of modern team sports. In the distant past, ball games moved freely about between villages as inhabitants competed against local rivals. Now it is more common to watch paid imported athletes 'serve' the big city for whose team they play, and even cities as large and as traditionally supportive of hockey as Winnipeg and Quebec City are thought to be too small and economically insignificant for the NHL. Sociologist Henning Eichberg says sport has been cheapened by such changes as the removal of laughter, the standardization of the body, the hierarchical and exclusive pyramid structure of sports leagues, as well as the fact that 'the relevant sports space has shrunk towards a standardised plastic field serving the production of "goal results" and the time orientation that modernity calls "tension."'[34] Rivers and ponds do not naturally fit International Ice Hockey Federation standards, and in some ways shinny contradicts sporting modernity.

Against the obsession with time in most modern sports, shinny games are often played to a specific score – if score is even kept at all. Playing to a score of 10 or 20 offers more internal coherence than playing against time. Theologian Michael Novak argues that sporting time is different, akin to 'sacred time [with] its emphasis on life as possibility [because] as long as there are seconds on the clock, anything can happen.'[35] This common sports cliché regarding the possible is wild overstatement in a critical work; it is better suited to television commentators coaxing the audience to stay tuned for the final period (and advertisements) of a one-sided game. Only if the score is relatively close is there any real hope for the losing side. An NHL team down by three goals plays with one eye on the clock, and the same time obsession that regulates the mundane world of postal delivery and the punch clock is intensified in the game world. In contrast, a breakaway in shinny is not cut short by a buzzer marking the end of a twenty-minute period.

In *Dreaming of Heroes: American Sports Fiction, 1868–1980,* Michael Oriard points out that, 'in baseball, time is in a sense defeated, for the length of a game is nine potentially limitless innings not governed by clocks'; although no such endless game has ever occurred, many games have been interrupted by darkness, by 'the kind of time that functions in nature.' Birk Sproxton's poem 'Playing Time Is a Fiction' calls such time 'the gap between clock time and game time.' It is outside of any real concept of temporality. Paul Quarrington refutes this sort of thinking as he ruminates on organized hockey's rigid stopwatch mentality: 'That's another reason I like hockey: that big clock. It hovers above the ice like a god and ruthlessly eats up seconds.' It is a truism to say that we cannot live outside time – it 'is what we exist in, it is our element, and out of it I feel like a beached whale.' Nevertheless, the attraction of baseball and shinny is that we can more easily embrace the illusion of this possibility.[36] (Sudden-death overtime gives us a rare glimpse of this relation to time, but even then the game clock breaks time down into twenty-minute parcels.)

Dreams

David Adams Richards is fiercely unapologetic about his love for hockey in his autobiographical *Hockey Dreams: Memories of a Man Who Couldn't Play.* He establishes the tone early on, admitting that he fled a snow-bound host's house during a promotional book tour because the 'son of a bitch doesn't like hockey.' He later takes us into the world of shinny and childhood NHL dreams. It mattered little that not all players could skate properly and that some were financially or physically burdened; what mattered was the dream of success, of skating from the frozen Miramichi River to hockey glory. When we consider the harsh realities of Richards's fiction set in similar surroundings – such as the alcoholism, poverty, and social pariahs in novels like *Mercy among the Children* or *River of the Broken-Hearted* – the desire to escape through bodily movement and imagination takes on a greater import.[37]

The shinny games in *Hockey Dreams* are inclusive, communal, and harmonic playscapes. Youngsters of all ages participate, with the older ones schooling the more tender ones on how to avoid collisions and injury. The author, with a damaged left arm, and his friend, who is a diabetic (and therefore considered an athletic impossibility in the early 1960s of

the book), both get to play. Nowadays small players are a rarity in the
NHL, and not even the goalie is allowed to be rotund. In the shinny
setting there is no standardization of the body. The 'big kids,' the pro-
totypically large, hyper-masculine players, are there, but they share the
space with other mortal shells.

Depictions of shinny often overstate the case by portraying shinny as
democratic, gender-blind, and fun for all. Patricia McGoldrick Goldberg's autobiographical sketch 'Growing Up with Hockey' recalls that
females were, at best, just barely a part of the game:

> My sister and I tagged along to the outdoor rink, hoping to get a chance
> to skate around before the big game began. Often, we were recruited for
> net-minding as well, depending on the turnout of players.

The girls can play, but only when the boys are in a pinch. This is closer
to the reality than musings that this part of hockey culture is not concerned with gender or sex. Shinny culture may be more accepting of
women than mainstream professional hockey, but literary glorifications
of shinny are often disingenuous in describing how boys and girls play
together. Peter Gzowski, in his generally laudatory views of hockey and
Canada, notes honestly that even those young women who wanted to
play back in his era were excluded, along with 'those few of our own sex
who chose not to play hockey at all, and were branded forever as outsiders.' Not wanting to play shinny can have social consequences
beyond the ice.[38]

Richards recalls a far more democratic scenario in *Hockey Dreams*,
noting that 'one of our goalies was a girl,' while the other net was
tended by a rather effeminate character, 'a huge boy with fresh-pressed
pants and the smell of holy water.' In terms of traditional gender constructions, this text sends mixed signals: though even the cherubic,
effeminate boy and the girl can play, the other players never forget that
they are somehow 'different.' There is a sense that they are less talented, but Richards does not dwell on that. Yet Richards does not place
the game in a social vacuum: one boy 'had all the talent in the world but
did not own a pair of skates until he was twelve ...' Many of those who
played regularly on the Miramichi had never played in the local arena.
Pond or river hockey means space, room to move. Indoor hockey is
independent of the weather since artificial ice can be produced year-
round; however, the conveniently roofed arena also comes with strict
dividing walls that leave many out in the cold. Others, not least

Richards's penniless childhood peers, approach those arena walls with
the desire of Kafka's K, the perennial outsider looking to gain entrance
to the castle. The frozen Miramichi on which these children play is a
place of wonder that is accessible and open to all.[39] It is for this reason
that shinny is a far more widespread Canadian experience and a more
accurate touchstone than organized team hockey. For pickup hockey or
shinny there is no need to adhere to a specific schedule; arriving an
hour late will not usually prevent one from being allowed to play at all.

Escaping the Prison of Organized Play

Frank Paci's novel *Icelands* offers a realistic glimpse into the world of
youth hockey at the highest level, often mixing sociological critique of
hockey culture with literary narrative. In these hockey circles, many of
the young players (usually at Dad's behest) begin thinking seriously of
a professional career from the age of eight. Organized hockey in *Icelands* is often a particularly cruel milieu: children are berated and belit-
tled by coaches and parents, and kept from the playing surface for
minor mistakes; violence often intrudes as referees and coaches are
physically and verbally abused by parents; daughters are neglected as
fatherly eyes follow the son's career; and focus on the financial burden
of hockey as well as on the tremendous time investment exposes
hockey's opportunity cost. This is supported and perpetuated by hockey
parents who live through their children and use them to compensate
for what they themselves have not achieved. The children are sometimes dehumanized as they become mere tools in the hands of the
parents.

For the children, the fragile balloon of play is punctured because it is
often mandated. *Icelands* offers a concrete example of hockey as a
national imperative. While Vince, a hockey father, revels in his son
Stevie's on-ice successes, the young player mopes about before games –
as if 'hockey was the worst chore imaginable.' Hockey and play proper
can coexist; play and 'the worst chore imaginable' cannot. Much of the
blame for this is the father's: '[Vince] knew he was pushing his son too
much. But he couldn't help it.' This tragic flaw springs from a love of
the game, a desire to see Stevie succeed, and a corresponding inability
to comprehend that Stevie might see things differently, or enjoy hockey
under different circumstances.[40]

The novel has several protagonists, including three young players of
whom Mike Horseford is by far the most talented. Paci describes Mike's

talent in Trinitarian imagery: 'Mike and the stick and the puck were one. Mike was totally in the game. Mike was the game.' In addition to being a 'natural' and perhaps semi-divine in his talents, Mike has an undying love for the game, including practising. He has everything it takes to make the NHL. This novel evokes the tropes of juvenile sports fiction, in which talent, hard work, and a dose of moral gumption usher in a happy ending. However, by focusing on a group of protagonists, Paci mitigates the rampant individualism of past sports novels. As well, Paci saves Mike from becoming a caricature or stock figure by providing social context: hockey may be a potential career path, the arena a place for recognition and development for Mike, but it is also a regular and dependable break from his miserable home life. The boy's father is absent, and his mother is an alcoholic. Lacking role models at home, Mike identifies himself completely with hockey, and as always when one over-identifies with an activity, ideology, or person, this has dangerous consequences for the individual. Hockey-mad Mike has no time for school. After nearly drowning in a backyard pool one summer during a hockey banquet (a hibernal creature, he has never learned to swim), he longs for winter and the chance to show up those peers who look down on him for his inability: 'He'd make them forget the summer sun. In all those arenas of the Metro area he'd show them his *real* self' on the ice. This belief that he *has* to succeed adds an uncomfortable sense of urgency.[41] It taints the purity of his enjoyment of the game because, as a result of his talent and his career ambitions, he has already adopted a professional attitude.

Despite his avid love for league hockey, Mike often pines for another type of play. This other variety is the chaotic, loosely organized game played on the local outdoor rink: 'Here hockey was so different than on the confined ice arenas. Here you were free to do anything you wanted. There were no rules.' This attitude is representative of the Edenic views of shinny in Canada, and, like many a paradisiacal vision, it reveals a limited outlook. Compared to the confined areas of the Toronto-area rinks on which his competitive team plays, Mike is free. But Mike is mistaken in thinking there are 'no rules' just because there are no referees. Any game depends on rules for its existence, and even shinny requires that a certain number of rules be accepted by all players. The rules of shinny go unnoticed simply because they are less restrictive. Referees are often accused of intruding too much, interrupting the flow of the game and taking the game away from the players. On Mike's outdoor ice surface, justice and rules are rigid enough to let the game exist, but loose enough not to infringe on creativity and a sense of freedom. In shinny, as journalist Jack Falla has written concerning his own backyard games in *Home Ice: Reflections on Backyard Rinks and Frozen Ponds*, rules and justice are 'built in, not added on.' The hockey referee determines how the game is to be played, but he or she is outside of it. Anarchic shinny, says Beardsley, is self-governing, managed solely by the players and their communal sense of limitations and how to behave:

> Wherever and whenever shinny is played there are never any referees; players are always on their own honour and various unwritten codes of conduct prevail. It is left to the players themselves to work out things between them.

This is the freedom that Mike enjoys on the outdoor rink and also the reason why he believes there are 'no rules.' These games are guided, in fact, by social rules about who gets to play, but they are unwritten and forgotten by the adults who reminisce and simply not seen by the fictional child in *Icelands*.[42]

In *The Grasshopper*, Suits provides advice for those who create games, and his advice seems to have been taken by the god of shinny:

> The gamewright must avoid two extremes. If he draws his lines too loosely the game will be dull because winning will be too easy. As looseness is increased to the point of utter laxity the game simply falls apart, since there are then no rules proscribing available means.

In shinny, everyone wins. Though rules are scaled back, the game is not loosened beyond all form, and the driving competitive element remains. In *The Game of Our Lives*, his non-fiction book on the Edmonton Oilers and hockey's cultural contribution to Canada, Peter Gzowski outlines the few sparse rules that give birth to shinny:

> The essential rules were the same everywhere: no goal-sucking [i.e., waiting near the opponent's goal for a long pass and ensuing scoring opportunity], no raising [the puck], unless whoever's younger brother was stuck in goal was also foolish enough to wear shin-pads, no long shots, no throwing your stick to stop a breakaway.

These rules have both a moral and a constitutive authority. They make the game and its prolongation possible, but they also cultivate a playful

spirit that demands fair play, as opposed to more arbitrary game rules
that simply plant obstacles to be overcome. 'Goal-sucking' is banned
because there are neither offsides nor referees to judge them. Since
there are often no goalies in shinny, 'long shots' are frowned upon
because they are too easy and upset the flow of the game. 'Raising' the
puck off the ice is wisely banned when most players have no protection,
as too many injuries would destroy the game. If hockey is a sonnet,
shinny is free verse – there are rules, but they are less formal and are
more issues of style than mathematics of lineation and rhyme. Both the
sonnet and free verse belong to the genre of poetry, yet the differences
between the two are significant. Shinny is a sport, but it comes close to
carefree and arbitrary frolicking with a stick and puck.[43]

Despite not being consciously aware of any rules, Mike in Paci's *Icelands* would easily glide off the fictional page into a game of shinny with
Gzowski. If the awareness of rules recedes or disappears altogether,
Mikes notes that it is replaced by other types of sensibility: '... you had
to be aware of everyone on your team because there were no team
sweaters.' Since people often wear their old hockey jerseys, each shinny
side will be a motley crew, with none of the hints of militarism and uniformity cynics may see when individuals are homogenized by team shirts
and numbers on their backs. And the rule stipulating six players per
side is thrown out, which can mean dozens of players with no distin-
guishing team sweaters. (It is this on-ice chaos that gave birth to Jack
Falla's definition of shinny occurring when 'you don't know for a half
hour who's on your team.') Because one's identity is not determined by
shirt colour – and game plans and set plays are basically unfeasible in
the mass of bodies – shinny is more individualistic than organized
hockey.[44] Yet, as an emblem of becoming, dreams, and potential,
players often wear the shirt of their favourite player or exclaim 'I'm
Gretzky!' before play starts. The game exists as much in the unfettered
realm of the imagination as on the ice.

Becoming Something or Someone Else

Although Roch Carrier's 1979 'The Hockey Sweater' was originally
written in French, the English translation by Sheila Fischman has made
it easily the best-known Canadian short story. The National Film Board
produced a popular cartoon of the tale, and a bilingual quotation from
the story sits in millions of Canadian wallets. 'The Hockey Sweater'
reveals how all the boys of a small Quebec village revered the great

Maurice Richard, and how each boy 'wore the same uniform as he, the red white and blue uniform of the Montreal Canadiens.' Discerning who is on which team is difficult:

> ... we were five Maurice Richard's playing against five other Maurice Richard's; we were ten players, all of us wearing with the same blazing enthusiasm the uniform of the Montreal Canadiens. On our backs, we all wore the famous number 9.

Sports are not just a distraction from the pain or humdrum of daily life; they are also an imaginative way of becoming someone or something else. It is for this reason that Roger Caillois sees *mimicry* as one of the key categories of games and play. In Carrier's tale, Maurice Richard represents the zenith of what these young boys could hope to achieve or be. As Carrier writes in the biography *Our Life with the Rocket: The Maurice Richard Story,*

> Nothing is impossible. Maurice Richard has won. The Canadiens have won. We have won. Under the blue sky we're taller now, stronger, more important. Maurice Richard has scored two goals. We have scored two goals.

In both the short story and the biography, the young boys' adulation is excessive, and they even try to copy Maurice Richard's hairstyle. Here, their exuberantly imaginative identifying takes them beyond the bounds of their provincial village, demarcated by church and school (which the young narrator is convinced are merely creative parental punishment). For the length of their time on the ice, their existence is not controlled by parents or teachers; the vicar becomes a referee, overseeing divine justice by judging offsides instead of catechisms.[45]

This sort of imagining can become delusion. When the understandable wish to be like a hockey hero becomes an imperative – 'I *must* become like him' – there is a problem, one which arises often enough in hockey fiction. When parents sacrifice other activities by expending too much time, money, and effort for their son's career, they kill the play spirit. Hockey is no longer a place of escape but an encroaching or determining force in one's life. The details of Carrier's story, with the boys combing their hair like Richard and following him through the press with the passion of star-stalkers, are charming because the reader assumes that this is but a phase of childhood. They have, presumably, since moved on to adulthood and other pursuits. Still, glimmers of such childhood dreams flash into adulthood whenever hockey or shinny is played, and most will agree with Jack Falla that 'anyone who bulges the netting without imagining he is scoring a goal in the NHL is lying, unimaginative or a terminal grown-up.' When a middle-aged man stands alone and shoots tennis balls into an empty net, dreaming of NHL goals, there is the satisfaction of a temporary return to childhood. What is more, this dreaming cannot be tainted by any professional attitude because at some level this imaginative grown-up knows that he is too old for the NHL.[46] He is recapturing the sweet bird of youth.

Such dreaming and hero-worship is not limited to the also-rans. Former NHL goalie Ken Dryden describes the same fascination with becoming someone else in *The Game*. While older brothers and friends retreated from the backyard playing area to concentrate on homework, Dryden would play by himself:

> It was a private game. I would stand alone in the middle of the yard, a stick in my hands, a tennis ball in front of me, silent, still, then suddenly dash ahead, stickhandling furiously, dodging invisible obstacles for a shot on net ... I was Frank Mahovlich, or Gordie Howe, I was anyone I wanted to be ...

Through the power of his imagination, the boy Dryden could be anyone he wanted, capable of overcoming any of the 'invisible obstacles.' Because the imagination perfects the shortcomings of the body, each player is complete in these private games (perhaps even more so than in a game of shinny, when others can shine more brightly), can be more dominant and skilful and therefore more like Howe or Mahovlich. 'The backyard,' explains Dryden, 'was not a training ground ... I don't remember ever thinking I would be an NHL goalie, ... I dreamed I *was* Sawchuck or Hall, Mahovlich or Howe; I never dreamed I would be like them.' Obviously, skills sharpened in the backyard helped Dryden become a professional athlete, but it was primarily a play area for him; skills were functions and spin-offs of the simple urge to have fun.[47] In Dryden's memories, the backyard version of the shinny rink is a magical world apart that is a world of presence – the players' eyes were on the ersatz-puck ball, not the future. Not a training ground, which smacks of professionalism and careerism, this makeshift hockey arena was a place where dreams came true.

Peter Gzowski's *The Game of Our Lives* describes an Edmonton Oilers shinny game which includes some of the best players in the world:

The action swirled back and forth, as I skated in wide arcs around its periphery. Because of the unpredictability of the tennis ball, passes launched with perfect accuracy arrived like bounding jackrabbits. The various speeds of the players made organized rushes difficult. And there were games within the game: Peter Driscoll, rushing to clutch [Doug] Hicks in an illegal but friendly embrace, would suddenly have to swerve to avoid a tottering child or a stationary middle-aged man.

Here the presence of less-skilled players, some disadvantaged by age, means the game is even more chaotic than usual. While there is an element of suspense regarding the outcome of each play in every game, the inclusion of the 'middle-aged man' and the 'tottering child' means play is less predictable because passes will probably not be received perfectly. As well, there is no uniform tempo or flow to the game because the skaters move at different speeds. These professionals will go easy on both the toddler and the codger. Using a tennis ball instead of a puck adds an element of bouncing *alea*, or chance, because passes will not slide smoothly across the ice. Organization breaks down because of 'the various speeds of the players,' and the 'games within the game' provide a heterogeneous and merry carnival atmosphere in which amusement, not winning, is the main attraction. The essence of the sport moves away from competition, edging closer to the higher justice or fate of the roulette wheel or lottery. Destiny, not *agon*, becomes the sole arbiter of victory.[48]

This style of hockey, as Mike from Paci's *Icelands* notes, is 'different than on the confined ice arenas.' The difference, however, is not just one of architecture. Dryden's backyard, the Edmonton Oilers' shinny game on a regulation rink, and Mike's outdoor rink in *Icelands* show that imagination, not geometry, is what frees one from a feeling of circumscription. In *The Game,* Dryden praises the Canadiens' fleet-footed Guy Lafleur by suggesting he plays as though he were unconfined by boards. This is because he grew up playing on the wide-open space of a river – a space that is temporary or liminal because, come spring, the ice will melt (this heritage is disappearing as more and more players develop their skills indoors). Players skate specific drills in cramped spaces, and the game ultimately becomes more entrenched and static in its patterns. When such patterns take over the game, the necessary creativity and spontaneity with which we respond to chaotic shinny is lost. 'The river,' believes Dryden, 'is less a physical space than an *attitude,* a metaphor for unstructured, unorganized time alone. And if the game

no longer needs the place, it needs the attitude.'[49] It would not be a dis-
tortion of meaning to replace 'river skater' here with 'play' attitude. An
attitude towards time and space in hockey that stresses organization and
structure is a professional attitude, one that potentially limits spontaneous, joyful play.

One could easily apply Dryden's claim to *Icelands* and Mike's relation
to the space on the outdoor rink. Even artificial outdoor ice is marginally more natural than an indoor surface, and therefore more easily provides the illusion of a connection with the land – inviting or renewing
myths of cold, snow, and space in Canada. The real difference, however,
is in what one can do during a game of shinny:

> ... you could do stupid things, like flop down on the ice in the middle of
> the game and let the snowflakes fall on your tongue. Or make long cross-
> the-ice passes. Or take a golf swing at the ball. Or stop shots in the crease
> when your goalie was out of the play. Or roughhouse in the corner long
> after the ball had been kicked away.

When not playing organized hockey, Mike can act like the child he is.
The shinny environment allows for the 'laughter and popular carnival-
ism' that Henning Eichberg maintains are absent from modern sport.
In such atmospheres, the chances of enjoying oneself are greatly
increased. Mike is most aware of this; after a disappointing league game,
he feels the need to head out to the shinny rink to achieve a sense of
release. Part of the hockey family, shinny is also an antidote for its more
restrictive indoor brother.[50]

Foolishness is fun, but it is especially fun in games because the silliness usually goes unpunished. When Mike uses the adjective 'stupid' to
describe harmless fun, he reveals much about restrictive hockey environments. Tasting snowflakes during a hockey game is 'stupid' only
because it is irrelevant to the game. Mike is not even a spoilsport here
because the play atmosphere is kept intact and the game itself is not dis-
turbed, as long as other players chase the puck instead of the
snowflakes. Birk Sproxton's prose poem 'The Pastoral Tradition'
includes two types of play co-occurring: at one end of the rink, 'kids on
defence ... tilt heads back to catch snowflakes on the tongue'; at the
other, 'bundled-up skaters ... flock around the puck.'[51] The beauty of
shinny is that there is *time* to do such things, as we take time out from
play to play in another way. Paci's two subsequent examples of 'stupid'
actions shed light on the restrictions of organized hockey: making a

long pass and taking a wild golf swing at the puck are moves for which Mike would be chastised in his regular hockey world, as they are erratic actions that might endanger the team's chances of winning. Controlled, safe passes are the norm there. Mike's team may be punished by the opponents' resulting scoring opportunities, and, more likely, Mike will not see much ice time if he continues making long passes that are easy for opponents to intercept. In the organized world of *Icelands* there is no time to 'play around' when playing hockey.

The final two examples Mike provides – stopping the puck in the crease and roughhousing away from the play – are illegal in hockey. In organized hockey, the referee's play-squelching whistle would stop the fun immediately. What is expressed here is a double retreat from the real world that is often postulated as hockey's opposite: a movement from one type of hockey to another. The work-play binary is misleading because it implies no fun can be had at work or that any instance of playing a game involves no reward. It is, however, a convenient metaphorical opposition if play is always more enticing than work. As the literature shows, shinny is the more enticing version of the national game. Fooling around with the puck, stopping to catch snowflakes or to roughhouse with your friends, is playing within a game. As in a cadenza or free improvisation, the performer is temporarily freed from having to read the notes, can show off a little bit, but nevertheless plays with a view to the structure and flow of the composition. The spirit, rather than the letter, of the score or game is respected.

The longing to retreat from rule-bound hockey is a desire to move from one play pole to the other, from what Roger Caillois has called the *ludic* to the *paedic* end of the play continuum. *Ludus* satisfies the 'taste for gratuitous difficulty,' while *paedia* 'is the indispensible prime mover of play [that] remains at the origins of its most complex and rigidly organized forms.' Allen Guttmann's *From Ritual to Record: The Nature of Modern Sports* neatly bridges the gap between earlier works on game and play and modern sport by focusing entirely on sport, even while incorporating the theories of Huizinga and Caillois. Guttmann illustrates the difference between play and sport by comparing a 'child's unpremeditated leap over a bush or a rock' with the 'soaring, televised jump over the standardized crossbar' or by comparing 'a pebble skipped across the water of a pond with the complicated technique and awesome force of the hammerthrow.' In a word, whereas play is characterized by the instinctive, sport is highly regulated and planned. To use Caillois's vocabulary, the 'unpremeditated leap' is *paedia*; the 'soaring, televised jump' is *ludus*.[52]

Hockey fiction shows that the focus on *ludus* in organized hockey threatens to strangle the primal play spirit, which is why shinny is more easily romanticized than versions of the game that seem to require fighting, that motivate parents to violence, and, at the highest level, give rise to lockouts and strikes. In shinny the playful core of hockey is retained, while the overly confining rules and restrictions are discarded.

The Playful Core: Searching for Hockey's Essence

If one considers the various types of hockey, the looseness of shinny, and the simultaneous need for a certain number of constitutive rules, the question arises: where does hockey begin? An image of hockey's essential, playful core appears in Paul Quarrington's *King Leary*, which won the 2008 CBC Canada Reads competition over heavyweights such as Mavis Gallant's lyrical *From the Fifteenth District*. The novel's hero, Leary, is sent as a young boy to 'The Brothers of St. Alban the Martyr' to be reformed. Young Leary is not a stereotypical delinquent, and, to be fair, his crime of arson occurred when he was cajoled into burning a bag of canine manure on a neighbour's doorstep. The dog had a peculiar radish diet, the results were explosive, and the neighbour's house burned down. As no animal or person was harmed in the carrying-out of the prank, Leary's punishment was light. (The cajoler, naturally, escaped punishment.)

Hockey is part of the Brothers' plan for making difficult young boys road-ready and socially acceptable, as their motto pleasantly intones: 'To Keep A Boy Out Of Hot Water, Put Him On Ice.'[53] In other words, hockey is supposed to improve the moral fibre of a young man by delivering him from evil. The motto and the philosophy of the Brothers constitute a torch for muscular Christianity, the belief prevalent in nineteenth-century English private schools that participating in sports, along with religious instruction, provides benefits in the moral upbringing of children – 'young gentlemen would develop a hearty character and strong-mindedness to complement healthy bodies.' In Quarrington's novel, the Brothers are only partially successful. Although Leary turns away from petty misdemeanours and develops into an NHL star, the clear allusion to Shakespeare's Lear, with all his kingly faults, is also a reminder that the reform was not complete. In this way, *King Leary* is a satire of much sports fiction of the past because Leary's moral character remains questionable. Leary's taints remain with him long after his honours have been forgotten by all but him. And, in case there is any danger of his prowess being forgotten, Leary brags incessantly about his long-ago exploits.[54]

One night the boy Leary looks out the window at the reform school and sees the Brothers playing a strange game on the ice:

> The moon was so bright that I do believe I squinted up my eyes. I have never seen it like that since ... There were five of them. I watched from a distance at first. I couldn't understand what sort of game they were playing. The action would move erratically within the circle, and sometimes the five would split so that three men would rush two, or four would rush one, and then sometimes the five of them would move in cahoots, the idea seeming to be to achieve a certain prettiness of passing. Then a man would break from the pack, and another man would chase him around the circle, and as quick as that happened they'd rejoin the three in the center. There were no goal nets on the ice. Just five men, a puck, and a lot of moonlight.[55]

The bright moon adds a romantic tint to the scene, uniqueness. Although Leary knows hockey and its various vernacular offshoots inside out, this particular form of the game bewilders, yet entraps him with the attraction of the strange. It is not the entirely different that unsettles but the slightly skewed. When a complete stranger to the sport watches hockey 'from a distance,' the actions can be dismissed as chaos, even nonsense.

Leary's reactions to this type of hockey are almost an echo of William Faulkner's 1955 essay for *Sports Illustrated*, entitled an 'An Innocent at Rinkside.' The essay focuses on the confusion this 'new' type of sporting spectacle represents for the neophyte spectator:

> To the innocent, who had never seen it before, it seemed discorded and inconsequent, bizarre and paradoxical like the frantic darting of the weightless bugs which run on the surface of stagnant pools. Then it would break, coalesce through a kind of kaleidoscopic whirl like a child's toy, into a pattern, a design almost beautiful, as if an inspired choreographer had drilled a willing and patient and hard-working troupe of dancers ...[56]

The idea of beauty emerging from confusion exists in both Faulkner's and Quarrington's passages. The difference is that the Southerner Faulkner had little knowledge of hockey (which is one of the reasons why he was selected to give his 'innocent' impressions of a game whose appeals, unlike baseball's or football's, are immediate). When confronted with a different sort of hockey, the frustration Leary feels is that of not understanding someone who supposedly speaks the same language as you. Leary watches what is obviously a hockey vernacular, yet he feels excluded from this game even in intellectual terms. This exclusion is justified. Because the braggart Leary is more of a Felix Batterinski–type in his excessive play attitude, he does not belong with the Brothers and his friend Manny on the midnight ice. He is a mere spectator to the scene, and not even an invited one at that.

The scene, with its unpredictably beautiful order, is idealistic. Though the tension and balance required for modern sport are not there (there is an uneven number of players and they switch teams constantly), and the players 'move erratically,' even goal-driven Leary recognizes the beauty and symmetry of this pageant. The game has been broken down into its base elements: 'just five men, a puck, and a lot of moonlight.' There are no 'goal nets' to distract them, and the players are taken over by the true goal of play, which is to have fun. The removal of physical goals means the removal of scoring and the way to judge winners and losers – that final mathematical simplicity that makes sport easier to understand or interpret than most art. This means that there is no danger of the competitive aspect of play spilling over into ruthless goal-driven ambition, such as happens when joy and fun are relegated to the go-for-gold mentality so common in sport. The players become artists, with the simple goal of trying 'to achieve a certain prettiness of passing.' Unimpeded by the time clock, but in touch with the moon (the primary symbol of the calendar and natural time), the Brothers seem both entirely in 'time' with nature while enjoying a slice of eternity – of which the circle of their play is an obvious symbol.

The game flows freely, unhemmed by the boards that will later mark out Leary's workplace in the NHL. Instead there is the geometrical perfection of a circle. Commands and set plays are replaced by a tacit understanding of what to do, not just on an individual level, but as a group that communicates wordlessly as they revel in this denuded, entirely free hockey variation. Here we sense a rebirth of hockey, and a return to a place and time when hockey was uncorrupted by lucre, the need to win, or even a desire to show off. The scene takes place in the first half of the 1920s, but since the novel was published in 1987, and since Leary complains throughout that the game as played in the 1980s is a watery version of real hockey, the comparison is inevitable. Whereas so much sport is now packaged in modern arenas, here it is returned to natural ice and the natural magic of moonlight. Since the monks are unaware there is a spectator, they are clearly not just putting on a show with their pretty passes and splendid, flowing symmetry. This is truly intrinsic enjoyment, even *l'art pour l'art*.

While the focus on shinny is often on chaos and lack of organization, in this scene Quarrington reduces shinny to its joyous lowest common denominator. It is as if Quarrington is answering the question of *at what point* a game of shinny or hockey begins. In this case, Leary views a minimalist version of the game that possesses a purity lost in more goal-driven and rule-restricted hockey. Most hockey games require great organization: phone calls must be made, a playing space reserved, and so on. In areas where ponds freeze over, one can simply show up. There is

> a kind of unplanned but inevitable blending where groups and individuals come together spontaneously – not by invitation of the group or intrusion by the individual but by a kind of insinuation of each to the other. You chase down a stray puck on a pond, pass it back to a player in the game and the next thing you know he's passed it to you and the most anyone might say is, 'He's on your team.'[57]

In *King Leary* this spontaneous, wordless, yet intuitively understood harmony reaches aesthetic heights with the midnight play of the Brothers. They enjoy themselves and communicate solely through their common object, the puck, like jugglers who achieve complicated patterns of control and beauty solely through the batons they exchange.

Overcoming Gravity

The midnight hockey game played by the Brothers of Saint Alban is decidedly dreamlike. It is played at night, has its own internal logic, and makes an impression on Leary despite his lack of understanding. If hockey dreams exist mostly in the minds of the players, skates help humans achieve a certain supernatural movement on the ice. While we may not be able to leave the ground, on skates we stretch gravitational limitations by moving about as fast as we can under our own power. We become just a little bit faster, a little bit 'better' than we normally are. There is the illusion of overcoming the ballast of the body.

The fascination with skating has a long tradition in Canadian literature. In Charles G.D. Roberts's much-anthologized poem 'The Skater,' which first appeared in 1901,[58] the link between skating and the land is made evident. The poem begins with a forthright comparison to Hermes:

My glad feet shod with the glittering steel
I was the god of the winged heel.

Skates provide the feeling of ecstasy, giving the user a hint of the divine because abilities are heightened. Aided by the steel blades of his skates, the speaker of the poem can better explore Canada's vastness on his joyous feet:

Here was a pathway, smooth like glass,
Where I and the wandering wind might pass

The connection with nature is explicit, as the skater becomes brother to the wind. Skates turn him into an almost spiritual shape-shifter who can surpass the limitations of the body. Although the skater in this poem does not wield a hockey stick, the poem establishes and, when read today, helps perpetuate the Canadian trope of hockey as a natural link to the land. The freedom of movement felt by the speaker of the poem translates into movement into the landscape and the typical romanticized man-in-motion delight (seen in everything from quest novels to road movies) – until he is overcome by fear in the concluding couplet:

... I turned and fled, like a soul pursued,
From the white, inviolate solitude.

'The Skater' ends with a presumed return to civilization after the fears of truly facing nature on skates.

Almost a century later, Frank Paci expresses similar feelings of freedom in his 1982 novel *Black Madonna*. Again there is the image of a solitary skater exploring endless spaces, as the hockey player Joey has

his familiar dream of skating on a limitless expanse of a lake as huge as Superior. He thought it was a lake because it was so huge and he was alone with only the sky above him. He was skating slowly against a light cold breeze, keeping the puck ahead of him in regular pit-pats of his hockey stick. His hockey uniform felt snug and protective on him, although the sweater wasn't the familiar colour of any of his previous teams. There seemed to be no hurry to get anywhere. Only the secure feeling that he was protected against the cold and he was moving in hard sure strides against the Northern expanse. He felt invincible, and the odd colouring of his sweater seemed to substantiate this. The dazzling white light, which issued from under the ice, made the translucent surface glow with incredible beauty.[59]

There are several ways to read this passage. Phrases such as 'moving ... against the Northern expanse,' and the expressed beauty of that expanse, imply simultaneous colonization and appreciation of nature, as well as the myth of naturalness. The focus in this passage, however, is on freedom, on skating as a release from typical restraints. Limits are eradicated, even the limits of the boards around the hockey rink, and Joey can travel wherever he wants; time slows down for him, his uniform feels 'snug and protective,' and 'protects' him against the cold; he is 'invincible' yet fully aware of the beauty that surrounds him. Here we have seamless fusing of aimless play and appreciation of nature's splendour, and, as an image of hockey's essence, the scene is even more concentrated than in Quarrington's midnight game. The communication is with nature itself, and Joey, with no opponents to slow his progress, enters into the solipsistic realm of the imagination (not unlike those solitary men envisioning NHL goals when shooting into empty nets in the backyard). Alone on the ice, he is pure self, purely individual. There is no pressure to play the right way or to adhere to team plans and goals.

Paci's fanciful vignette is yet another contrast to the rigid world of organized hockey. Against this freedom on the open ice, the hockey arena seems a rogue's gallery of limits. A game is always hurried, and one cannot go far before hitting the boards that surround the rink. Nevertheless, there are times when Joey, even when playing league games, 'felt so light on his skates that he thought he could fly,' with that 'smoothness under his feet that could lead him anywhere he wanted to go. Only the boards could restrain him.' At such times, the freedom most often reserved in the literature for shinny is found on the serious playing surface, reminding us that strictly structured games and the spirit of play sometimes do coincide. This natural high comes to an end quickly during a league game:

And when he unexpectedly found himself crashing into the wood he felt cheated that there wasn't as much room as in his dream. As much space as the whole of Lake Superior.

This sense of levity and flight before crashing into the boards symbol-izes play's fragility.[60] In common terms, the fun can stop at any time. Paci also shows the distance between dream and reality. While it is only in dreams that such flight is possible, it is the less rigid forms of hockey that open the doors for imaginative flights of fancy. Visions of Eden are crucial to understanding even the negative portrayals of hockey in Canadian literature because they remind us of how hockey is 'supposed' to be.

Taking the Game Back Outside

In his history of modern hockey *Putting a Roof on Winter: Hockey's Rise from Sport to Spectacle,* Michael McKinley notes how hockey played out-doors was changed drastically by the move to indoor arenas:

> It would be indoors where hockey became a sport, gaining definition and character by the very fact of its physical confinement. The 'temporary world' of each game in each arena spilled over into the next game, and into the next generation. Hockey would become refined in its structure and rules, it would develop standards to surpass, and it would populate the ice with heroes and their exploits to fire our hearts and minds in the coldest, deadest season.

One hundred and twenty-five years after hockey moved indoors, slowly became professionalized, and sometimes devolved into pure spectacle, the NHL went back outdoors. On 22 November 2003, *Hockey Night in Canada* broadcast a game between the Edmonton Oilers and the Mon-treal Canadiens. The regular season game was dubbed 'The Heritage Classic' and took place on a regulation-sized rink built on the frozen football field of Edmonton's Commonwealth Stadium. Just a few months before the labour lockout that would mean the cancellation of the 2004/2005 NHL season, more than 57,000 fans paid to watch multi-millionaire players (who grew up playing on artificial ice in indoor arenas) compete in minus-twenty-degree temperatures. When Montreal goalie José Théodore wisely decided to wear a toque with the team logo in addition to his goalie mask, Canadiens toque sales sky-rocketed. In short, the event was a marketing success, not least because it tapped into Canadian nostalgia about the way hockey was before it became an over-regulated sport. It is easy to argue that this event, like professional hockey as a whole, was a commercialization orgy. But this rationalized regard would miss part of the story. Michael Kennedy conveys a sense of tension between cognition and emotions when he writes, '… the outdoor nature of the game attracted people from across the country in an illogical yet understandable way.' Cynically rejecting the event just because it made some money devalues the involvement of those that travelled vast distances.[61]

In Paul Quarrington's other hockey novel, *Logan in Overtime*, the same sort of anachronistic hockey migration occurs. The novel is about a semi-talented goalie who labours for the Falconbridge Falcons, a terrible team in a Northern Ontario industrial league. Logan's one strong point as a goalie is that he is very difficult to score against in overtime, when hockey moves away from clock time towards the self-regulating 'sporting time' of sports like baseball or cricket. When the Falcons have a playoff game against a team from the town of Hope, overtime continues for hours (with daily interruptions because these semi-professional players all have day jobs). Eventually they decide to complete the game outdoors:

> The Falconbridge Falcons supplied the actual equipment, but all that amounted to was a bucketful of pucks and the two goal nets. The spot on Round River was just about as wide as a hockey rink, bounded on either side by high banks of snow. The Falcons judged the distance between the nets by eye and anchored them with stones and chunks of ice.

The players return to the shinny of their youth.

The rules and conventions of indoor hockey are ignored: 'There were no lines painted on the river,' and 'one of the highlights of the afternoon occurred when [rival goalie] Bram Ridout made a one-man rush the length of the ice.' The two rival goalies meet and roughhouse like children. The loosening of rules provides the optimal circumstances for enjoyment, and as the sun sets on their laugh-filled game, 'they looked like shadows and they looked like angels.' The game, the novel, and this chapter end with an image of transcendence through joyful, unregulated, Edenic play. Judging by Canadian hockey fiction, this delightful play atmosphere can only occur when hockey becomes more like shinny.[62]

Chapter Three

Representations of Hockey Violence

> I reminded myself that his wounds were hockey related. They were enter-
> tainment wounds, and nothing to get emotional about.
>
> Don DeLillo [aka Cleo Birdwell],[1] *Amazons*, p. 36

Writers of hockey fiction seem most concerned with violence, and this chapter is thus the longest in this study. Being a hockey player or fan means physically or intellectually confronting violence. This history of violence makes it seem natural and understandable that players beat each other up and do not necessarily harbour any ill will afterwards. Violence in sport is generally difficult to define, but in hockey fiction it is always clear and usually extreme. Fights and stick attacks form a central part of the narrative, and the reader cannot forget them or dismiss them as a footnote to the game. Such literary scenes, however, remain realistic in professional hockey terms, as fans will remember horrific on-ice incidents of the past and place the literary fight into that context. As an old-time NHLer once quipped while a bumbling referee searched for the puck, 'Never mind the god-damned puck, let's start the game!'[2] In other words, let the fighting begin. Though fighting is not integral to hockey, it has a history of acceptance, and Doug Beardsley chose a variation on this bon mot as a tone-setting epigraph to his non-fictional *Country on Ice*. This anecdote about one player's desire for puckless hockey, argues Beardsley, 'best examines the natural toughness of the game.' Violence is a boon for writers since they do not have to invent a possible world where fighting is accepted and applauded – in hockey fiction, no one needs to be convinced of the plausibility of that world. It is pre-existing.

If sports accurately reflect individual societies, aggressive hockey is the 'wrong game' for Canada, a country that imagines itself to be peaceful. In this chapter, after considering hockey as an unsuitable game for Canada, I provide definitions of aggression and violence within hockey culture, while giving literary examples of characters who are alienated by hockey that is too rugged.[3] Historically, violence has been a male specialty, and in hockey literature it is always the males who are aggressive and violent. The chapter thus moves on to show the importance of violence, including violent sports, to constructions of traditional or heroic masculinity (also referred to by academics as 'orthodox' or 'hegemonic' masculinity), for which the bullfighter, the warrior, and the hockey player stand. The subsequent four sections show how violence is understood and justified in hockey culture: violence does 'not count' because it occurs on the ice; fighting is a necessary means of catharsis that preempts more serious attacks; fighting is regulated and therefore controlled violence; lastly, there is the denial of violence through linguistic means such as euphemism or often humorous understatement. The chapter then shows literary examples of violence as it affects hockey fans and forces them to reconsider their love of the game. The remainder of the chapter focuses on specific aspects of hockey's culture of aggression: learning the unwritten rules that govern violence; violence as a public display; violence as a sort of justice; violence as a destroyer of idyllic play surroundings; and resorting to violence as a symbol of athletic failure. The penultimate section shows how instrumental violence can be an effective way of ensuring victory, and the final vignette in this chapter is of a dovish hockey player who is required to fight – in spite of the fact that he is playing a game and should be free to play the way he wants.

The Wrong Game for Canada

Henning Eichberg writes, '... show me how you are running, and I can see something of the society in which you are living.' The comment on the link between sport and community or nation is both exaggerated and cautious. Though running is a universal human activity and therefore essentially the same around the world, even this basic action indicates 'something,' however small, about our society. Christian Messenger says that sport 'is an institutionalized game that may be an external expression of the order of society responding to or underscoring a national pattern.' This is more than the truism that a nation's culture, including its sports, somehow reflects its surroundings and history; it argues for the exploration of sports and games as an inroad to understanding regional or national cultures. All sports have commonalities, but it is a mistake to lump soccer culture in with hockey culture, or to assume that the ethos of cycling will be transferable to that of basketball or football. If we can merely replace hockey with another team sport, it has little cultural value for Canada because it is choice, not randomness, that provides value.[4]

Canadians spend much of their leisure time watching a game that is often rough, and this raises questions about a particularly Canadian connection to a particularly Canadian type of violence. Engaging with hockey culture means engaging with violence, which reveals something about Canada. When a fight breaks out in an NHL game between two reputed 'tough guys,' or between siblings in a shinny game, it is significant. However, because the variables that led to the fight are so knotted, interpreting the meaning and causes of a single fight is difficult. Was it caused by weakness of character? the specific sporting surroundings? a bad childhood? a rough day? Is it all for show? The schoolyard argument that it 'just happened' does not explain hockey violence in general, even if it is really meant as a way of saying that the myriad factors that led to the fight are too muddled and varied to be comprehended. In literature, on the other hand, violence is never an accident. Even if the fight resembles those we have witnessed in the NHL, the author has chosen to include, depict, and shape violence in words. This is articulated violence, and it is the best-represented theme of those examined in this book.

John Ralston Saul applauds hockey as a fitting sport for Canada and claims, '... every Canadian male has played hockey at some age or ends up believing he has.'[5] This minor male self-deception stems most obviously from a desire to join in the conversation and be part of the Canadian crowd, while showing the tremendous influence sports culture has on the individual. For those bombarded with hockey talk, hockey images, and hockey fantasies for years, creating a fictional hockey past is easy. Despite its humour, Ralston Saul's remark in no way ridicules the game or denies its importance to Canada. Rather, it illustrates the widespread desire for a complete immersion into hockey culture. This complete identification with the game is ironical for a generally amenable country because it means willing complicity in an often violent sporting culture. That real or believed hockey past includes fists.

Canadians are far too often described as a colourless group qualified by the tepid adjective 'nice' – which implies that hockey is actually the wrong sport for us. Irving Layton's 1956 poem 'From Colony to Nation' includes the acerbic observation that we are 'a dull people / enamoured of childish games.' For a country that prides itself on being '*not* American,' and whose other well-nurtured myths include pacifism, peacekeeping, and tolerance, aggressive hockey does not seem the appropriate sport. Nevertheless, it is hockey rather than curling that captures the Canadian imagination. To aggravate matters of identification, unlike European hockey and North American university hockey, Canadian professional-style hockey has always found ample space for fighting. Canadians have both sought out and created the more violent form.

Definitions of Aggression and Violence

In everyday life, 'aggression' and 'violence' are near synonyms, indicating forceful or injurious actions. Michael Smith, in *Violence and Sport*, points out that 'physical violence represents the end point on a continuum of aggressive behaviour [and] is the most extreme form of aggression.'[6] Continuum or not, neither is allowed in the cafeteria line-up. Within the arena's hallowed walls, however, aggression and a certain type of violence are demanded. Every team sport involves some sort of aggression beyond the etymological sense of 'moving forward,' as there is always someone who wants to block his or her opponent from gaining a spatial advantage, and the differences are only in degree. We may speak of 'aggressive play' in curling, but this does not mean combativeness or rough physical contact. Sports like rugby, American football, and hockey celebrate aggression because tackles and bodychecks are allowed by the rules.

In hockey, the line between harmless aggression and physical violence is thin, and even the concept that violence includes an 'intent to injure or hurt' is difficult to prove. Minor slashing and crushing bodychecks regularly occur with no thoughts of physical harm. Michael Messner's *Power at Play: Sports and the Problem of Masculinity* clearly shows how sports culture promotes traditional concepts of masculinity, including violence and aggression. 'Much of the violence commonplace in sport,' he writes, is a matter of socialization, meaning that over time, 'males often view aggression, within the rule-bound structure of sport as legitimate and "natural."'[7] When body contact is integrated into the rules of a sport traditionally played by men, such as American football or hockey, some level of violence is a necessary component of the game.

But even if we accept this as violence, bodychecking is never the main issue when hockey violence is portrayed in literature.

American football, with its rationalized, militaristic force, carefully limits the escalation of violence: a single punch means ejection from the game. The same holds true for soccer, Europe's and South America's epitome of masculinity. Football, baseball, and soccer players are hardly pacifists by nature; it is merely that winning is sacred, and fighting damages their team's chances for victory. In hockey a fight can often mean nothing more than a short stint in the penalty box, and so it continues. It is the presence of fighting which differentiates professional hockey in North America from all other ball games and to which hockey owes its violent reputation. Hockey literature generally problematizes violence by specifically considering the role of fighting in the game, and the acceptance of fighting as an understandable, natural, and even required part of the game. Of course, much organized hockey is played without any fighting, and even international hockey, such as that of the Olympics, is relatively fight-free. But these other types of hockey are less widely watched in Canada, where the NHL reigns (and almost all literary depictions of hockey violence focus on NHL-style hockey). As Patricia Hughes-Fuller notes in her PhD dissertation 'The Good Old Game: Hockey, Nostalgia, Identity,' '... the NHL has, in a negative sense, functioned as a kind of Master Narrative.'[8] The dominant form of hockey, NHL hockey is also the norm.

Some NHL players never fought, though such heroes were few and far between. They were players like the extraordinarily gifted Wayne Gretzky, whose talent came with protective Dave Semenkos and Marty McSorleys to drop the gloves for him. Unlike Gordie Howe, Maurice Richard, and Bobby Orr (formidable fighters all), Gretzky did not play 'Canadian-style' hockey. In a delightful irony in light of Canada's hyper-masculine hockey mythology, one of Canada's greatest players was sometimes accused of being effete or 'gay' because of his non-aggressive style. In Dave Bidini's short story 'Why I Love Wayne Bradley' (which appeared earlier in the *Village Voice* under a somewhat more recognizable name), the themes of hockey greatness, the need for a protector, and homoeroticism merge. After Wayne Bradley is attacked, the goalie narrator rushes to his aid. Neither is a fighter, and each loses badly. Proud nonetheless, the narrator notes, 'We looked fucking cool' with our 'noses and mouths bloodied and broken, arms weak and defeated at our sides.' For such players, winning the fight is not important for constructions of manliness; it is the participating that matters. In the dressing room after the two are ejected, Bradley explains how it started: 'He started in with the fag stuff, you know? Christ, I don't mind being called a fag, but not by some fucking pussy like him.' The 'Great One' considers himself manly enough to be called a fag because the accusation is so palpably false. The goalie misunderstands the message and seizes the moment: 'What happened out there,' he says, 'I did ... because I love you.' After a brief fantasy scene including deep tongue kissing and groping, Bradley shakes the narrator back into reality by telling him about his trophy girlfriend Janet. Bidini's story is unique in hockey fiction because it directly portrays homosexual attraction.[9] It also invites us to reconsider the assumption that masculinity is a 'package deal' that includes heterosexuality, while casting a different light over players rushing to stick up for their teammates.

While sexual orientation remains a taboo topic, hockey fiction is saturated with statements about the required masculinity. In Bill Gaston's *The Good Body*, which is about a player who spent twenty years in the NHL's feeder league before attempting to go back to school, we learn that a minimal level of toughness is required for any high-level hockey. It is this toughness that 'give[s] you dignity as you walk your chin to the dressing room to get it stitched, no freezing, so you miss no more than one shift.' Not showing pain is a traditional marker of masculinity, and Canadian hockey players are reputed to have this resilience in abundance – though, Gaston's narrator admits, '... you can see its birth in some Europeans over the course of a few seasons.' Allegedly, Canadian hockey players are born with this manliness – epitomized by an attraction to aggressive play and pain, whereas Europeans have to develop it. This reveals the parameters of hockey discourse in Canada: in the typical Canadian understanding, 'physical' hockey excludes the bodies of those who refuse to fight.[10]

Occasionally, hockey literature shows what happens when hockey meets with an Other, when those unfamiliar with the game see how Canadians play. Many of the towns in which *The Good Body*'s hero played had no hockey tradition, and fans were thus puzzled by the aggression in this Canadian game. Gaston's narrator, Bobby Bonaduce, recalls a stint in Oklahoma, home of tough men of the John Wayne variety:

[It was] a strange place for a Canadian to be ... Strange to be the home team here, trying to beat the shit out of a busload of fellow Canadians while all the cowboys in the audience hollered ... Safe in the dressing room, they enjoyed constant mock cowboy talk. *Well-sir, I reckon it's 'bout tam we should take and work up a lather out thar on the frozen ceement pond...*[11]

This speaks volumes about violence and aggression in sport, traditional concepts of masculinity, and cultural export. When taken away from Canada and its naturalized hockey violence, stripped of all rhetoric and motive, hockey is reduced to groups of Canadians abusing one another for the entertainment of others. The glorious national game of Canada has turned these particular Canadians into circus geeks for macho cowboys in what the narrator regards as a backwater American town. The sense of foreignness is heightened by the put-on accents and the reminder that here there is no natural ice, just 'ceement ponds.' From the safety of the dressing room, the players may make themselves feel more at home by mocking the macho cowboy locals, and suggesting the 'hollering' audience will never understand the game, but here the laugh is on Canadians. (The players feel 'safe in the dressing room' because they are somewhat nervous about venturing out into the gun-happy surroundings.) Unlike most literary representations of an Other, which serve to valorize the self or the home group, Gaston uses the Oklahoma residents to show a dark side of hockey culture. When the Canadians leave the dressing room, it is to provide vicarious thrills for cowboys who clearly find this on-ice fighting bizarre. For such a specta-tor, violence is the essential attractive feature of hockey.

Violence in sports attracts many, but it also repels. For those not on the diet of Canadian-style hockey, fighting can upset the stomach. Any game we play or watch without fully understanding the rules is disturb-ing because, although we know clear rules and goals exist, we lack the ability to make sense of it and thus feel left out. It is like not knowing the words when a group breaks into song at a social gathering. Such alienation provides the material for a 1995 sketch by Steven Michael Berzensky, which was published under the pen name 'Mick Burrs.' In 'My First Hockey Service,' a foreign priest watching his first hockey game is excluded by the atmosphere and attitude of the other specta-tors, as well as by his minimal understanding of how this game works. He wonders at the 'secular worshippers in their community sanctuary,' including hockey mothers who bellow, 'KNOCK HIS GODDAMN BLOCK OFF!' at the 'cherubs in uniform.' In *The Grasshopper: Games, Life, and Utopia*, Bernard Suits argues that 'the games we play in our non-Utopian lives are intimations of things to come.' A heavenly existence consists of games because playful occupation without the burden of necessity or work could fill our endless time. The priest in Burrs's story would disagree with this assessment, at least when it comes to hockey. The 'service' in the story's title already denotes religion, and the story itself provides for violence. Since this is youth hockey, there are 'no fights, no violence' on the ice during the game – although a punch is thrown after the match and there is no post-game handshaking ('to make sure' that the priest does not leave the rink 'with any wrong impressions' about non-violence).[12]

The game in Burrs's story takes place on Boxing Day. There is, however, no holiday spirit, and after the game the priest remarks that the atmosphere is that of a funeral parlour. The story ends with a balanced reflection on the attraction of hockey:

> I know this is a sacred sport played and watched in every city and village in Canada. It has winners and losers who all pray fervently for grace and violence and victory. But now you can see why I am also assured: they don't play hockey in heaven.

The various puns throughout the tale add irony to the uncomfortable marriage of play and violence (a tension poet Al Purdy called a 'combination of ballet and murder'). The townspeople pray for 'grace,' including gracefulness on the ice, but the priest sees only violence and their misguided 'religious' fervour. Still, he is aware of hockey's spell. Though new to the game, he knows all about the sacred and unifying effect the game has on Canadians, or at least on his fellow townspeople. But by failing to see any gracefulness on the ice, the priest exposes himself as an outsider, thereby highlighting the communal role of hockey to Canadians. In Burrs's view, part of being the standard Canadian hockey fan means approving, or failing to see, aggressive acts on the ice. The outsider's viewpoint forces the reader to look critically at what is often taken for granted, to regard with another person's eyes. In the arena the priest is a deviant, but his baffled reactions remind the reader that those individuals out for blood would be the asocial ones in any other environment. His direct, unembellished, unapologetic and un-theorized critique of what he sees makes us question the violence so blithely accepted in Canada's national game. The message is that cheering for and promoting aggression among children is immoral, and the fact that it takes place on the ice is no excuse.[13]

Manliness on the Ice

For all the stereotypes and jokes about hockey's essential violence, a fight is at best an intermezzo. Players interrupt the main event to assault each other. For the duration of the fight, all sublimated sporting aggression is concentrated into a real fight. Canadians often view this as an honest, pure act. Rightly or wrongly, the assumption is that the 'less physical' Russians and Swedes prefer sneak attacks with sticks and skate blades – attacks that, more often than not, will escape the referee's attention. It is for this reason that David Adams Richards, in an essay simply called 'Hockey,' derides international hockey, where Europeans (including anti-Canadian referees) 'want to prove to a watching world that their game is more "moral" than ours.' Canadians fight it out 'like men,' and expect to be punished by the referee.[14]

The great Gordie Howe famously stated that hockey is a 'man's game,' and he saw no reason for apologizing for his rough tactics on the ice. In *The Arena of Masculinity*, Brian Pronger refers to Howe's comment and supports its validity with a quotation by Frank Rose: 'There is an undeniable *frisson* to the sight of blood on ice – the spilling of the very warm onto the very cold, perhaps – that not even [American] football can match.' This striking red on white evokes the Canadian flag and at the same time implies that hockey is a modern-day bloodsport because the bloodshed is not incidental but expected, accepted, and encouraged. Hockey is clearly more physically combative than most sports, but it is by no means uniquely confrontational. Team sports like rugby and American football are also regularly evoked as examples of manliness, precisely because of their 'physical' nature, including necessary aggression. Brian Pronger points out that there are other ways of playing hockey, but that its real significance, unfortunately, is as a 'man's game.' It rejoices in 'orthodox masculinity [by] emphasizing the conventional masculine values of power, muscular strength, competition, and so on.' Many areas of North American society, from politics to the business world, extol the same values, but only in sports circles – whether played by men or women, boys or girls – are those values represented and displayed so obviously for the crowd.[15]

American football adds an element of theatre to these values by providing outward markers of manliness: the equipment donned by football players helps to 'amplify the ritualized display of hegemonic masculinity by making big men even bigger, larger than life.' Hockey equipment does the same thing: the shoulder pads make every player look like a bodybuilder, and the skates add an extra inch or two of height. Yet even while pumping up the player's profile, hockey equipment conceals the body entirely. Whereas the short sleeves and three-quarter trousers of American football uniforms reveal and allow us to revere muscular arms and calves, those muscles are hidden in hockey. One cannot immediately tell the men from the boys, or even the men from the women. It is partly because of this concealment that, for all its emphasis on physicality, body image and size are less important in hockey literature. When the players are on the ice, spectators cannot tell who has the biggest biceps, the most developed thighs, or the lowest body fat percentage. As shoulder pads and hockey pants exaggerate musculature by increasing size, they also add the aura of dress-up; female hockey players also look hyper-masculine when they wear shoulder pads. When Hugh Hood asks in the Foreword to *Scoring: The Art of Hockey*, 'What is the sex of the goalie?' the answer is not obvious to the naked eye, even if tradition has taught us to see a boy or man behind the mask.[16]

In Roy MacGregor's *The Last Season*, Felix Batterinski provides a taxonomy of masculinity in sports. Those games that do not require protective equipment fare poorly:

> A long time ago I decided that hockey was the masculine game. Sports go roughly like this, from masculine to feminine: hockey, football, baseball, soccer, tennis. Hockey requires both strength and thought. Football requires strength, the thought they send in from the sidelines. Baseball would qualify higher if they allowed body contact, but they don't. Soccer requires a weak mind that won't get bored while running up and down a lawn never scoring. And tennis, of course, rewards those with limited skill with the illusion that they are actually playing properly.

The list is comical because of the obvious gulf between Batterinski's limited intellect and his bragging about how simple other athletes are. The arbitrary 'I decided' and 'of course' betray a mind blithely free of doubt; the belief that only hockey players need to think is as original as it is wrong; the wistful 'if only' regarding baseball makes one wonder how more 'body contact' could be injected into that sport (while overlooking the many collisions between base-runners and catchers and other infielders that occur in each game); associating soccer with a feminine 'lawn' instead of a field is perhaps intentional, perhaps another indication of how isolated Batterinski's hockey culture is; and, lastly, the suggestion that tennis players lack skill and are therefore not 'playing properly' seems written expressly to annoy the beefy Nadals and the Williams sisters of the world. Many hockey fans may agree with the ordering of the sports, and concur that hockey is more 'masculine' than 'tennis,' but Batterinski's shaky arguments reveal how narrow such viewpoints are.[17] The reader is led to question rather than confirm hockey's masculinity.

Batterinski's list has obviously been created only to trumpet hockey as a masculine sport. His neglect of rugby and combat sports shows a slanted argumentative approach, since in the hierarchy of traditionally masculine sports hockey is well behind boxing or judo's gentle ways. As Joyce Carol Oates writes,

> Professional boxing is the only major American sport whose primary, and often murderous, energies are not coyly deflected by such artifacts as balls and pucks ... It survives as the most primitive and terrifying of contests: two men, near naked, fight each other in a ... space roped in like an animal pen.

Oates makes quick work of Batterinski's hierarchy by explicitly mentioning a boxer's nakedness (as opposed to shielded hockey bodies) and 'pucks.' She emphasizes that boxing is not just 'a stylistic mimicry of a fight.'[18] But there is a 'but' in comparing the masculinity of boxing and hockey. When two men or women box, the event is preplanned; when hockey players fight, even if they have been told to fight by their coaches, there is a constant sense that the violence is more intense *because* it is spontaneous and illicit. A hockey fight always looks like things have temporarily got out of control, and the ordered game-world has been given over to the purely animalistic and masculine.

No sport is intrinsically masculine. Masculinity is a socially constructed cultural concept or range of concepts validated only by tradition (though tradition can weigh as heavily upon us and determine our way of thinking as much as intrinsic qualities do). Women can also play hockey in a masculine way, can be 'called ballsy [...] for going into the corners, for standing up to guys trying to intimidate,' as the female narrator of *Amazons: An Intimate Memoir by the First Woman Ever to Play in the National Hockey League* insists; but in order to do so, they would have to find ice time. Although women have been playing hockey for over a hundred years, they have been excluded from the myth of hockey as a binding element in Canada. Moreover, as Elizabeth Etue and Megan K.

Williams write, the 'underlying pro hockey mentality only intensifies the benign neglect and patronizing attitudes that continue to keep women off the ice, away from sponsors and absent from the media.' In terms of hockey non-fiction, the harmonic and inclusive sketches of shinny cited in chapter 2 distort the reality. The collective drive to point out that women played, too, misrepresents the typical make-up of a shinny game. In hockey fiction, the exclusion pointed out by Etue and Williams is more faithfully represented, with the majority of that fiction focusing on hockey played and watched by men, as well as on hockey culture as a male realm.[19]

Lisa Kulisek's sketch 'The Queen of Cottam Pond: A Memoir' concretely shows that a gender separation persists not only in shinny, but also when boys and girls adhere to the same orthodox masculinity. Kulisek recalls her desire to play pond hockey as a young girl, and being considered '"too fragile" to be in the fray' by the boys who control the game. She is allowed to play only on those rare occasions when too few males show up, and then she is stuck in goal – in the game, but not of it. Cottam Pond should promote the same sort of democratic and inclusive shinny in which players are gentle towards smaller or less-skilled friends and everyone has a chance to possess the puck. 'My greatest moment,' writes Kulisek, 'came on the glorious day I was checked so hard that I flew off the ice ... I'd finally made it. I was playing hockey!' Being hit with a vicious bodycheck is a sign of acceptance and equality, and a reasonable hockey initiation within the accepted logic of the narrator. More importantly for constructions of masculinity, the check was a test of her ability to take physical punishment.[20] Were Kulisek just another prepubescent male playing shinny without shin pads or shoulder pads, she would be justified in complaining that the check was unfair and improper. For a young woman out to prove she can 'play with the boys,' this option does not exist; given her 'sex deficit,' Kulisek has to try harder at being masculine in order to play hockey the Canadian way.

Female sportswomen long posed a threat to the 'female frailty myth and the illusion of male supremacy.' However, since they rarely played against men, there was rarely a danger of losing one's masculinity by losing to a female team or opponent. In Thomson Highway's 1989 play *Dry Lips Oughta Move to Kapuskasing*, the women from the Wasaychigan Hill Indian Reserve form a hockey team, symbolically appropriating a primary realm of masculine power and hegemony. They destroy the frailty myth and make some of the males question their role as men. As

one character responds to the situation, 'I hate them fuckin' bitches.
Because they – our own women – took the fuckin' power away from
us ...'[21] Even when taken from the play as a whole and looked at in isolation, these lines show the absurdity of the indignation. The sense of
betrayal inherent in 'our own women' does not accord with the posses-
sive pronoun, much less the fact that the women merely asserted themselves in sporting terms. Furthermore, power that perches itself on a
hockey puck is especially wobbly.

Violence on the Ice, or Violence That Is Not Itself

Participating in sports almost always means inviting aggression into our
lives, and, as already mentioned, aggression that would be scorned off
the ice is allowed in sports culture. Sometimes this allowance means
that we fail to recognize obvious violence. Moreover, on-ice violence is
openly glorified in hockey culture. For players and fans in the more
'masculine' sports, violence is not recognized because playing the game
at all means implicit agreement that injury and bloodshed are a real
possibility. The usual definitions of violence are set aside as we favour
the arbitrary rules and conventions of sports.

A.J. Liebling's *The Sweet Science*, a collection of essays on boxing first
published in the mid-1950s, looks at the relationship between levels of
aggression or violence and the parameters allowed by the rules of the
game. He describes a powerful punch that

> knocked Joe [Louis] through the ropes and he lay on the ring apron, only
> one leg inside.
>   The tall blonde [spectator watching the fight] was bawling, and pretty
> soon she began to sob. The fellow who had brought her was horrified.
> 'Rocky [Marciano] didn't do anything wrong,' he said. 'He didn't foul
> him. What you booing?'[22]

Here Liebling economically shows the expectations and exceptional
morality of boxing culture. The informed male observer is not 'horri-
fied' at the punch, or the sight of a man lying helpless, but at his date's
naively weeping response. In boxing terms, no unusual aggression had
occurred, as the blow was entirely in keeping with the rules and conventions of the sport's violence. The 'tall blonde' had embarrassed her
companion by applying the outside world's moral standards to boxing,

attracting undue attention by not watching the fight in the 'right' way. There is no cause to hiss at something that is usual, and the direct quotation of unrefined, ungrammatical English highlights this. Even a seemingly uneducated individual can understand this matter-of-fact aggression within the rules. Hockey is not boxing on ice, but a spectator who shed tears at a hockey fight could similarly embarrass his or her more knowledgeable rink companion.

Liebling's essay concentrates on the reception and perception of aggression and violence. The issue in hockey is similar since most aggression in hockey, including bodychecks and incidental or minor stick violations, would not qualify as violence to most fans or players. Since such actions are part of the game, players do not recognize them as something out of the ordinary. Despite this (sometimes wilful) overlooking, caused by long immersion in certain types of hockey culture, any definition of violence should include the 'more direct confrontation of fighting, when the hockey itself is put aside for a one-on-one punching match.' At such times, hockey becomes what Joyce Carol Oates, describing boxing, calls 'the very soul of war in microcosm.' Yet even when this descent occurs, Weinstein et al. observe bad faith among players. This attitude is clearly reflected in the fiction, since protagonists rarely speak of violence, even as they swim in a sea of it. In the abstract, the players may have 'acknowledged that fighting, body contact and stick infractions ... are forms of violence'; in reality, even fighting is included in the violence 'overlooked.'[23] Through exposure, hockey culture desensitizes players and fans and diverts their ability to recognize the obvious.

When fights are no longer recognized as something unusual, there is tacit agreement that they are an intrinsic component of the game. The difference between a real hockey fight observed on *Hockey Night in Canada* and a fight depicted in a novel is that printed words always encourage further reflection. All hockey fights have meaning and can be interpreted, but a fight in a hockey novel or story has more meaning because there is no possibility that it arose spontaneously. Since the novelist chose to include and shape the fight, the reader is invited to interpret and reflect on the role of aggression and violence both within the novel and within broader societal contexts. Furthermore, we are more intimately linked to fictional hockey heroes not only because of the intimate nature of the reading process, but also because we have insight into their thoughts, are aware of their personal histories, and understand the financial imperatives to fight.

Catharsis Theory

The need for catharsis is the prime excuse given for hockey fights. More specifically, limited violence is thought to prevent greater violence. Konrad Lorenz's *On Aggression* defines aggression as 'the fighting instinct ... which is directed *against* members of the same species.' Although his focus is zoology, Lorenz believes that aggression helps explain the role of sport in society. Boxing and other contact sports may represent the antithesis of civilized behaviour, but, if aggression is indeed innate, they are attractive precisely for that reason. Usually repressed feelings are given free play and put on display. According to Lorenz, this is a positive and useful biological occurrence, since 'the main function of sport today lies in the cathartic discharge of aggressive urge.' The danger level of this discharge is strictly controlled by rules and circumstances, and those who lose their tempers or lose control are penalized accordingly. Boxers who get angry are ineffective, and controlling anger is part of most athletes' training. In novels like MacGregor's *The Last Season* and Lynn Coady's *Saints of Big Harbour,* fighting and aggression among athletes is promoted and even trained; that is, aggression itself is the education.[24]

Among sociologists, theories about innate aggression and its necessary release are widely disputed, along with the role sports play in this discharge. Whereas Norbert Elias and Eric Dunning believe that 'mimetic leisure forms have replaced aggressive or violent forms' – that is, modern sports have helped the 'civilizing process' by supplanting even more violent bloodsport antecedents – others are less enthusiastic. In the contrasting view, aggression is something we learn. Gruneau and Whitson, writing specifically about hockey, argue that such behaviour is by no means innate and 'aggressive environments serve to arouse aggressive responses, even among spectators.' This means that hockey players fight and behave violently because they have grown up watching other players do the same. This belief that aggressive sporting environments can lead to aggression among fans is less obvious in North America, where, despite the popularity of sports like American football and ice hockey, hooliganism is an almost unknown phenomenon.[25] There is no personal danger in attending an NHL hockey game.

Colourful hockey commentator and former coach Don Cherry is easily the most vociferous public supporter of fighting in hockey. Basing his arguments on his vast hockey experience, he argues that emotions will inevitably boil over and that fighting is simply the best way of letting off steam. As he explained to journalist George Plimpton in *Open Net* (the middle-aged Plimpton was allowed to play goal for the Boston Bruins at a time when Don Cherry was the team's coach), 'You've got to allow a definite reaction. If not, you're going to get sneaky, far more dangerous stuff.' More formally: 'The catharsis hypothesis suggests that fighting in sports provides controlled and symbolic outlets for aggression that might otherwise manifest itself in more serious forms.' This 'more dangerous stuff' and these 'more serious forms' usually refer to stick attacks, and catharsis theory adherents have great respect for the damage a hockey stick can cause. The argument is that since attacks and retaliation are inevitable, they should take the form of straightforward fist fights, in which both players are on the alert.[26] This argument seems reasonable, at least if we do not question the inevitability of retaliation.

Fighting may be against the rules, but it continues because the penalties for dropping the gloves are often minimal. Even Wally Harris, an NHL referee employed to enforce the rules, has a seemingly relaxed attitude towards fighting:

> ... nothing can happen when two guys are squaring off against each other. They haven't got good balance to begin with [because they are on skates]. Someone's going to go down fairly quickly. Then you step in. But you've got to let them get it out of their systems.

There is a firm sense of control here. As long as the players are standing, the potential for injury is limited ('nothing can happen'), and it is usually only when a player falls that the referee stops the fight. In this philosophy, which clearly follows Lorenz's assumptions about innate aggression and an inability to harness it completely, fighting is a highly regulated, salubrious safety valve. Harris cautions that the referee has to know exactly when to step in: 'If you interfere too early, they haven't let the steam out. They'll fight again.' Even Ken Dryden, a former NHL goalie and lawyer who in theory is firmly against fighting in hockey, concedes that fights are 'little more than a harmless burlesque of threats, sweater-pulling, and off-balance punches, leaving the losers often unmarked' – which is why fighting, rather than other means of releasing aggression, 'becomes the tolerated channel.'[27]

This concentration on and acceptance of fighting as a necessary release takes us back to the issue of why hockey is the 'wrong' game for 'a dull people.' Novelist Hugh MacLennan sees hockey violence in Canada as both understandable and fitting. In a 1954 article entitled

'Fury on Ice,' he introduces hockey to neophytes and deals with the question of violence in cultural terms:

> Natives of Spain and Mexico find incomprehensible the initial reaction of most foreigners to the bullfight. Canadians feel the same way when strangers express horror at the violence of hockey.

MacLennan believes that, on the whole, Canadians overlook this violence because it is a typical ingredient of hockey. Again, the rules and the tradition of the sport relax our view of what constitutes violence, or at least acceptable violence. One of MacLennan's hockey heroes, Maurice Richard, was a goal scorer also known for his frequent retaliation with fists and sticks. Richard openly admits, 'J'étais violent, oui. Mais je n'étais pas méchant.' Outside of hockey (or war), it is hard to imagine violence without malice.[28]

MacLennan's essay relies heavily on national stereotypes, such as when he remarks, 'This is one Irishman who would rather play than fight.' He also says that Canadians rank alongside the Swedes and the Swiss for cool-headedness, while 'Americans often seem as volatile as Latins. Yet the favourite sports of Americans are neat, precise games like baseball and college football' (this was before the rise of NFL football and NBA basketball). Against the argument that sports reflect individual cultures, MacLennan claims that hockey is the cultural activity *required* to maintain the peaceful national character. He tries to show that hockey and the hypothesized Canadian denial of aggressive urges are one and the same: 'To spectator and player alike, hockey gives the release that strong liquor gives to a repressed man. It is the counterpoint of the Canadian self-restraint ...' Like Konrad Lorenz, MacLennan believes that we are full of innate aggression and that watching or playing hockey provides for catharsis or a communal cleansing. In these terms, the CBC's Saturday *Hockey Night in Canada* is a reward of over-indulgence after a week of good behaviour. Similarly, in his essayistic short story 'A Nation Plays Chopsticks,' Mark Anthony Jarman writes about hockey culture's relation to the 'civilized veneer' that keeps our 'rage' hidden most of the time. Some types of hockey culture allow 'behaviour [that] is frowned upon in my other worlds, and this may be why I get a kick out of time lost in this world.' Such views add zest to Roch Carrier's five-dollar-bill-gracing claim that 'our real life was on the ice' because the postulated essential core of Canada is not mature calm but capped aggression.[29] In this variation on essentialism, Canadians need hockey because we are repressed.

This view of hockey as a 'release' takes us into Aristotelian territory, shifting the concept of catharsis to the literary world. As the philosopher argues in *Poetics*, we can witness staged events that are violent and tragic, yet still feel good. His famous conclusion was that drama, in imitating 'incidents arousing pity and fear,' facilitates and enables the 'catharsis [purification or purgation] of such emotions.' Actors speaking a rhythmic script aloud manipulate our emotions. The spectator identifies with the characters on stage, suffers vicariously, and then moves on. But despite the similar ring of MacLennan and Aristotle, sport and theatre are not the same. Though spectators may consider the hockey rink a stage, hockey is not art in the traditional sense because even the violence is real. For this reason, sports are not dramatic or cathartic in the same way as traditional art forms. A fightless peewee hockey game contains more actual aggression than bloody *Macbeth*. If hockey, rather than theatre, is the national passion, Canadians clearly prefer honest aggression and violence to mere shadow actions and emotions. MacLennan fuses 'spectator and player' in his catharsis argument, and this focus on the spectator is useful because fighting has been supported by hockey fans' enjoyment of and complicity in on-ice violence. Hockey fans watch fights in order to feel a release, or at least enjoy vicarious thrills, like the Oklahoma cowboys yipping at Canadian geeks in Bill Gaston's *The Good Body*.[30]

The previous subsection discussed how those immersed in hockey culture often overlook violence on the ice. The theory of catharsis is equally widespread, even though it contradicts the idea that violence in a sporting realm usually does not exist. Justifying the utility of and need for violence as an outlet of aggression means accepting it as a required, benign part of the game. Thus, hockey culture is rife with doublethink: on the one hand, we overlook violence; on the other, we argue that it is required. That this sort of catharsis is difficult to prove is moot in much hockey culture because it is taken as an accepted, unquestioned fact. Hockey fiction reopens the debate in aesthetic terms.

Hockey Violence as Controlled Violence

Fights are thought to be harmless because the potential for serious injury is low and there are strict limits to the violence. Violence is expected, which is why the rule book has to outlaw acts such as 'spearing,' 'slashing,' 'boarding,' and the catch-all 'roughing.' In organized hockey, the referee enforces these rules, which helps uphold the idea of sports as a separate world or society that is free to determine its own laws and govern itself. Not much on-ice violence has been contested in the courts (which is why the handful of exceptions are so well known). The referee capably conducts affairs, including discerning the amount of pressure the safety valves should release before he steps in to break up a fight.

In his autobiography *If You Can't Beat 'Em in the Alley*, the late Toronto Maple Leafs owner Conn Smythe writes bluntly about who really controls hockey violence. After a referee doled out gentle punishment for an infraction against the Leafs, Smythe 'blasted him' and 'never allowed [him] to referee again.' This might imply that Smythe was anti-fighting. Hardly. When the court of law took action against an NHL hockey player for an on-ice incident, Smythe again grew explosive:

> When I blasted Ontario Attorney-General Roy McMurtry for interfering with hockey by laying assault charges, do-gooders thought my intention was to brutalize the game; actually, I was only standing up for what I knew, that hockey could manage itself.

A team owner talking moralistically about his business 'managing itself,' without legal or governmental interference, is suspect. Smythe's attack against McMurtry is hypocritical in light of his earlier decision to use his clout as an owner to ban a lenient referee (who had sinned by calling only a two-minute penalty). Smythe's memoirs confirm the belief that businessmen manage the way the game is played, including the level and regulation of violence.[31] Stopping violence altogether could be bad for business, and perhaps prevent growth into less traditional hockey areas, where the visceral attraction to legal violence is thought to be an inroad to more refined appreciation of the game.

Lawrence Scanlan's book *Grace under Fire: The State of Our Sweet and Savage Game* contains a long letter from novelist Guy Vanderhaeghe:

> Outrage is frequently expressed by hockey people when violence which would never be condoned on the street is threatened with prosecution in the courts. Hockey is assumed to somehow be exempt from the rule of law. And hockey culture is unlikely to change because there is so little internal criticism.

Harsher penalties would probably eliminate violence, but, warns Vanderhaeghe in a playful reversal of argument, hockey would then become 'a pansy game.' The novelist's reference to hockey's manliness reflects Mordecai Richler's view of writing, including why he and his ilk chose the pen over the puck: '... we settled for writing, a sissy's game, because we couldn't pitch a curve ball, catch, deke, score a touchdown, or "float like a butterfly and sting like a bee."' Vanderhaeghe and Richler, 'sissy' writers both, are also hockey fans, and when Vanderhaeghe revokes his criticism of hockey culture, he points out how even cultured hockey fans – unlike honest Don Cherry – pay mere lip service to eradicating fighting.[32] He and other fans may 'know better,' but the continued approval of fighting clearly means that most fans do not really want to make hockey less violent. The general stance seems to be that hockey violence is part of the game, and that the game can control itself. Fiction, however, does not uncritically accept positions like those of owner Conn Smythe.

The goal here is not to prove or disprove sociological theories about catharsis or controlled hockey violence; I present these concepts because they form the necessary background for understanding hockey fiction. Though some fictional works indirectly criticize the role of violence in the national game, few philosophize about the need for violence or the extension of violence into the world beyond the rink. Hockey literature is parasitical in that it portrays a realistic space where grown men can beat each other up to the delight of spectators. There is no need for authors to create that unusual world, and the intellectual justification for otherwise aberrant behaviour is pre-existing.

Linguistic Denial of Violence

Hockey writing often denies or diminishes violence through choice words, ambiguity, and euphemism that imply violence has not occurred. Instead of overlooking the violence, writers rein it in linguistically. Since hockey is regarded as the essentially 'masculine' and 'violent' game in Canada, one would expect the same in the language used to describe it (and to some extent commentators and journalists comply, as players regularly become 'warriors' or 'gladiators'). Yet when fights break out, the opposite – preciosity or euphemism – is just as common. In rugby, references to violence are systematically included in the terminology and the writing on the sport,[33] and the entirely militaristic vocabulary of American football includes terms like 'long bomb' or 'coffin corner.' In hockey, there is a constant stream of euphemism, understatement, and archaisms that suggest that the fighting is not really taking place. Hockey journalism has always been full of terms like 'plucky' or 'spirited' to refer to an apparent thirst for blood. Nevertheless, when a spectator watches what is obviously a fight, no amount of linguistic wizardry can deny that a fight is what it is.

Brian Turner, in a free-flowing essay belonging to the genre of literary sports journalism in the style of A.J. Liebling's *The Sweet Science*, Norman Mailer's *The Fight*, and Lorna Jackson's 2007 *Cold-Cocked: On Hockey*, describes a mistake he made early in his career. Covering his small college's ice hockey team, he chose the wrong word to describe a brawl, embarrassing the institution's authorities. After a heated game in which there was an altercation between players and fans, he called a local news station and stated tersely, 'A.I.C. beats Salem State, 12–10. There was a riot.' When the news spreads like wildfire and reaches his boss, the young reporter is taken to task:

> '... there is a word that does not exist in the lexicon of public relations. And that word is "riot."'
> 'Sorry.'
> 'You can call it an altercation, you can call it a spirited encounter, a melee, a brawl, a fight.'
> 'O.K.'
> '*But never, ever a riot–!*'

The young journalist has given the lie to concepts of sport as a controlled, playful, enjoyable, and apolitical realm. A vocabulary more suitable to the ideal of play, although less honest to the reality of sport, must be used.[34]

Commentators often use the language of theatre and performance to describe hockey, and Ken Dryden is not alone in calling this very real fighting a 'harmless burlesque' because it takes place on ice. After a fight that involves much blood and continues for longer than usual, commentators might refer to a 'real tango' or to 'putting on a good show,' and a player looking for a fight might complain, 'No one wants to dance!' Even when a fight does take place, it is usually more of a 'clownish wrestling match' that unfolds according to plan. Comparing grown men to tussling clowns implicitly states that fights are faked performances.[35]

Violence and the Viewer

Diane Schoemperlen's 'Hockey Night in Canada' and Hanford Woods's 'The Drubbing of Nesterenko' show fans' individual responses to watching a hockey game, including its violence. The first story portrays a healthy attitude and distance towards the game, whereas Woods's tale is a classic case of over-identifying and becoming too involved in the spectacle. Schoemperlen's spectators have a more aesthetic relationship to the game, while in the Woods story, the narrator opens himself up to harm through his emotional involvement.

Schoemperlen's story is about a one-child family and centres around a possible affair between the father and Rita, a family friend who enjoys hockey. Every Saturday, father and daughter enjoy the Canadian ritual of sitting down to watch *Hockey Night in Canada*. Though the mother is present while the television blares, she has no interest in hockey. She remains in the background as an archetypal maternal figure, 'ripping apart with relish a red-and-white polka dot dress' in order to give it a new life as a feminine blouse for her hockey-loving daughter. Despite their loyalty to the weekly show, the father and the daughter maintain a disinterested attitude towards hockey:

> We were not violent fans, either one of us. We never hollered, leaped out of our chairs, or pounded ourselves in alternating fits of frustration and ecstasy. We did not jump up and down yelling, 'kill him, kill him!' Instead, we were teasing fans, pretend fans almost, feigning hostility and heartbreak ... sometimes just to get a rise out of my mother ...

These 'teasing fans, pretend fans almost,' barely qualify as sports fans. To be a fan there must be a psychological attachment to the team, as well as an absolute bias; one has to care about the outcome of the game. Such a leap of faith is required to submerge the individual into the physical or imagined mass that is fandom. The father and daughter are engaging in the ritual of being fans, acting as they think fans should act, pretending that the game propels them to uncontrolled behaviour and aggression. The description of what they did *not* do reveals the way fans act when driven to frenzy by the aggression and violence on the ice. This lighthearted attitude shows their awareness that the game is not important – they watch it out of habit more than any perceived need.[36]

The mother's friend Rita relates differently to hockey: 'Unlike my father and me, was a *real* fan, a serious fan who shrieked and howled and paced around the living room' – like Kurtz's 'savage and superb, wild-eyed and magnificent' mistress prowling the shore in Joseph Conrad's *Heart of Darkness*. In both the feigned and 'real' fandom, watching the game is associated with a loss of control and coincident potential danger. As Daniel L. Wann et al. note, '… the emotional arousal engendered by the outcome of a game, be it joy and ecstasy or grief and anger, leads to loss of normal restraint, or disinhibition.' It is because of Rita's fandom, and obvious romantic desire for the husband, that the narrator's mother feigns interest in the game whenever Rita is there. The reason for this pretense is clear: the mother senses a risk of losing her husband to Rita because of the supposedly meaningless game they share. Brought together by the game, the story strongly suggests that they have an affair. The mother is made to feel that she has to pay attention to the game if she wants her husband to pay attention to her. Though leisure time should be free of necessity, the *playing* is a forced and concrete acting out in miniature of the national imperative: Thou shalt enjoy this game, including its violence.[37]

The distant spectacle of hockey encroaches on the narrator's life outside hockey in Hanford Woods's short story 'The Drubbing of Nesterenko.' Violence brings the spectacle all too close to the narrator, traumatizing him, so to speak. Despite the real names and events described and its naturalistically detailed examination of hockey violence, 'The Drubbing of Nesterenko' is a work of fiction. Woods shows that a one-sided fight is more likely to be labelled violence, regardless of whether both agreed to the ritual by dropping their gloves. As the title indicates, the story is about a fight between the narrator's hero, Eric Nesterenko, and the Montreal Canadiens' John Ferguson. Though each is a role player rather than a star, the difference between them is enormous (in fact, the real-life Nesterenko wrote and published poetry). The ageing Nesterenko excels at controlling a game when his team is short-handed. According to the story, Ferguson lacks any talent and is almost criminal. Ferguson has been hired to fight rather than kill penalties, and he performs this duty earnestly. In short, the difference between the two players is this: John Ferguson is generally recognized as the first 'enforcer,' that is, the first NHL hockey player to be employed primarily on the basis of his ability to fight and intimidate (though he did pile up reasonable offensive statistics, too). The role that Nesterenko plays is directly related to winning games by preventing goals against. Ferguson is pure 'value added' or, at best, an indirect means of gaining an advantage. Because this takes place before the fight-happy NHL of the 1970s, Ferguson still seems exceptional – and he sticks out especially on the Montreal Canadiens, a team known for its skill, speed, and finesse.

Under normal circumstances, Woods's narrator argues, fights in the NHL are harmless. They are an innocuous ritual that consists of a 'foolish bout of punching, shoving and grabbing.' The players, once separated by the linesmen, may threaten each other, but less out of a real desire than because 'they must blindly follow rituals. By performing in this tedious denouement they console themselves that their pride is intact.' The entire fight process is an exhibition of masculinity, with values such as 'pride' and 'honour' exhibited through strength and power. Because this is all 'stylized activity,' the violence is not real and 'people who find hockey brutal are unnecessarily squeamish.'[38] Merely a display, the violence is thought to be feigned, like shadowboxing or glamour-ridden professional wrestling – simply a performance and 'denouement' to be watched.

In his sociological work *Men at Play: A Working Understanding of Professional Hockey*, Michael Robidoux examines the voyeuristic aspects of hockey. He recalls attending a game and the crowd's 'horror' when a spectator was hit in the mouth by an errant puck. This is in stark contrast to the absence of 'noticeable concern that [a player] likely would need stitches to repair the cut on his face' incurred during a fight. Since there is no intent to injure, an accidental injury caused by a puck obviously does not constitute violence. Still, real concern for the injured player is commonly put aside merely because the injury takes place 'out there' on the ice and is an occupational hazard. Robidoux concludes: '... the horror with which the fans watched this woman in her predicament is the horror of spectacle and reality coming together as one.' Hockey is a spectacle in the sense that, although real, it is mass entertainment. Robidoux's example is yet another reminder that fans wilfully forget that real punches are thrown during a hockey fight, and even though the referee is present to keep things under control, real stitches are sometimes required.[39]

'Spectacle and reality' coincide in 'The Drubbing' as well, albeit on the ice. The fight between Ferguson and Nesterenko breaks the usual pattern; there is nothing clownish, burlesque-like, or feigned about it:

I can still hear the voice of [play-by-play announcer] Danny Gallivan ... *Ferguson and Nesterenko race after* [the puck], *they contest it along the boards ... now Ferguson has dropped his gloves, Ferguson is going after Nesterenko, they're going at*

*it ... Ferguson pummels Nesterenko with a series of right hooks, Nesterenko is on his
knees, he's not fighting back, he's cut, he's bleeding badly ... linesman Pavlitch is
struggling to pull Ferguson off Nesterenko, they can't get him off ...*[40]

The horror comes from seeing Ferguson cross the line of accepted violence, and is worsened because Ferguson attacks a favourite player. The
attack becomes an aggravated assault when Nesterenko stops and Ferguson abandons all decorum and sportsmanship by continuing to throw
punches. Under normal circumstances, a hockey fight ends once a
player falls (and often the player who is winning the fight will not continue to punch a player who has fallen to the ice – he has already been
seen to be the victor and has 'proved' his masculinity). The degree of
violence in this fight is unusual, and its extremity is indicated by the
play-by-play announcer's shift from the usual euphemisms to more
direct language. 'They're going at it' is a socially acceptable way of
saying players are fighting. Only when Ferguson begins to dominate do
the words 'pummel' and 'not fighting back' appear, along with the
hapless linesman 'struggling' to regain control. There is no longer an
attempt to reduce the violence: the reader is presented with an image
of a bleeding man 'on his knees.' The scene is horrific, even for the narrator who had earlier accused others of 'squeamishness' when it comes
to hockey fights. By focusing on hockey violence, the story forces the
reader to consider the brutality at the heart of Canada's favourite
pastime.

The pseudo-fans in Schoemperlen's 'Hockey Night in Canada' have
ironic detachment towards the game. Woods's narrator does not. He
undergoes a transformation from a generic hockey fan to one who has
to rethink the limits of on-ice violence. The fight is so frightening that
it eradicates his earlier indifference towards hockey violence – horror
and the detached viewpoint that engenders irony do not coalesce. Presumably others watching the fight would have retained emotional distance, and thus not be haunted by the violence. Woods states that, years
later, 'the blows with which Ferguson hammered Nesterenko ... are not
of the past,' though they are 'buried in the sacred soil that nourishes all
repressed events.'[41] This is the language of trauma, the antithesis of
catharsis or healthy, redemptive release that Aristotle and MacLennan
espouse for tragedy and hockey, respectively. Whether it is drama or
sport, some sort of identification is required for a release of emotions to
take place. If we do not care about the event or people involved, no
identification can take place, and any emotional upheaval and catharsis

is nipped in the bud. Woods's narrator goes too far in the other direction by identifying too strongly with Nesterenko and (negatively) with Ferguson. As a result, the narrator admits he would like to see Ferguson injured. 'The Drubbing' does not promote the catharsis theory. Rather, it argues that hockey violence, even if gazed at from the gallery, encourages further violence.

This desire to see Ferguson injured stems not only from the pummelling of the narrator's favourite player. Describing another game, the narrator nonchalantly outlines and applauds – though 'not entirely free of shame' – the Boston Bruins' strategy of intimidating Montreal through aggression or instrumental violence. This may be an indirect road, but it still leads to winning the game. The narrator ignores all sense of strategy in Ferguson's case, focusing on the individual and ignoring the idea of planned violence. Ferguson attacks for the sake of it, 'not in response to any real or imagined aggression,' and is therefore a pure corruption of the game. He corrupts the game because he does not abide by the unwritten rules that keep violence under control. He is an animal, 'a beast in its fury'; 'his opponents were at a disadvantage: they had long since mastered this fury and could not counter it with one ... of their own.' This mastering shows that, in the narrator's mind, an important part of this culture of masculinity means being able to control oneself (though this is less pronounced in hockey than in other sports).[42] The other, more predictable, players and fighters are stronger moral characters because they know and respect limits. They fulfil the traditional, stoic hero role.

Learning the Rules

Ferguson's sin in 'The Drubbing of Nesterenko' was to continue attacking when his opponent was down. Though this was a clear transgression, the unwritten fight rules are as subterranean and tangled as any social codes, and, like social codes, they are easier to sense than to explain to the outsider. Codes determining how a man should behave on the ice are complicated by factors such as on-ice passion, directives from team officials, fear of losing one's job by being regarded as 'too soft,' and even the desire to be considered a little crazy and therefore unpredictable. As well, there are those few players who are beyond codes, the type that 'depends on everyone's fear of the unknown. The game of hockey is license for some truly crazy men to inflict pain,' as the narrator of Bill Gaston's *The Good Body* observes. Though certain players in the NHL are employed primarily as fighters, and fighting is entrenched within the professional game, it is rare that a coach will actually tell someone to fight. Journalist George Plimpton in *Open Net*, writes of 'the curious code that enforcers went by – that what they were to do on the ice was always suggested by inference and innuendo.' Though it is an open secret that most orders to fight come from behind the bench, if no direct commands are given, only the fighter is to 'blame.' Management can always fall back on the illusion of fights breaking out solely through the free actions of the individuals involved.[43]

Justin Bryant's short story 'Hakkanen's Move' is about Doug Kazlor, an enforcer whose world is administered by hints and nudges. Though not quite as inept as Woods claims Ferguson was, Kazlor has, like most enforcers, 'a flaw or two in [his] game. Doug's was skating.' When Kazlor tries to imitate the patent move of his flashy Finnish teammate Hakkanen, the result is comical ineptitude. Bryant provides a clear account of the type of unwritten rules governing the enforcer's life on the ice – including the one stipulating that enforcers, rarely the most agile skaters, should not adopt the role of goal scorers or creative forwards. Their job is to fight and intimidate. When Kazlor finds himself next to his counterpart Stonewald, the reader expects an immediate fight. Instead Doug Kazlor is calm as can be:

> Doug turned his head and waited for the face-off. He knew they weren't going to fight yet. He'd just come on the ice, while Stonewald was finishing a long shift and was gassed. That was one of the unwritten Tough Guy Rules: don't square off with a guy who's at the end of a shift. Doug took it seriously, along with other maxims such as no headbutting, no sucker punches and no jumping on non-fighters, unless they're asking for it. From what he'd heard around the league, Frank Stonewald didn't always abide by the Tough Guy Rules. But even if that were so, Doug wasn't lowering himself to cross that line.

The series of clichés indicate a certainty about how a fight between 'tough guys' is supposed to transpire. In hopes of guaranteeing a fair fight, all enforcers have a deeply moral obligation to avoid fighting when the opponent is tired. Fighting in hockey looks like a descent into warfare, into a battle for survival, but that is only part of the ritual. Doug clearly believes in the warrior's honour. The unwritten Tough Guy Rules may be nebulous, but they are, as a matter of honour, 'absolutely binding' to Doug. They provide some limits to the chaos of war or fighting. Rules such as 'no headbutting' or 'sucker punches' are in place to protect the fighters in hockey, to control the violence, if only to let them fight again in the near future.[44] Kazlor will heed them, refusing to 'lower himself,' and the result is the system is kept intact; the violence can continue.

In the mind of Woods's narrator, Ferguson was dangerous because he jeopardized the system of controlled violence by ignoring the unwritten rules and codes. Doug Kazlor is sincere in his hockey role, but when Bryant writes that Kazlor 'took it seriously,' he is referring to the ultimate respect Kazlor has for the capitalized Tough Guy Rules. If reputation counts for anything, Frank Stonewald endangers this system in which Doug Kazlor so firmly trusts. There is a contrast between Kazlor's certainty – 'he knew they weren't going to fight yet' – and the actual statements decreeing who should fight and when. For example, when Bryant points out that attacking non-fighters is taboo, 'unless they're asking for it,' the reader realizes just how nebulous these rules are. As hockey and far more abusive and dangerous circumstances have shown, 'to be asking for it' is open to gross misinterpretation. (When, for example, is a non-fighter provoking violence? By scoring too much?) When misinterpretation comes into play, along with obvious flouting of unwritten rules by characters like Stonewald, Kazlor's firm system should fall apart, yet his faith in the system does not waver.

Limits, unwritten rules, and codes seem to be intuitive in Canadian hockey circles. Lynn Coady's 2002 novel *Saints of Big Harbour*, a sad and comic meandering coming-of-age story in which hockey plays a minor role, shows how codes are in fact a learned behaviour. Hockey is a man's game in Big Harbour, Nova Scotia, a place where violence makes sense, is endorsed by most, and regularly on display for all to see. The novel is peopled by various small-town heroes, would-be heroes and anti-heroes, but dominated by Isadore Boucher, a violent, alcoholic uncle to the teenaged narrator, Guy. A born hockey fan, one would imagine, but though he was involved in hockey in the past, Isadore has avoided the game completely for twenty years and 'wouldn't even come over to see [the television] when there was a fight' (he does, however, slip up to Halifax and Montreal for the occasional fix). When the unreliable and often absent uncle discovers that his nephew Guy plays, he makes a gallant return to act as advisor, mentor, and unofficial coach. Power motivates him: 'For the first time since he had played as a teenager, he would have some measure of control over the outcome' of some aspect of his life. Unfortunately, Isadore's sense of power and domination is both surrogate for and entirely dependent on fighting, as opposed to other skills. He encourages fights and violence on the ice, offering such gems as 'Fuck the penalty! This is hockey!' when Guy is slow to respond to an attack on a teammate. For Isadore, this is a clear situation demanding a clear course of action. Guy's friend was abused and the unwritten rule requires immediate retribution – 'That was your goddamn teammate! You go get him!' yells Isadore. His words reveal the code that perpetuates and escalates violence.[45]

Under Isadore's tutelage of Guy, the local team plays what fans jokingly and euphemistically call 'old time hockey.' The atmosphere of aggression spreads beyond the rink come playoff time: 'The town became a carnival of violence and the hockey rink was the main attraction, like a big tent pitched in its center.' Guy, whose fists the townspeople so avidly follow, remains aloof. Like many literary hockey protagonists, he is paradoxically detached from the violence that is now the centre of his life: 'Guy took it all in. He noticed how everybody pretended to mind [the violent atmosphere], how everybody seemed to be bubbling with outrage, but nobody did anything to quell it.' This is the lip service so commonly paid to ridding hockey of fighting. In reality, 'everybody' rewards both Guy and Isadore for the on-ice fisticuffs, and there is no impetus for them to stop. After his first fight, the thirteen-year-old accompanies his uncle to the bar, and 'men asked if they could buy Guy beers and stood talking to Isadore about him.' Isadore is a classic manipulator, and as the men gather around to talk *about* Guy, even in his presence, the uncle is the bar's focal point.[46] Isadore happily basks in this reflected glory. Guy is a puppet as Isadore, the man behind the violence, provides an education in aggression and reaps the rewards.

Despite all the attention and opportunities for the boy to be a man by drinking in public, Guy is not happy with his role as a hockey enforcer. Instead of just cleaning up his style of play, however, he decides to quit hockey altogether while his team is competing in the playoffs. The boy narrator's lack of perspective and awareness of other hockey options reflects the broader belief that fighting and violence are part and parcel of hockey and the only way to play the game. Later in the novel, months after Guy has quit playing, an older boy jumps and pummels him for no apparent reason. The ex-hockey player Guy compares this vicious attack to another one that had occurred the year before: 'At least I knew what [that attack] was about ... It was about hockey, so it made sense.'[47] This recognition of the 'sense' of that attack baldly expresses that violence and abuse in hockey are reasonable and acceptable, and thus forgivable; even if the earlier attack took place off the ice, which is a transgression of unwritten hockey rules, Guy can accept it. An attack that is not related to hockey in any way disturbs Guy precisely because of its randomness.

Codified violence is not intrinsic to the game, but Canadians have naturalized it through acceptance and exposure. Bill Gaston's 1998 short story 'Your First Time' contains the mildly comical and highly illustrative character of Dil Carnback, a Swedish goal scorer who lacks Guy Boucher's culture and education of hockey violence. Like the enforcer Frank Stonewald in 'Hakkanen's Move,' Dil Carnback adds an element of danger because he does not abide by the unwritten rules. Whereas Stonewald presumably chooses to ignore the rules, the Swedish player is a cultural misfit in a game where the written rules are more or less the same around the world. The European 'misse[s] the point' because

> ... he had no sense of appropriate force. Blind to the flow of a game, he'd absolutely cream a guy, a non-threatening nobody, face in the glass, for no reason, in the neutral zone, and he'd wonder not only why he got a penalty but also why he got no accolades back on the bench, where he'd look around for the praise a good smear could get you. Or during that brawl, everybody dropping their gloves and a few guys going at it but mostly just orderly shoving – Dilly speared the guy he'd partnered off with.

Gaston's short story is a departure from the 'chicken Swede' label that foments the belief that European players are less gutsy because hockey in that neutral country is fight-free and has a lower bodycheck count. Dil's actions are beyond both strategy and decorum: when he draws a penalty for hitting 'a non-threatening nobody,' it is clear that his team will not benefit from any intimidation factors and that the hit is therefore foolish and superfluous. 'Spearing' is frowned upon at the best of times, but entirely unseemly when players drop their gloves to box (especially when there is mere 'orderly shoving'). Gaston provides a simple explanation for Dil's behaviour: 'Dil couldn't respect a fair fight because he was too freaked out to see one.' Because of Dil's native hockey environment, he is not able to see anything 'orderly' about the 'shoving,' or differentiate between types of roughness. He is like the foreign spectator of a ball game who cannot follow the path of the ball or predict where it might be headed, and therefore witnesses only chaos. The irony is that Dil is playing 'his' game, just not the old-time, NHL, Canadian way.[48]

Hamming It Up: Violence on Display I

Whatever their stance towards fighting in hockey, few will identify with the hero of Roy MacGregor's novel *The Last Season*. Highly critical of some hockey surroundings, the novel centres on the aptly named Felix Batterinski and his role as an enforcer or 'goon.' *The Last Season* is primarily an indictment of violence in hockey, especially in 1970s NHL hockey and its feeder leagues. It has the classic form of a *Bildungsroman*, less the maturity and moral or intellectual growth typical of the genre. MacGregor leads Batterinski from his boyhood in the Ontario bush to a successful career as a 'Broadstreet Bully' playing for the notoriously aggressive Philadelphia Flyers of the early and mid-1970s, and on to his final season as a player-coach in a fight-free Finnish league. In between the bush and Finland, Batterinski becomes the NHL record holder for penalty minutes. Whenever Batterinski plays outside of Canada, it is never forgotten that he is Canadian. (Batterinski, meanwhile, wrestles with his Polish heritage, and his father's accent embarrasses him.) For example, the adoring Philadelphia fans call him 'Canucklehead.' After Batterinski is caught on film seemingly attacking a spectator while playing for the Finnish team, the photograph circles the globe. He learns from a Canadian reporter: 'You've become a symbol overnight for what's wrong with Canadian hockey.'[49] The comment is bewildering for Batterinski because he has not changed his playing style over the years. Hockey culture has changed greatly, but Batterinski fails to take notice.

Batterinski's desire for audience applause does not neatly fit the catharsis theory of violence as a boiling over of emotions. In fact, his violence rarely arises from anger. There is an unsettling air of calmness in his description of one of his first fights:

> [The other player] came at me swinging and my linesman wouldn't let go, so I ducked and could hear the crack of the defenseman's fist on my linesman's head. I take things like that personally. My linesman released me, perhaps deliberately ... Pulling up his sweater over his head so it tied his arms, I drilled him right through the Parry Sound Shamrocks' crest, a direct hit on the mouth. Twice more and I could see the sweater staining red through the crest and, mercifully, both linesmen fell on me and pulled me away.

This passage bristles with hints of the controlled violence discussed previously in this chapter. Batterinski speaks with an odd intimacy of 'my linesman' and attacks in earnest only after that linesman is punched, an action he takes 'personally' – as though the Shamrocks player's real guilt lies in accidentally striking the sacred official. Temporarily restrained by the linesman, Batterinski even claims, 'I was willing to let things die,' to peter out without a fight. This is false magnanimity since Batterinski's earlier attack on a smaller player is what led to the fight in the first place. Despite the bloody result of the fight, Batterinski shows that the linesmen are in control of the situation. The fight starts when Batterinski is released, 'perhaps deliberately,' by the linesman and concludes through the 'merciful' intervention of two officials. Batterinski implies that the linesmen are like stage directors or even puppeteers, complicit in the violence. This reveals, not limits of violence, but yet another hockey narrator's limited viewpoint – the sense that the officials control the scope of the violence, including the use of the word 'merciful,' is ambivalent because it means that Batterinski separates himself from his own actions and responsibility for these actions. Here he relies on an external force to corral his own violent actions.[50]

Batterinski's sense of control of the situation is in sharp contrast to the need for referees to regulate fights. The young fighter masters fights by mastering his anger, though this does not lead to less violence. Unlike those who win fights through rage and anger, Batterinski wins them by means of eerily calculated calmness. He revels in the attention that a fight garners, finding there an audience and a chance to be in the spotlight he does not enjoy off the ice. The description of the fight is a description of a specific process, which is the epitome of control (as though Batterinski were dealing with a problem by breaking it down into more manageable elements). What happens during the tumultuous seconds of a fight is carried out with clear intent, and Batterinski explains, with an instruction manual's detachment, that he pulls the sweater up in order to disable the opponent's arms. Batterinski describes his feelings and amazing sense of self-awareness when in a fight:

> When attention was on me, time slowed down. In a fight, I relaxed. I could sit in the dressing room in the hours before a game and twitch so bad sometimes a foot would jump right off the floor. But when my defenseman charged I was aware even of my own breathing. He came in flailing, but to me it was like watching someone swim toward me doing the crawl. I could sense his intention and I could feel his blind fury.

When not under the lights, away from a fight, he speaks objectively about 'a foot,' as though this limb jumping 'right off the floor' were disembodied or detached; yet he speaks of 'my defenseman' just as he had spoken of 'my linesman.' Batterinski appears to have more control over the opponent than over his own body. Whereas the other fighter is overcome by 'blind fury' and attacks with a resulting 'flailing' randomness, Batterinski is calm and able to use this tranquility to abuse the opponent.[51]

The best athletes in team sports always seem to have more time on the field or ice. When Batterinski is fighting, he is blessed with the same ability, as is clear from the comment that the opponent seemed to be 'swimming.' Again and again in *The Last Season*, the reader sees that Batterinski's viewpoint is woefully skewed and his skills misused, distorted by his own awareness of fighting as a spectacle. This clearly comes through in his description of the fight, as he proudly notes that a stretcher was needed for the other boy: 'the ultimate proof that I'd won.' In addition, Batterinski claims that finishing the fight quickly was 'an act of charity ... and I ended his humiliation quickly for him, even hiding his face under his sweater when it happened. He should have thanked me.' Batterinski knows that he has won the fight, and the need for proof can only be for the audience; similarly, the talk of 'charity' and 'humiliation' only makes sense if we share Batterinski's horror, not of losing or of injury, but of losing in front of a crowd. For Batterinski it is less important to win a fight than *to be seen* winning the fight. Batterinski is only a teenager at this point in the novel, but unlike Guy Boucher in *Saints of Big Harbour*, he does not renounce violence or grow out of it. He makes violence his career and thereby suffers from what David L. Vanderwerken, in an article on MacGregor's novel, calls 'Terminal Adolescent Syndrome.' Growing pains remain with this player: 'The ice becomes Batterinski's refuge, where his monstrousness not only is approved, but also economically rewarded.' His hockey world makes it financially irrational to grow up and move away from violence – only within the confines of this hockey culture are violence and the refusal or inability to mature understandable options. In *The Last Season* there is no real growth, progress, or meaningful education.[52]

Mark Anthony Jarman's *Salvage King, Ya!* is about a boozing, journeyman minor league player comically named Drinkwater, who is just one expansion shy of making the NHL and striking it rich, as Batterinski did. Like Batterinski, Drinkwater understands the unwritten rules of hockey violence. He is, however, blessed with far greater insight than

Batterinski, which makes his complicity in the culture of violence all the more acute. On the other hand, he is better able to exploit his awareness of hockey codes to prolong his career as a player. Although Drinkwater does not delude himself into believing he is in control of his life on or off the ice, he is well aware of the wherefore and the why of his hockey culture:

> I was traded for losing a fight in front of our bench. No one cared how I came out, only that it was bad psychologically for the team. I was gone in hours. Another suitcase open, my cheekbone killing me, double-vision.

Drinkwater is not complaining, and he does not bewail his fate like the narrator of Jarman's story 'Righteous Speedboat.' As a role player, he is expected to do more than just 'show up' for a fight, and he knows that his job is to win fights; furthermore, he realizes that the individual is entirely relegated to the needs of the team. Again we see the importance of spectatorship for hockey fights, since here the teammates and coaches become a second audience. Batterinski expresses his aggrandized understanding of his purpose as a player, namely 'to exhibit strength' and 'appear superhuman to the rest of the team.' For the violent show to go on there must be a series of spectators, ranging from other players to coaches to owners to paying fans.[53]

Drinkwater, unfortunately for his career prospects and health, is far from 'superhuman' and a poor fighter. Coming back to clarity after losing yet another fight, the trainer asks if he know where he is. Drinkwater 'look[s] around,' takes stock of his surroundings, and says, 'Yeah. The fucking minors.' Hockey fans will read this as more than an easy wisecrack. It is a reminder that the minor leagues can be tougher than the NHL because an extra aggressive, even violent, edge can literally make a million dollar difference in salary. Given similar skill levels, NHL managers will invariably take the player with a reputation for 'toughness.' At the same time, there is Drinkwater's own realization that he is no goal scorer and that a tough guy who loses fights is not going to the NHL. Drinkwater's clarity about his position in hockey life dovetails with an anecdote related in *Lions in Winter*, Goyens and Turowetz's history of the Montreal Canadiens. After losing a fight in a preseason game – that time of year when the individual players are battling for positions on the team – a player vows, 'I'll get you for that next game!' The winner ungracefully replies, 'I'm not worried, you'll be in the minors by then.' For all but the most skilled players, turning down a fight is not an option. Drinkwater knows he belongs to the hockey proletariat and cribs from the Communist Manifesto at one point to proclaim, 'Grinders of the world unite, you have nothing to lose but your teeth.' He knows, too, that this is an odd way for a grown man to earn a living, and he is equally aware that all those lesser-skilled players who literally have to fight each other to keep their jobs are in fact of the same guild, even as they hit each other. Nor are things likely to change.[54]

How the enforcer behaves when not on the ice fascinates fans because it can show the contrast between a normal individual and a violent hockey player. Jarman takes another tack in part of *Salvage King, Ya!* Though most of the novel concentrates on Drinkwater's confused personal life, Jarman also takes us into the head of the fighter on the job. In one fight, Drinkwater absent-mindedly hums to himself while 'some steroid headcase [is] wailing on' him. The pop song, perfectly revelatory of both his lot in life and his awareness of that lot, is cotton candy Tiffany's 1987 hit 'I Think We're Alone Now' – which begins, 'Children behave, that's what they say when we're together.' The song is appropriately inappropriate (unless we allow the parallel that randy teenagers are also inclined to engage in the wrong activity for their age) and provides a witty comment on the fight scene; the adult hockey players are behaving like scuffling schoolchildren and unlikely to grow out of it.[55]

Elsewhere, Drinkwater actually wins a fight and is lucid and detached enough to provide his own commentary:

> The ref wouldn't let me at the other guy and I was so wound up I clocked the ref to get rid of him and then clobbered the other joker who thought he was scot free. Sweater down, punch up, punch up, punch up. This should make Don Cherry's video, I thought ...

The euphemistically playful terms 'joker,' 'scot free,' and 'clocked' make it seem like Drinkwater has internalized the benign language of hockey journalists. Contradicting this is the mechanical, repetitive 'sweater down, punch up, punch up, punch up,' which shows the athlete's body as a tool or machine going through the motions – a common trope in sports literature and journalism, where the athlete's body is a 'complex machine whose performance can be enhanced, and which can break down and be repaired, just like any other machine.'

Machines do not think, however, and here the abuse of the body is coupled with self-reflection.[56]

Also-ran Drinkwater's wish to make Don Cherry's hockey highlight video is not just a wish for a few seconds of fame. Don Cherry is the most recognized advocate of fighting in hockey, and though his series of *Rock 'em, Sock 'em* videos also shows saves and goals, viewers will remember them primarily for the bodychecks and the fights. Cherry is mentioned in hockey literature of the past quarter century more than any other figure in or around the game – as proof of both his onerous ways and his popularity, he has given Canadians something to write about. A *New York Times* article of 5 June 2004 set itself a difficult task: presenting Don Cherry to an audience who, for the most part, believes 'that to be Canadian is to shun controversy, ostentation or violence.' The article went on to explain the shock value of Don Cherry: 'He preaches law and order, warns about the threats of multiculturalism to Canadian society and argues that Canadians should back the United States when it goes to war.' In other words, hockey and its main media representative, Don Cherry, are deemed by this American newspaper to be ill-chosen Canadian icons because they reflect neither Canada's international reputation nor its self-image as a nation, becalmed by what Hugh MacLennan calls 'Canadian self-restraint.' The *Times* article includes a colourful quotation from Cherry, who earnestly noted, 'I am extremely Canadian to the extreme, which most Canadians aren't.' The eerie suggestion is that Cherry states clearly what many Canadians would like to say, only they lack the chutzpah.[57]

Before returning to Drinkwater and his dreams of video, two other literary references to Cherry and his hold on Canadian culture will prove useful to explaining his star-maker capabilities. Poet Richard Harrison examines the suitability of this national icon in 'Coach's Corner,' named after Cherry's immensely popular and ever controversial weekly CBC television show. Cherry, with his seemingly anachronistic, racist, and homophobic comments 'slams foreigners, / praises women in all the ways wrong for our time, / [and] rejects any wavering in the masculinity of his troops'; in short, he is 'everything a man should not be.' But he is not a hypocrite. He makes no pretense of the need to eliminate fighting and clearly states his reasons for why hockey should *not* become fight-free. It is, in part, because of this honesty and directness that he has become the 'priest' or evangelist of a rough style of playing hockey. 'Every sports bar / wills itself to quiet, turns up the volume on its dozen / [television] sets only for his words.' The priest comparison is a clever one, for when Don Cherry enters the picture to offer a few comments in between periods of hockey, a hush literally falls over the bar as drunken men listen like reverent and docile children.[58] Like hockey itself in MacLennan's view, Cherry offers Canadians a release by proxy.

Another literary comment on Don Cherry's status as a hockey expert and prominent Canadian underlines the importance of making it into his video for Drinkwater in *Salvage King, Ya!*, of making people watch as well as listen. In the novel *When's She Gone*, Steve Lundin's narrator recalls a dull NHL playoff series that was made bearable only by the presence of Don Cherry. For many, Don Cherry is not just an entertaining commentator but the embodiment of hockey and Canada. Lundin's passage continues with an apocalyptic vision of life after Don Cherry: 'I had a dream once, one night, that the CBC fired Cherry and the whole nation went up in flames, every city from east to west burned to the ground.' The CBC has an unearned reputation of being politically correct and generally reticent in its programming. Here Don Cherry is the saving grace of this public broadcaster and Canadian unity because he directly states the assumptions about hockey that are otherwise silenced in CBC discourse.[59]

Being praised by Cherry on *Hockey Night in Canada* or, better, making it into his video for a fight, is a very public stamp of approval for a certain type of hockey and a sure way of establishing, or accentuating, one's masculine image. For the fast-fading veteran Drinkwater, reference to 'Cherry's video' in *Salvage King, Ya!* suggests minor longevity in another medium. He will be made immortal, so to speak. This is a reminder that, as Michael Robidoux has written, 'violence on the ice can be seen as a highly expressive text that may establish a player's identity.'[60] Drinkwater provides a thought-out performance in real time for an audience, meaning that sport moves in the direction of art because Drinkwater is fighting according to a script that he controls. This refutes the home truth that violence is something that boils over when rationality deserts us and passion clouds judgment.

Hard-loving, hard-drinking and hard-bodied Drinkwater should be the epitome of traditional masculinity. However, he thinks too much and constantly maintains an ironic distance from his surroundings, even if irony and fighting are a strange combination. Drinkwater is a kibitzer in the game of his own life. At times, he has the same sort of distanced take on hockey as the 'pretend fans' in Schoemperlen's 'Hockey

Night in Canada.' The difference is that while the father and daughter observe the hockey world from afar, Drinkwater is directly involved. In response to a pep talk he says, amazed, 'The ex-goon coach actually gives a stirring speech without mentioning beating them in the alley.' The phrase Drinkwater has heard far too often is a quotation attributed to late Toronto Maple Leafs owner Conn Smythe, who surmised that a team that 'can't beat 'em in the alley' will not beat the opponent on the ice (Smythe denied having said this, though it did become the title of his autobiography). 'Such candor and metaphor,' says Drinkwater, as if his real calling were as a critic like his near-namesake Boileau, 'I see Pulitzers in his future.'[61]

As clumsy and hackneyed as the coach's speech may be, it will suffice to deliver orders to the players, and Drinkwater will heed those orders. The self-evident truth that crackles under Jarman's sarcasm is that these are men of action, and language is all but irrelevant to what they do. After explaining the coach's cryptically metaphorical speech to a team-mate, in which the coach demands, 'If I'm a gentleman and you're a gentleman, then who will milk the cow?' Drinkwater says,

> We're all gung ho but I notice when fastening the strap on my helmet, head tilted and hand up to the side of my head, that it's exactly like a woman putting on an earring. I try to do it in a different way but somehow I just don't feel quite as brutal.[62]

Here Jarman shows the gap between the life lived by Drinkwater and the life displayed for the crowd. Drinkwater is aware that he lives in a clichéd, atavistically masculine world. He is also aware of performing. He may *feel* less brutal, but few spectators would see anything remotely feminine in his hulking figure.

Fighting to the Gallery: Violence on Display II

There is a significant difference in reception between being on the ice and longing to witness displays of violence: from the fan's safely removed point of view, the violence is definitely a sort of text that can be interpreted (though this commonly occurs after the fact or on video). The relationship between the fans and the players, or a consideration of the difference between the man of action and the paying spectator, is also examined in *The Last Season*. When Batterinski's Broad Street Bullies face the Soviet Union's Central Red Army team, the game is heralded as a political clash. The spectators happily wave American flags, along with posters offering such encouragement as 'THE BELL OF FREEDOM WILL RING SOVIET SKULLS!' and groan-inducing mottoes like 'CANUCKLEHEAD JA, SOVIETS NYET!'[63] More directly: the Flyers from the City of Brotherly Love will intimidate and abuse the visiting Soviet team, even though many of the hired hockey guns from north of the border lag behind in skill.

Hockey fiction in general refers to and includes real-life incidents, and in this case MacGregor reworks an exhibition game that took place on 11 January 1976. At one point, the (real) Soviet team left the ice to protest the Flyers' style of play, including a hard but legal bodycheck by Ed Van Impe. The following summation of Ed Van Impe provides a sense of the hockey aggression MacGregor was criticizing in *The Last Season*:

> Athletes often have a Dr. Jekyll-Mr. Hyde personality, and Ed Van Impe was no exception. On a team full of tough guys, Van Impe was one of the toughest. Off the ice, he was a model citizen. Although Van Impe skated as if he were stuck in mud and his shot had the fire power of a cap gun, he was a hockey player through and through.[64]

This description from the Philadelphia Flyers' website (which has since been replaced by a less ridiculous assessment) corroborates the claim that hockey is more concerned with fighting than scoring.

One might expect MacGregor's fictionalized account of the Flyers – Red Army game to focus on cross-cultural misunderstanding. Instead, he provides an insightful literary analysis of violence on display, and though the players come from entirely different political and hockey cultures, at least one Soviet player immediately comprehends Batterinski and his role.

When Batterinski steps onto the ice for his first shift, the crowd roars its approval and begins chanting his name in anticipation of a fight. Batterinski is eventually unnerved by the Soviet star who lines up for a faceoff near him – Kharlamov, 'who less than half an hour ago had seemed on his death bed, courtesy of Eddie Van Impe.' The apparent resurrection after being bodychecked displays another perceived difference between NHL and European hockey; in Batterinski's world, 'diving' in hopes of drawing a penalty is frowned upon, but worse still is Kharlamov's pretending to be 'on his death bed.' (Meanwhile, the NHL's aggressiveness is surely despicable to the Soviet players – hence the very public and propagandistic voicing of disapproval by leaving the ice.) In terms of hockey philosophies, the two players seem miles apart, even if MacGregor makes it clear that they are both performers. Before a faceoff, Kharlamov looks at Batterinski, sizes him up, and winks: 'It caught me so off guard I blinked at myself and he kept smiling and nodded at me.' The wink signals near-approval of Batterinski's act. Although he comes from a hockey world that is supposedly more skill-based, Kharlamov immediately recognizes the cause of the cheering. He may be a faster skater and better shooter than Batterinski, but Kharlamov is only able to excite crowds through realization of his skills. 'I did it through expectation,' notes Batterinski, adding,

> It stunned me that Kharlamov understood this and was amused by it. Not only did he see the absurdity of the crowd from his elegant side of hockey as clearly as I saw it from the animal side, he had the nerve to share this insight with me.[65]

Perhaps also due to its sexual innuendo, Kharlamov's wink shatters Batterinski's illusion of being the quintessential Achilles type. There is multi-layered irony here. First, Kharlamov is not critical of this brutish hockey player; he understands that Batterinski has to make a living at the NHL game and that his role is just a reflection of the economics of hockey, which are remarkably well grasped by this army man from a Communist society. The more revealing irony in the scene, however, is that Kharlamov's outsider viewpoint spots in an instant something of which Batterinski had been ignorant: for all his assertiveness on the ice, and even with his recognition that he plays 'animal' hockey, he is merely an object of the fans' desire to see fights. Only during the course of the game does Batterinski become fully aware of his situation and his role as an enforcer.

Batterinski's role changes during this intercultural game, as do the unwritten rules, which leaves Batterinski confused and out of control. When he tries to attack an opposing player, he is surprised by the linesmen's preventative action. The Soviet opponent is not restrained because there is no need to restrain a man not looking for a fight. Batterinski is out of his league:

> I'd never been held this way before. Where was the mutual restraint? Where was the tug and release of so many previous battles, the opponent with his personal linesman, me with mine, the four of us sure of our roles,

what was allowable, what not, when to lunge and when to retreat, when to quit? Where was the old pattern?

The series of questions, culminating in the desire for a 'pattern,' clearly shows Batterinski's confusion. A pattern, including an awareness of what is 'allowable,' allows for comfort even in an extreme situation. With this predictable pattern of violence removed, the bewildered Batterinski is suddenly superfluous. Unable to fight, yet aware of the crowd presence and the cameras following his actions, he responds with lame theatre: 'I cursed as loud as I could, hoping [the cameraman] might have the pick-up mike on, and stared straight into the camera …' Since Batterinski cannot offer physical violence, he offers its verbal equivalent, 'cursing' for the public. With no opponent to concentrate on, just a camera and the spectators, Batterinski comes to clarity and reaches an unfortunate conclusion about his own life:

> I'd never been this close to my fans before, never seen what they looked like. Never cared. But I saw now, and I knew finally that I was not Batterinski.
> *They were.*

The scene is potentially traumatic because it means Batterinski's entire life has been one of self-alienation. Lacking self-awareness, he had been living in the shadows throughout his hockey career. The unfortunate truth in the novel is that Batterinski fights not solely out of self-will, or to compensate for off-ice clumsiness and injustice, but because the crowd wants it. A team not endowed with flashy goal scorers can always sell tickets, and perhaps even win a few games (or two Stanley Cups, in the case of the Flyers), by making fighting a central part of their strategy. Even his violence is not really his own; he is a puppet soldier reacting to the fans' whims. Not long after he comes to this realization, his world crumbles, and soon he ends up in Finland for a final hockey tour.[66]

Violence as Justice

Felix Batterinski takes out his frustrations while in uniform, when he is protected from the injustices and nebulous social laws and rules of everyday life. Beating somebody up on the ice is unlikely to land Batterinski in court because hockey controls its own justice. Connected to this is the fact that spectators often read justice into it a fight. The majority of fighters' unwritten rules support this sense of justice because they have been established in order to keep things even and fair, so that the 'best man' may win without any trickery. In 'Hakkanen's Move,' Dave Kazlor is not worried about Frank Stonewald because fighting a player who is tired from a long shift is repulsive to the honourable fighter (as is attacking smaller players, 'headbutting,' 'sucker-punching,' and so on). When his hockey world promotes fighting, Batterinski knows what is and what is not allowed. Yet as comforting as these codes may be, they are not all about keeping fighting safe for the fighters. One overriding code that leads to more fights is the retribution rule, which demands revenge on those that do not revere the unwritten rules. This is the rule – more important than any penalty – that Isadore Boucher invokes in *Saints of Big Harbour* when demanding his nephew Guy attack another player ('That was your goddamn teammate! You go get him!'). It was also this rule that led to Batterinski's gruesome fight as a teenager. Batterinski had injured a much smaller Parry Sound Shamrocks player (a young Bobby Orr), and the subsequent challenge to Batterinski is 'How about somebody your own size, asshole!'[67] The larger player has to try to restore the balance of violence by avenging Batterinski's attack.

Fans participate in this system of retribution and justice, but only as vicarious witnesses. This is best illustrated in Ray Robertson's *Heroes*, an ironically titled hockey novel about a lackadaisical graduate student in philosophy who accepts a magazine assignment covering hockey in Kansas. The novel includes reminiscences of the eternal student's upbringing in Toronto, which naturally includes watching the Toronto Maple Leafs and their enforcer Dave 'Tiger' Williams (the all-time NHL penalty minute leader). The narrator slips into a vulgar hockey idiom as he recalls the father's sense of on-ice justice:

> 'C'mon Tiger,' his father would yell. Dave 'Tiger' Williams, the best pure fighter the Maple Leafs had ever had taking to task some gutless sono-fabitch dumb enough to mess around with Salming or Thompson or any of the Leafs' other bread and butter players. 'Make that bastard pay, Tiger!'

Here, cheering for Williams represents more than a base attraction to violence because it is entwined with justice, retribution, and the breaking of codes. Something greater is at stake, as the re-establishment of order is on the line. Williams regularly fights in response to 'gutless' attacks on his teammates:

When the fight was finally over ... Bayle's father would smile and lean back
in his easy chair and nod his head with the satisfaction of knowing that at
least for tonight – at least at Maple Leaf Gardens tonight – *fairness and
justice ruled the world once and for all,* that the bad guys weren't going to get
away with anything they shouldn't, and that the good and honourable were
guaranteed the standing ovation they so rightly deserved. (My emphasis)

Inspired by watching justice prevail, the spectator feels personally
involved in the fight. The reference to the 'easy chair' is a reminder that
this involvement and identification is moral rather than physical. The
armchair athlete will never be injured. Like the smaller player on the
ice, he has Tiger Williams to fight for his cause; unlike the smaller
player on the ice, the fan does not contribute to the team.[68]
  While it is obvious that the spectator is not physically involved, the
above passage highlights the emotional or psychological investment in
Williams's fights. This is the satisfaction of seeing the right man and
home team player win. Robertson injects irony (though no mockery)
into the description of the father both by lowering the register to
describe the fight ('gutless sonofabitch dumb enough ...,' etc.) and,
later, reducing the sports world into a black-and-white representation of
good guys and bad guys. There is also the absolute contradiction that
undercuts this comfort, namely, the juxtaposition of 'at least for
tonight' with the finality of 'fairness and justice ruled the world once
and for all.' Bayle's father is obviously wrong about why Williams wins
most of his fights. He wins them simply because he is a great fighter, and
if he were to lose the next bout, the world would hardly be a less just
place. Nor would the bad guys be vindicated in 'getting away with' something. In emotional terms, however, Robertson shows how the satisfaction of victory bathes the spectator in a temporary sense of moral order.
  When asked about *Heroes* in an April 2000 interview for the University of Toronto's student newspaper *The Varsity,* Robertson further
explained the attraction of Tiger Williams. Bayle's father toils at a
working-class job all week, with little sense of honesty or justice in the
world: '... so Saturday night when someone's picking on one of the
smaller Leaf team-mates and Tiger Williams steps in, that's the only
kind of integrity he sees all week. It's real.' An additional factor is the
relative simplicity of a fight. The complicated patterns of the game
break down when a fight erupts, to be replaced by the concentration of
a duel. The father may not understand the world around him, but the
directness of hockey, especially the fights, is clear, genuine, and there-

fore comforting. Bayle's father can revel like spectators at a wrestling match who, as Roland Barthes observes, are 'jubilant at seeing the rules broken for the sake of a deserved punishment.'[69] However, the type of wrestling described by Barthes is spectacular because the wrestlers act out roles such that the 'good guy' is clearly differentiated from his less scrupulous opponent; this is not the case in hockey, where rooting steadfastly for the home team is the general moral impetus. Of course, any morality or sense of right that rests on the fans' bias is a kangaroo court verdict.

Sport requires equality and fairness before the rules, and skill determines the outcome. Mitigating factors, advantages of position, class, education, and politics are set aside, and competition is reduced to its barest elements. But the man most likely to win an on-ice boxing match need not be a pillar of morality. For this reason, it is common to demonize an opposing team's best fighter as a talentless player and corruption of the game, even while overlooking the same qualities in the home team's designated fighter. One's own enforcer is usually praised, even lionized, as a good soul, hard worker, and necessary arbiter of justice (as with the father's adulation for Williams in *Heroes*). Robertson's example nourishes the sense of justice because Williams 'corrects' a transgression by attacking a player who had done wrong. Had Williams simply gone skate-toe-to-skate-toe with another enforcer for no other reason than enforcers are expected to fight, it would still provide entertainment for many fans – but this could not be squeezed into a moral frame.

It is illogical to equate aggressive, and sometimes contemptible, behaviour with ideals of justice and righteousness. Hanford Woods's 'The Drubbing of Nesterenko' also touches on this theme. Though the narrator makes a convincing case for Nesterenko's innocence, the Montreal newspaper columnists are faced with the problem of justifying the Canadien Ferguson's atrocious assault to hometown readers. They have to put a positive spin on it, and resort to legalese and an intimate pet-name to do so:

> The columnists probed the wound mercilessly and brought down their verdict: Nesterenko had been guilty of some indefeasible incursion into Fergy's domain, he should never have been there, Fergy had acted within his rights.

The 'wound' is the narrator's reception of, and later trauma stemming from, the fight; the journalists provide no explanation for *why* Ferguson was 'within his rights.' This is because no reason for Ferguson's behaviour exists: 'The writers drew strength for the pronouncement from the act's utter inexplicability.' The act is so far beyond the expected and the allowed that it appears to the hometown crowd as if external forces, rather than human volition, is what guided Ferguson. Lacking a proper explanation, the sports journalists avoid specifics and merely assume that, because an attack occurred, it must have been in response to something Nesterenko had done. They have to bend logic to keep the system of justice in hockey intact and to invent a morality guiding the home-team player's actions.[70]

Instead of bending logic to justify the actions of the hometown hero, spectators can heap abuse on opposing players and the referee. Loudly voicing (biased) moral views is one of the few ways that a spectator can actively participate in a game. Morley Callaghan's novel *The Loved and the Lost* shows the reaction of a crowd when the provider of rule-book justice proves a little too blind:

> In the corner to the left of the Canadiens goal a Ranger forward was blocked out and held against the boards by a Canadiens defenceman, who cleared the puck up the ice. The Ranger forward, skating past the defenceman, turned and slashed at him, breaking the stick over his shoulder. The referee didn't see it.

When the inevitable fight starts in response to the slash, the Canadiens player who throws the first punch is given a penalty (as he knew he would be), whereas the Ranger forward goes free. The fans may reprobate the sneaky Ranger, but that is of little matter to him, as he has escaped the gaze of the regulating official. Callaghan concisely describes the cycle of violence in hockey. Escalation, fuelled by the rule of retribution, is sudden and chaotic: the slash is in response to the frustration of being blocked and held against the boards (a perfectly legal act); the fight is in response to the slash, and the reason that the original culprit is not penalized is that another player 'came out of nowhere and dived at the defenceman and tackled him,' perhaps because a smaller or particularly gifted player was being attacked; finally, 'all the players converged on one another, ... fists swinging, gloves and sticks littering the ice.' The transition from a single aggressive act to group violence is swift and assumes the form of a cumulative song such as 'There Was an Old Lady Who Swallowed a Fly...'[71]

When the referee finally restores order, the crowd that had 'howled in glee' at the fight suddenly turns sour because the player who instigated it all was not punished by the referee. The 'Two Solitudes' of francophone and anglophone Canadians come together in the name of justice to holler at the referee. Boos resound, and indignation reigns:

> The ice was now a small white space at the bottom of a great black pit where sacrificial figures writhed, and on the vast slopes of the pit a maniacal white-face mob shrieked at the one with the innocent air who had broken the rules, and the one who tolerated the offence.

The referee is accused of having actively 'tolerated' and not just missed the original offence, and in this passage it appears that violence is a fairer judge than is the referee. When two players fight, it is impossible for the referee to overlook or miss the transgression, and fighting is therefore more honest than a sneak attack. As well, there is the hope that corporal punishment will be administered to the deserving wrongdoer. In chapter 2, I mentioned Jack Falla's praise of shinny as a type of hockey that needs no referees because 'justice is built in, not added on.' Shinny does not require regulating officials because everyone plays with a regard for the wellbeing of all. In Callaghan's passage, the idea that the game is self-regulating remains, though 'justice' administered through violence is bitter.[72]

Violence as a Barrier to Utopia: Intentionally Injuring

While violence has its place in the NHL, it precludes any sense of utopian play in less formal surroundings. Hockey literature shows professional players who fail to adapt to the shinny rink, and intentionally injure another player – partly through reflex, partly through an internalized understanding of how best to inflict pain.

In Bill Gaston's 2000 novel *The Good Body*, Bobby Bonaduce has almost made the NHL; he has managed to make a living playing a game. On the one hand, he sometimes feels ridiculous for having 'dedicated his life to working violently hard at preventing people with a different-coloured uniform from putting a puck in his net.' On the other, he argues that this triviality is the essence of fans' attraction to hockey because they 'are drawn to the spectacle of who are the best in the land at using their bodies to fulfil *pure desire*. Pure, because these are guys who will basically kill to get at a puck ...' The desire is 'pure' also because there is no external motivation. The men seem entirely free as they expend their energy on a task that has no visible extrinsic rewards. This argument is obviously idealist and requires that we forget about salaries and endorsements. The shadow cutting into this utopian view is that these men will murder for a puck. When considering the problems a social worker faces on a daily basis, 'Bonaduce would see as if in a mirror the trivial ugliness he represented. Hockey.' The opportunity cost of using strong, healthy bodies and pure desire to create 'ugliness' or to 'basically kill' is enormous, and Bonaduce, like many athletes, has to confront the senselessness of what he does.[73]

'What kind of a game is this,' asks Lawrence Scanlan in the *Grace under Fire: The State of Our Sweet and Savage Game,* 'in which finesse yields so blithely to a menacing fist?' It is not so much the intrusion of a fist that is unsettling as the fact that it is so casually accepted by so many hockey fans. Casual acceptance is in fact part of the trivial ugliness that Bonaduce represents and which has become a major cultural symbol and all-pervasive myth in Canada. If myth, as Northrop Frye writes, 'draws a circumference' around a people, then mythologized hockey can trap Canadians within a circle of violence if we refrain from questioning it. When hockey is purported to be the essence of Canada, there is an accompanying imperative to enjoy the game, since that is what 'good Canadians' do, regardless of one's attitude towards fighting on the ice.[74]

A person weaned solely on hockey literature would be led to believe that all hockey involves fights. They are, in fact, overrepresented in fiction. This is because, outside of the NHL, strict penalties, such as automatic suspensions, make it impractical to fight or to use stronger physical aggression; and this is especially so in recreational surroundings, because the unwritten rules make it socially unacceptable. Whereas in structured hockey the unwritten rules or codes can often spur violence, the same sorts of codes limit it in more vernacular or relaxed forms of hockey. When playing a pick-up game among friends, one should not respond to an inadvertent high stick by punching the culprit in the nose.[75] The dangers of not adhering to the unwritten rules or codes have been mentioned, but even then there is the understanding that ignoring the unwritten rules may actually mean a faster trip to the NHL or an advantage gained. After all, if opponents are scared of a player, that individual has more room to manoeuvre on the ice, which is a definite advantage. Being unpredictably aggressive helps achieve this goal. Conversely, breaking the rules in a fun game is a tremendous taboo that means no subsequent invitations to play.

Returning to Bonaduce in *The Good Body*, we see he has problems switching between levels and types of play. As a former professional player, Bonaduce is used to a rough and aggressive hockey. The novel begins with his return to Fredericton, New Brunswick – ostensibly to study creative writing at graduate school, but primarily because he dreams of playing on the same university hockey team as Jason, the son he had abandoned twenty years earlier. (The family theme will be discussed at greater length in chapter 5.) The 'good body' of the title refers to how Bonaduce makes his living, but it also refers to the tragically ironic fact that he has muscular sclerosis: the source of his livelihood, profession, and sense of self is deteriorating. Intimations of mortality, including the awareness that the disease is hereditary, increase his desire for an on-ice reunion with his son.

Bonaduce has to wait a few months before he can play because university rules restrict the eligibility of former professional players. This waiting period is meant to prevent unfair advantages, while casting a glance at the noble British school tradition of amateurism that was transported to New World athletics. More important is that university hockey has a zero tolerance policy for fights and violence. The resulting penalties outweigh any gains in space that violence may produce. A tad nervous about playing this other type of hockey, Bonaduce wonders whether the coach of the team has played professionally – whether he has the trench training to be open to and appreciate Bonaduce's style of play. Bonaduce also has concerns about making the team at training camp, the time when decisions about whom to keep and whom to cut are made; in these surroundings (and at his age), his professional background is like the taxi driver's foreign medical degree. Since all players will eventually be on the same team, the style of play at the camp is less aggressive. In Bonaduce's view,

> you saved your bashing for the enemy. This was a concern because, from the look of things, he might be forced to go out and impress someone, show what he could do. And what he could do was bash.[76]

In this sporting realm, Bonaduce is metaphorically a stranger in a strange land (just as he had literally been while fighting other Canadians in faraway Oklahoma).

Not an official member of the varsity team, Bonaduce has a marginal coaching position and is allowed to participate in a fun Christmas match between university squad members. This game should be even tamer than training camp or an exhibition game because all players have made the team. There is no competing for a job. Bonaduce is aware of what this means: 'No hitting to speak of, an unwritten code. So lots of goals.' Such games are a chance to try things out, to try out fancy moves without fear of bodychecks, to take risks that one might not take during a real game. When an opposing teammate tries out a virtuosic move during this friendly game, Bonaduce sees it as an affront, an attempt to embarrass a somewhat rusty, much older player. His reaction would be dubious in any game, but in these playful surroundings, it is grotesque:

> Wonky as he [Bonaduce] was it wasn't hard to fall into a curl and get his ass out to submarine the guy, catch his knee just right, you could feel it bend in the wrong direction, hear the second or two of surprise before the scream.

Accidental injury does not constitute violence – it is unplanned and unintended. Here there is the same repulsion as when Batterinski beats up another player while in absolute control. The facility ('it wasn't hard') and the sense of process here ('catch his knee just right'), along with the objectively cold description, evoke the orchestrated pain of torture. The coach has to adopt the role of a referee, as he sends Bonaduce off the ice. Bonaduce shows no remorse at this point, and he even speaks sardonically of altruism. Batterinski referred to 'charity' when he ended a fight quickly; Bonaduce says, 'Little Christmas present for you there Jace' – by injuring the better player, the good father was securing more ice time for his son Jason. The cynical jest about a Christmas present is particularly grim because it is not in keeping with Bonaduce's personality, even as he spins an immoral act into an ethical good. Bonaduce may be limited in perspective, as the optimistically naive act of returning twenty years after the fact to resume fatherhood suggests, but he is nowhere near as dim as Batterinski. As Gaston remarked to Jamie Fitzpatrick in a 2005 interview, 'Bob Bonaduce ... acts dumber than he is. It's a strategic hiding place.' There are, however, parallels between Batterinski and Bonaduce. One of these parallels is violence as the beginning of failure. For Batterinski it offered a back-door route to a professional career; for Bonaduce it shows that he has slowed down and is less able to stop opponents more honestly.[77]

Violence as Failure

Hockey fiction often portrays fighting as a back-road path to a hockey career, as a marker of being a less talented player. Famous NHL fighters may become crowd favourites, but they will rarely be recognized as greats of the game. Even Felix Batterinski only lives up to his fitting name after it is made clear to him that his skating and passing skills alone will not carry him to the NHL. This realization occurs when a child Bobby Orr skates rings around him. At that point, with much encouragement from his Junior coach, Batterinski realizes that his fists are what can make a professional hockey player out of him. Poet Christopher Wiseman makes the same point in 'Phone Calls Home (John Kordic d. 1992),' a eulogy in verse for the NHL player whose life ended fighting off police in a cocaine-induced stupor. Kordic was a fairly successful child athlete who longed to make a career as a professional:

> YOU wanted more –
> the big time, to burn up the NHL.
> But you didn't have the leg-speed or the touch
> to be the star you were in Juniors,
> and you became the goon, the heavyweight,
> sent off the bench to intimidate and subdue.[78]

Calling 'goons' talentless is commonplace but an exaggeration, and Wiseman does not fall into this trap. All NHL hockey players were, like Kordic, stars at some point. It is therefore more accurate to speak, like Justin Bryant in 'Hakkanen's Move,' of 'flaws' in their game. Not quite fast enough, Kordic had to fight to reach the big leagues.

When *The Good Body*'s Bonaduce deserted his son as a young man, it happened almost by accident. He had left Fredericton to play for an NHL farm team in another city, expecting to become a star within a short period of time. Instead, he found himself toiling in lower-tier leagues for a number of years in towns like Kalamazoo, Michigan, and Tulsa, Oklahoma. When a tough, older player named Krieger (German for 'warrior') retired, Bonaduce's Kalamazoo team no longer had a 'policeman' and was soon bullied on the ice. This caused Bonaduce to change his 'outlook on hockey' and become a 'basher and crasher,' a decision for violence made nonchalantly: 'Bonaduce said what the hell and stepped up his grit to fill the void.' (His Italian name is perhaps a play on benevolent dictator or good leader instead of *Il Duce*.) The euphemistic aspect of this stepping up is exposed on the same page, as Bonaduce recalls that 'what had really fuelled his new violence ... was the sight of Krieger selling cars' to make a living. Moving from a career based on aggressive behaviour to a life of violence is a mild career change; it 'wasn't so hard: you'd been living on the edge of malice to begin with.'79

What looks like malice to the crowd is rarely a visceral desire to harm another person. When people commit violent acts outside the sporting arena, it is most often because emotions have boiled over to cloud rationality and self-control. In hockey literature, violence and aggression often occur with the bank clerk's insouciance. This emotionless stance is, as mentioned, highly ironical in fights where the involvement could not be more direct. For Bonaduce the decision to become a 'basher and crasher' is just a matter of changing the way he plays his game. In career terms, 'he had to try something. He hadn't climbed leagues and he was twenty-five.' But this decision has grave consequences for Bonaduce's body. It results in more scars, more injuries, and a 'face [that] got messier.'80

During a writing assignment in his new life as a graduate student in New Brunswick, Bonaduce reflects on this change. The decline intrudes on the spelling of the story, with 'almost' sliding into 'almsot':

> For a couple of years in Kalamazoo I was the best at being an asshole in front of the net. Was called The Zookeeper. I was a master. It was an act. Almsot worked though. Almsot got me called up [to the NHL]. I was almsot a famous asshole.

Again there is the theme of control, both over the on-ice violence and Bonaduce's own life (striving to be a 'famous asshole' is like choosing to reign in Hell rather than serve in Heaven). A Zookeeper's job is to keep even the rowdy animals in line, and Bonaduce's role is to curtail potential violence through pre-emptive aggression, acting as a policeman so that other players will not be harmed. Again there is the language of theatre, of playful mimicry, implying that the violence is all feigned and ends once the curtain drops. The 'messier' face, however, makes it clear this career choice is more than a job: the toothless hockey smile and the many scars cannot be taken off with the uniform after the game. When Bonaduce intentionally injures the younger player at the Christmas game, he claims to be entirely in control, though his statement in that context that 'the Zookeeper had appeared out of nowhere' belies this.

The act takes over the person, just as it had previously when Bonaduce 'rose from his seat ready for a beer' at the end of a game and, on remembering he was only a spectator, 'saw he was nothing but a dog, salivating at a buzzer.'[81]

Instrumental Violence

Aggression and violence may mark failure because they can mean that pure skills are lacking, but they are effective. Aggression beyond the rules is useful in slowing down faster skaters and intimidating smooth goal scorers; it allows weaker players to take control of the game. As with all aggression and violence in sports, this is a matter of degree. In Allan Safarik's comic short story 'The North Field Comets,' a team suddenly starts winning when it adopts a rougher, more intimidating style of play. In a twist on the meaning of sportsmanship in hockey, the Comets win the finals after lacing their opponents' pre-game snack with laxative. The narrator laconically remarks that the new 'methods had worked without degenerating too far into goon hockey.' They 'degenerate' into 'goon hockey,' but despite their macabre team motto – 'IF IT'S MOVING, IT AIN'T DEAD' – they remain within reason and do not go 'too far.' Hockey journalist Stan Fischler has commented on the highly subjective and minimal increments between required and excessive aggression: 'The difference between a dirty hockey player and a tough hockey player is about the same as the difference between sleet and snow.' Players thought to be dirty when on opposing teams can immediately be regarded as useful tools when traded to the home squad.[82]

Richard Harrison's poem 'Using the Body' eloquently expresses this fusing of control and violence in considering the enforcer's job. He starts by outlining a misconception: 'When a fight begins, we say it is emotion.' For the 'goon,' however, losing one's head to emotion is both dangerous and counterproductive. These fights are planned, with the comfort and intuitive understanding that feeds ritual, and

> ... after
> the game, the goon speaks calmly of the momentum
> of play, doing what he had to do, a strict account
> level in his head.

There are a few linguistic tags here that distance the ordinary non-participant from the fighter, who can speak 'calmly' of his job or 'doing what he had to do' while keeping a 'strict account' – the language of bookkeeping – of what often appears as chaos to the spectator.[83] If we apply this analysis and understanding of the fighter's role, and recall Woods's 'The Drubbing of Nesterenko,' it appears that Ferguson's loss of control and crossing the line of accepted violence was, contradictorily, a normal fulfilment of his job. Even the narrator concedes, while decrying the violent attack, that the fight allowed Montreal to win the series. Since the main focus of professional hockey is winning, this attack comes close to negating the claim that violence is 'value added' and superfluous because it is secondary to the goal of the game.

When players are employed to intimidate opponents, violence is instrumental. In such cases, 'players are also required to create trouble for opponents and to employ tactics that create anxiety in adversaries.' Violence can set the tone of the game, make opponents more reticent, inspire the home crowd, or otherwise influence the game. Whenever winning is the primary goal, aggression or violence 'always serves a utilitarian function.' The problem is one of escalation: if players are used to dealing with violent tactics, creating anxiety becomes difficult. Returning to the Harrison poem, the goon sees

> ... how the game, flimsy
> as a wing, could be held at the socket where
> the wing joins the body, and broken.

The image is horrific because it means that calculated use of force alone can usurp control of the game and lead to victory. The game is 'broken' in two senses. Sports journalists and commentators often talk of 'breaking up' another team's game plan, and imposing one's own plan. Yet at the same time the beauty of the game can be crippled, damaged, and made ugly through violence.[84] This is a major departure from the belief that the game world is self-enclosed because here the consequences of what happens on the ice are carried off the ice. Here the skeletal image of a socket conjures up a literally broken limb (with a pun on left- or right-wing) as the game comes crashing down.

Calvin Daniels's 'Beyond the Ice' handles this theme extensively by showing the repercussions of a violent on-ice act for the rest of life. In this story, Hank is a former prospect who, like Drinkwater and Bonaduce, does not make it to the NHL and resigns himself to playing for a local team. Despite his declining skills and dwindling contributions, the amateur hometown team finds space for him. He earns the nickname

'Hacksaw' for the way he uses his stick to his advantage. The narrator states,

> Of course, as the years went by, the stickwork seemed to become a bigger part of [Hank's] game. The younger players were so damn fast, but a little jab in the ribs or a well-placed slash across the shins slowed them down to his speed.[85]

The phrase 'were so damn fast' sounds like a pensioner speaking, and one wonders if opponents tolerate Hank's jabs and slashes precisely because he is older and slower. Such minor stick attacks are incidental violence, since there is no obvious intent to injure. Nor are they instrumental in the usual sense, since Hank slashes and jabs to control his own game, not to guide it on behalf of the team.

Under normal circumstances, hockey insults are ignored; they may even be a sign of the 'intimate companionship and ... friendliness' that Hugh Hood sees residing in 'locker-room kidding.' But when called a 'washed-up has-been,' Hank responds immediately and brutally. In Harrison's poem, the game is metaphorically crippled by violence; here the player who insults Hank is literally crippled. This attack 'had just been reflex. He swung the stick like an axe. It hit Taylor right across the face. He went to the ice like a bag of potatoes dropped out of a truck.' Violence may be common in the national game, but losing control of oneself in this way is unforgivable. Hank is duly punished for his actions, and most of the disciplining takes place 'Beyond the Ice.' Though he manages to escape a prison term for assault, he becomes a social outcast in his hometown. Customers avoid his sports shop, and his marriage ends in divorce. (When he travels back to the arena with suicidal intentions, the wheelchair-bound opponent appears *deus ex machina* to convince him not to pull the trigger.) Despite his nickname, Hacksaw Hank is not a psychopath, and he claims that the attack was not premeditated but simply a rash action.[86] It seems that Hank, like Bonaduce, is unable to make the transition from a highly competitive professional background to a type of play with few consequences for the rest of life. Instrumental violence, usually used to help the team, returns as a marker of individual failure. Here violence is an outward marker of a failure to keep up, which simultaneously indicates Hank's refusal to accept his age. There is a lack of awareness of the self, or at least inordinate frustration at the fact of ageing, a split between what one thinks one is and what one really is.

Many hockey novels and stories follow players on the downside of their careers. Of the works looked at in this chapter, this theme of decline is a major one in *The Last Season, The Good Body, Salvage King, Ya!*, 'Beyond the Ice,' and 'The Drubbing of Nesterenko.' Since playing hockey depends almost exclusively on the body, and the body loses strength and suppleness as we age, it makes sense that players will employ other techniques to further their careers or to keep up with their younger playmates. When these other techniques are aggression and violence, regression occurs: whereas most learn to control their emotions as they age and mature, some hockey players remain volatile. Children who presumably learned to 'play nice' forget this as they age.

Required Violence

Frank Paci's *Icelands*, the final work to be examined here with regard to violence, is one of the few adult hockey novels to focus entirely on young people. It is about a trio of young, gifted hockey players as they skate their way towards the voting age, though not necessarily towards the NHL. Although *Icelands* has several lenses, it is more of a classical *Bildungsroman* than MacGregor's *The Last Season* because it ends with the boys' integration into society as adults. Hockey is an important part of their lives, but it is not the only career option open to most of these youngsters. There is no sour taste of decline in this novel, and the players' lives do not literally or figuratively end when their competitive hockey days cease, and they develop healthily into adults.

In *Icelands* hockey violence provides for the sour taste. Near the end of the novel, Paci depicts a scene at a Juniors training camp. Andrew, after scoring a pretty goal, is taunted by a much less capable player and challenged to a fight. A non-fighter, he sees this as 'the wall his whole hockey career had been inching toward' and realizes he can 'no longer skate away... If he wanted to go to a higher level in the game, there was no getting around this cold impenetrable wall of ice.' This 'wall' is like the glass ceiling that keeps women out of management positions in some companies. Here, however, the job requires participation in anachronistic rituals of masculinity. Andrew sees in the beckoning Goliath all that is wrong with hockey, including the fact that, on the ice, Canadian society condones fighting. The very freedom of sport, the metaphorical escape from everyday life, becomes an entrance into a violent other world that moves in a different orbit from the utopias postulated by Huizinga and Suits. One key play condition remains unfulfilled: because Andrew is compelled to fight, the fight is not voluntary. Also, though Andrew feels that the hockey rink is not ordinary life, there is no joy or freedom. Andrew 'was just a piece of meat on the rack, whether he fought or didn't fight.' This is his anagnorisis, as Andrew recognizes what is wrong with competitive hockey culture. Fighting seems to contradict true play, and the reader expects a change of narrative direction when Andrew sees this. Instead, like Bonaduce nonchalantly stepping into a violent role that will scar his face, Andrew says, '... what the fuck!' and drops his gloves to take on a skilled fighter. Like Bonaduce, he has weighed his career options in a reasoned manner.[87]

In *Salvage King, Ya!* Drinkwater exhibits a similar careerist attitude at a training camp, though prolongation of employment rather that upward mobility is his motivation. 'I agree to go primitive,' he says, because 'The Powers That Be like to see us peons duke it out, a feeding frenzy, a big 'roid rage.'[88] The resignation and critique implied by agreeing to be 'primitive' shows his awareness that there is something wrong with the way the sport is being played, but also his pragmatic complicity. Since Drinkwater realizes he cannot change the situation, he attempts to use it to his advantage. The hyperbolic reference to 'Powers That Be' underscores the hopelessness of his destiny, which almighty management controls. The same sort of violence that is tacitly or openly applauded in real hockey is represented as a corruption of the game in fiction.

Chapter Four

National Identity and Hockey

They always say, 'We.' They don't say, 'You did this.' We as Canadians did it.
Paul Henderson, in Dryden and MacGregor, *Home Game*, p. 215

In Richard B. Wright's 2004 novel *Adultery,* a visitor finds himself in a small Ontario town. There is talk of someone 'leaving an arena,' and the narrator remarks that this 'meant that he must play hockey, or coach it or watch it or do something with it.' In Canada, the implicit question 'What else can one do with hockey?' is not rhetorical. Beyond playing, coaching, or watching it, we spend a great deal of time ascribing meanings to the game, pondering its cultural importance, and mythologizing it as the essence of Canada. This is a matter of belief, not empirical truth, and every Canadian knows deep down that hockey is not what makes the nation tick. Roy MacGregor emphasizes that hockey is an essential metaphor for Canada because 'everything that happens in hockey tells us something about who we are and where we came from and where we're going.' Poet Birk Sproxton highlights media's role in the hockey story: 'Photographic images still and moving fracture the universe, cut it into bits and pieces' (in other words, make it more manageable but rob it of context). A 'film clip ... compresses space and gives the illusion of present action. It also sketches the future.' In these views, the game contains time present and past, and even has oracular qualities – if we know how to read it properly.[1]

In *National Dreams: Myth, Memory, and Canadian History*, Daniel Francis examines a number of collective Canadian narratives that have been handed down through history textbooks and popular accounts of stories that he 'had been taught to believe in.' Nordicity is central to many of these stories, and hockey is a 'corollary of the northern myth' because like 'nothing else, hockey allows us to celebrate our norther-ness.' Whereas Francis focuses on myth's ability to idealize as it twists truth, Benoît Melançon, on the example of Maurice Richard, points out a rule-of-thumb difference between legend and myth: it is impossible to live in Quebec and not know who Richard was. In addition to being all-pervasive, hockey myths are malleable because they change through the years and according to the needs of the times. They are thus less stable than traditional cosmological myths; more obviously, hockey myths do not deal in time out of mind. Hockey played in the sometimes recent past is near enough to be real, close enough to be remembered and reshaped in each fan's memory.[2]

Martin Laba writes that hockey, whenever people have claimed it to be naturally and organically linked to the land, 'has served as a virtual creation tale' for Canadians. As opposed to more entrenched creation tales, no sane Canadian believes that we were born of hockey. Never-theless, our collective delight in hockey has led to some unusual conclusions. Michael Kennedy recalls the ubiquitous 'hockey *is* Life' 't-shirt[s] seen throughout Canada in the late 1990s' and surmises cau-tiously, 'At the very least, the sport has attained significance beyond that of a recreational pastime.' Roch Carrier links ontological present and mythological past to claim,

> In terms of being Canadian, hockey is the best metaphor for life, for history … You can explain anything through hockey … you have something very complicated to say, you think, it's like hockey and everybody will understand.

This is perhaps optimistic because explaining complicated issues through hockey invites oversimplification, and perhaps jingoism. As well, the game can be put to manipulative political purposes (no savvy politician misses a photo opportunity at a hockey game). Most often hockey is used as a simplistic symbol of Canadian identity, which is why there is great rhetorical strength to comparing tough economic times or even war to a hockey game: 'We're all in this together,' say such hockey references. As outlined in chapter 1, distilling the Canadian mosaic into a hockey uniform can be reductive, but it is convenient. Also, because this practice is so blatantly reductive and slanted, there is often some humour or irony involved. In the essay 'I Am Hockey' (which clearly refers to the Molson Canadian 'I am Canadian' beer advertisements and their hockey motifs), Michael Kennedy considers the rationale behind travelling the great distance from Saskatchewan to Alberta just to watch the 2003 Heritage Classic hockey game in Edmonton. 'Logic?' he asks. 'The logic is there, of course, as any real Canadian would know. Hockey is Canada. I am Canadian. Therefore it is crystal clear ... I am Hockey!'[3] The emphasis on logic is comically and playfully contradicted by the entirely phatic, or emotional, reasoning. Desire cannot be explained away.

After the positive and the negative aspects of hockey discussed in chapters 2 and 3, this chapter examines literary uses of hockey as a synonym for Canada. It begins with an examination of how hockey is woven into Canada's popular mythology in writing (as opposed to the more general symbolism of hockey examined in chapter 1); it then looks at the ambiguity of literary language, including how hockey comments in fiction add nuance to, or undo, the facile 'hockey is Canada' equation. The chapter's subsequent focus is on some resounding literary portrayals of hockey as the essence of Canada, and it moves on to consider hockey as a means of integration and of becoming Canadian. It concludes with a look at literary manifestations of the fear of losing hockey and, by extension, Canada.

Writing Hockey, Writing Canada

Though hockey now competes with dozens of other entertainment options, and though fewer Canadian children grow up playing the game, Canadians seem to be attributing more value than ever to hockey. Hockey is an entertainment media bulwark of Canadianness against the tempting American television shows we watch the rest of the week. In Canada, hockey is not autotelic; the goal is identity, and often national unity, which helps explain the results of the CBC's 2004 quest to find the Greatest Canadian. The final list and winner were determined by popular voting, and, predictably, hockey figures were lionized. More than one in ten of the top one hundred Great Canadians were hockey players, and the top ten included both hockey commentator Don Cherry and former player Wayne Gretzky (the winner was socialist Tommy Douglas, the 'father of Medicare'). The populist poll was not kind to producers of high culture, and Shania Twain danced right past Glenn Gould, while Pamela Anderson was well ahead of Margaret Atwood and Mordecai Richler. The poll's results reflect, or project, a keen sense of community established through hockey. As superficial as this hero-worship may be, the presence of Quebec hockey stars as Great Canadians – along with Parry Sound, Ontario's, Bobby Orr, Floral, Saskatchewan's, Gordie Howe, and the like – confirms the idea of hockey as a community builder or cultural glue that traverses the country.[4]

No artist who sings, acts, or writes primarily in French made the top one hundred, but Quebec-born hockey stars Maurice Richard, Mario Lemieux, Jean Béliveau, and Patrick Roy did. In contrast to Hugh MacLennan's 1945 novelistic claim that Canada is made of 'two solitudes,' of parallel yet discrete English and French existences, the CBC poll shows that hockey promotes fleeting acquaintance or fair-weather friendship. Anglophones are most familiar with the Quebec Other when that Other is on the ice. In addition, hockey can help us temporarily suppress bigoted attitudes. In Diane Schoemperlen's 'Hockey Night in Canada,' for example, the narrator notes that Rita, a diehard Montreal Canadiens fan, 'did not consider her everyday dislike of those Frenchmen (as in, "I've got no use for those Frenchmen, no use at all") to be contradictory.' Rick Salutin's *Les Canadiens* has us look in the other direction when a player comments that a woman 'doesn't like us when we're English, but she likes us fine when we're the Canadiens.' Another anglophone player argues that Montreal's team is a promising example of 'French and English working together.'[5] Being a fan means being impartial, and this stronger prejudice of allegiance to the home or favourite team dispels other prejudices.

Salutin's play differs from most anglophone hockey literature because it includes the exaggerated rebuttal that hockey is the 'only example in the history of the country' of French and English coming together. Hockey fiction in English generally ignores hockey as it helps split identity *within* Canada. This could be a lack of familiarity with Quebec, but it could also be a wilful ignoring: as Quebec does not fit the Canadian story of commonalities, it is apparently rejected from the discourse. Such is the case in Sheldon Posen's *626 by 9: A Goal-by-Goal Timeline of Maurice 'The Rocket' Richard's Scoring Career in Pictures, Stats and Stories*, a sort of catalogue to the Museum of Civilization's 2004 exhibit. That the Rocket was a 'French Canadian hero' is emphasized less here than in any other Richard biography – and, in this regard, Posen's work is entirely in line with hockey fiction in English. A reader familiar only with English-language hockey fiction could easily overlook that Richard was presented as a hero of the Quebec people. Posen does not stir up debate, or interpret or theorize on our behalf. He simply displays

Richard arm-wrestling *indépendantiste* singer Felix Leclerc or entering the Order of Canada and lets the spectator consider 'how important he was, not only to hockey, but to Canada's history and sense of self.' The spectator can decide whether Richard is consorting with or battling separatists – the player himself is an empty vessel into which we pour meaning or significance. Mythical thinking allows for simultaneous 'truths,' and hockey heroes may thus be received and celebrated differently among various groups. Benoît Melançon points out that Maurice Richard was adopted by both federalist and sovereigntist camps, while devoting an entire section of his study of Le Rocket to reception among anglophones.[6]

That so many 'Great Canadians' were culled from our leisure time evokes what Brian Sutton-Smith calls the 'rhetoric of play as identity,' according to which play often functions as 'a means of confirming, maintaining, or advancing the power and identity of the community of players.' In Canada, this 'community of players' embraces those who stand and watch, and you do not have to skate to be part of the hockey group. The ritual of watching *Hockey Night in Canada* usually suffices to make one Canadian through entirely mediated and physically passive armchair celebrations – by means of which we can become what Lorna Jackson calls 'robot[s] guided by television's morbid fixation on the puck.' Hockey is transposed from a private game community with its internal rules and logic into a manifestation of Canadianness. This does not mean that an NHLer from Alberta is thinking about passports and flags when he tries to score against the Anaheim Mighty Ducks, or that Vancouver Canucks fans will only cheer if a Canadian-born player scores the winning goal. On television, however, games are given meaning as the viewer reads and makes sense of them as texts. As texts, they can be interpreted in many ways, but the common denominator is an acting-out of being Canadian. Regardless of the level or the 'vernacular,' the Canadianness of hockey is a constant, even though it may not necessarily be foremost in the mind of the player or fan involved.[7]

Hockey literature, like much literature, is a significant factor in nation-building and constructions of identity. As Timothy Brennan writes, it is not just founding documents such as constitutions and declarations of independence that determine the form of a nation: 'The rise of the modern nation-state in Europe in the late eighteenth and early nineteenth centuries is inseparable from the forms and subjects of imaginative literature.' While heterogeneous Canada obviously does not qualify as a traditional nation-state, the role of literary texts is equally important to shaping the country. Don Morrow argues that hockey literature is

important in that [it] take[s] the giant-ness of the land that is Canada, its snow and darkness and compresses them into 'winter tales' of a needed literature of near-legends, legendary memories and heroes.

Though they both point out the importance of literary narratives in constructing identities, these two assertions are not entirely synonymous. Whereas Brennan refers to literature of the past, of a time when an allegedly uniform nation-state was the Romantic ideal, Morrow is writing about Paul Quarrington's *Logan in Overtime* and *King Leary*, two hockey novels written in multi-ethnic Canada at the end of the twentieth century. Morrow is not heralding a return to reductive concepts of nationhood, but his words do point to Canada's latecomer status in terms of national literature.[8] It is hard to imagine Americans or Austrians talking about a 'needed literature.'

Morrow's praise of hockey novels like Paul Quarrington's *King Leary* (1987) comes close to the claim that the Great Canadian Novel must be about hockey. In spite of this widespread belief in the importance of and need for hockey fiction, biographies, autobiographies, exposés, and popular histories overwhelmingly outnumber fiction. Most hockey writing has a truth claim and refers to real-life players of the past, but even that body of non-fiction has a collective (though perhaps unconscious) agenda because it elevates already famous players to national heroes, immortalizing them in print as well as the collective imagination. In Birk Sproxton's formulation, hockey 'stories are hand-me-down gifts you wear that don't wear out.' Especially in the popular press and in children's literature, stories about Maurice Richard, for example, perpetuate and augment his legacy.[9]

Hockey has long been a provider of heroes in a country almost devoid of traditional folk heroes. It fulfils the same role in Canada as baseball literature does in the United States, by providing 'a vital source of myth in a nearly mythless country.' Patricia Hughes-Fuller, referring to 'Top Ten Canadian' Don Cherry, argues convincingly that his entire raison d'être and 'intent' as a hockey commentator 'is to reinforce the heroic/chivalric tradition and idea of adherence to a code, one which exalts, among other things, the values of loyalty, fraternity and mutual respect' – that is, the often aggressive value system of traditional masculinity discussed in chapter 3. In the CBC poll, Cherry, the old-fashioned mythmaker and shaper of one vision and version of Canada, was celebrated as a Canadian icon, along with the peacekeepers and universal health care proponents, who also buttress our sense of national identity and mythology.[10]

Journalist Robert Fulford argues that 'Canadians are authorities on mythology' in the way that 'residents of the Sahara grow learned in the location of water. It is what we spectacularly lack and what we yearn to possess.'[11] Though all mythologies are shaped and changed over time, hockey differs from most because – unlike that nation-building imaginative literature of the eighteenth and nineteenth centuries – its story is constantly and speedily being rewritten in the compressed history of daily newspapers, the latest player biographies, and general conversation. We may regard hockey as a Canadian 'creation myth,' but the earliest accounts of the game are just a century old, and most of our hockey heroes have been created in just a few years. It is common for hero-confirming biographies to be published before the player's career has ended. In some exceptional cases, such as Terry Jones's *The Great Gretzky* (1982) or Gare Joyce's *Sidney Crosby: Taking the Game by Storm* (2006), they appear not long after the professional career has begun. The plethora of biographies for players who retired decades ago – such as Maurice Richard, Gordie Howe, and Bobby Orr – reflects a public ever hungry for new assessments of its hockey heroes, of its popular mythology.

Hugh Hood's biography *Strength down Centre: The Jean Béliveau Story* was published in 1970, shortly before Béliveau retired. The final chapter of this nuanced hagiography is entitled 'More than Ordinary Powers,' which Hood commences with a definition:

> *Hero:* ... 3 (lit.), the central personage in an epic narrative or drama, possessing more than ordinary powers, and expressive of the aspirations of the society he represents.[12]

Hood accentuates the mythological dimension of his task, while his focus on societal aspirations clearly places Béliveau in the tradition of previous Canadiens heroes. This is primarily a story about a great player, but by providing a dictionary definition that emphasizes both the literary and the social connotations of a hero, Hood clearly points to the fact that he is making a contribution to broader cultural history.

Michael Robidoux reminds us that building and 'defining a national identity is a creative process that requires constructing a shared history and mythology(ies) that best suit the identity *imagined* by those few responsible for responding to this task.' Writers are definitely among those 'few responsible,' and, sometimes softly, sometimes not, they capably express the link between hockey and Canada. For example, novelist David Adams Richards asks

> ... if we can make the claim that we play hockey better than any other country – if we can make that claim, without having to listen to apologies about why we made it – then who speaks for *us*, as a HOCKEY nation ...?

Though Richards is speaking more globally about cultural loss in an era when most Canadian hockey players work for American teams, his entire memoir *Hockey Dreams* stands up for firm personal beliefs about the importance of the game to Canada. The voice of the people examines Canadians' favourite topic.[13]

Canada has no clear historical national poet or authorial voice. Whereas each Italian town has a Via Dante, and each German one a *Goethestraße*, our closest parallel to such national poets would be Margaret Atwood, who is alive, writing and promoting Canadian culture. She even has a cameo appearance in the short story 'Love Is All around Us,' in which author Mark Anthony Jarman includes more hockey than love, while poking fun at Atwood's cultural presence and voice. The story begins with an epigraph by poet David McGimpsey: 'Once, the snow was so deep you almost couldn't hear Margaret Atwood.' Atwood haunts the story, appearing in many guises, though not in disguise. A selection from this five-page story: Atwood's voice controls the narrator's answering machine ('*You have no new voice mail; you have no new voice, male*'), and resounds over an airport's P.A. system; with shades of Mephistopheles in the famous scene from Goethe's *Faust*, she takes to the stage at the 'Ratskeller Klub' to sing Neil Young; she has a chat with Don Cherry; and – as a key symbol of her status as Canadian cultural arbiter – she referees a shinny match, before finally departing. Despite the anti-Atwood sentiment throughout and complaints of her ubiquity, the story ends with 'Don't go! *Without you we are lost.*'[14]

Some of the humour in 'Love Is All around Us' is in imagining Atwood as a referee. This is less a statement about Atwood than it is a tapping into stereotypes about high culture being poles apart from sport. Lorna Jackson recalls a bunch of writer friends imagining 'Atwood and Alice Munro dropping the gloves, the size of their thighs, the style of play,' as well as a crude pun about 'who'd go down first.'

Neither Atwood nor Munro refers often to hockey in their work; Atwood, however, has been seen by thousands on the ice. On 31 January 2005 she appeared on CBC's comedy show *The Rick Mercer Report*, spectacularly decked out in full padding to offer goaltending tips. In between telling viewers how to stop a puck, Atwood notes that, like the 'world of literature, sometimes hockey's not pretty.' Atwood uses the athlete's idiom, even referring to herself in the third person (saying, 'You don't deke Margaret' and 'Momma can get nasty'), before finishing off with a description of a technique commonly known as 'stacking the pads, except where I come from they call it an Atwood.' This is mock self-aggrandizing because it is inconceivable that even she could have a hockey save named after her – that is, that a producer of high culture could be bigger than hockey. The performance is multi-layered irony, but the main background is the humour of Atwood, *the* defender of and spokesperson for Canadian culture, bragging that she is also an excellent goalie. A playful postmodern mingling of the high and the low, this sketch brings together two Canadian icons. Atwood, often seen as the quintessential Canadian writer, must be linked to the 'quintessential Canadian game.'

Since modern hockey arose in Canada, and since Canadian players long dominated the sport, calling hockey Canadian is not essentialist mythologizing or chauvinism but a reflection of fact. But overemphasizing hockey's role in identity can be misleading because, as Mary Louise Adams reminds us, it 'is part of the obfuscating construction of the so-called "ordinary Canadian."' Though Canada could teach many countries how *not* to posit 'ordinariness,' critics often point out that hockey's dominance comes at the expense of female and non-white Canadians. Yet there is also sporting exclusion. In a short personal essay, M.T. Kelly writes, 'Hockey always made me feel like an alien in my own country [for] the sports I excelled in, didn't have the mass tribal appeal that ... hockey did.' 'Tribal' is a word used fairly infrequently in Canada (though to great rhetorical effect), but in hockey discourse there is an intense sense of belonging that often, on the surface, smacks of kinship. In much hockey writing, foreign players are robbed of any hockey pedigree, and non-Canadian players and teams who excel at the game, or who play a slightly different style, are often accused of 'not really' playing. European leagues are accurately depicted as last-ditch playing options in stories such as Dave Bidini's 'Cortina,' in which a career minor-leaguer travels to Italy to finish off his career (and, as it turns out, his life). The ubiquitous references to hockey as 'our game' imply that foreigners who play are just borrowing it from Canada, the rightful birthplace, home and keeper of the hockey flame.[15]

The introduction to Doug Beardsley's anthology *Our Game: An All-Star Collection of Hockey Fiction* begins with the language of loss:

> Our game? Our game?! With Russians travelling like Soyuz rockets over white spaces of ice, and Europeans avoiding the corners and bodychecks as if all Canadians were contagious, and American businesspeople buying our game away from Halifax, Quebec City, Hamilton and Winnipeg to exotic faraway places such as Tampa Bay, Florida ...?

Defining oneself entails defining the Other, and to do this Beardsley employs both stereotypes and facts that Canadian hockey fans will immediately recognize. There is the familiar reputation European players have of avoiding 'corners' and the rougher aspects of the professional game; behind the reality of Winnipeg and Quebec City having lost their NHL teams to 'American businesspeople' is the fear of Canada being 'sold' to the southern neighbours. Although critics have taken Beardsley to task for basing his 'discussion on an idealized, organic conception of hockey as a natural Canadian cultural resource,' he is merely exploiting, albeit flamboyantly, a pre-established discourse. Through his hyperbole and epic list of hockey injustices against Canadians, Beardsley may be reinforcing stereotypes about foreign players, but he is not inventing them. In fact, many of the stories in his *Collection* focus on the shady sides of hockey, and are critical literary examinations of violence, commercialism, and the social exclusion of those who do not enjoy the national game. The Introduction to *Our Game* replays the nationalistic mythology; the anthology itself undermines this mythology. The hockey tale may be 'ours,' but hockey fiction consistently shows that it is neither glorious nor benign.[16]

Dale Jacobs's *Ice: New Writing on Hockey* (1999), as well as Michael Kennedy's *Words on Ice: A Collection of Hockey Prose* (2003), include some of the same stories as Beardsley's. Though the editors' introductions are more subdued than Beardsley's, each focuses on hockey as something essentially Canadian. Jacobs begins with a nostalgic positioning of the narrator. He writes his Preface from the sort of 'exotic faraway place' that has attracted Canadian professional teams:

> Now that I live in North Carolina, I seldom see temperatures below freezing; such infrequent events cause a spate of news stories ... And, consequently, there isn't much talk of hockey here.

The careful self-positioning through the statement of geographical location and the nostalgia it promotes is typical of hockey writing: for the most part, personal memoirs and essays express longing for bygone times, when children played shinny on natural ice or families gathered around the television to watch the original six NHL teams play each other. In the Introduction to *Words on Ice*, Kennedy evokes this past more explicitly:

> Whether playing the sport, watching it live or on television, or merely being aware of its effect on the community, Canadians by the millions and others who have come to understand the game have grown up with hockey as a part of their common memory.

Kennedy points out the obvious, though often forgotten, fact that non-Canadians can also comprehend the game, and he is therefore less exclusive than the other two editors. Indeed, he notes that hockey is now just one entertainment option among many – and perhaps this 'common memory' is a fading concept in a world of video games and play-on-demand Internet services – and that 'the sport has had a significant effect on young and old in increasing numbers within the United States, Sweden, Finland, and Russia,' among other places. After all, if hockey is to have any value at all, it must appeal to other nations. Celebrating hockey solely for its Canadianness would be like eating an unpalatable national dish for the sole reason that it is a national dish. The successful export of hockey is proof of its value.[17]

As mentioned, writers often handle this 'hockey is Canada' equation with humour or levity. This is surely because waxing philosophical and poetical about a game that is trivial invites bathos: there is a dash of the mock heroic when sport is taken too seriously. So when a fine novelist like David Adams Richards resorts to capital letters and refuses to apologize when talking about 'HOCKEY,' or Doug Beardsley uses a stentorian nationalistic tone in a preface to a literary anthology, one suspects posturing or histrionics. Just as humour or irony can nip charges of sentimentality or rueful nostalgia in the bud, so have Richards and Beardsley found a stylistic means of bridging the gap between trivial game and cultural emblem of a nation. Each author moves towards the mock serious at such times in their prose on hockey. For a nation whose other mythological conceptions of the national character include tolerance, cool-headedness, and a penchant for apologizing, it is difficult to accept apparent statements of rage and disbelief such as Beardsley's 'Our game?!' entirely at face value. Regardless of how many professional teams head to Texas or Arizona, Manitobans will continue to play and embrace hockey.

Literary Language

The ambiguity of literary language gives it an advantage over non-fictional works. In fiction, even the clichéd language often used to describe hockey in newspapers makes us look more closely. Just as euphemisms for violence in literature stand out all the more precisely because they are in print, so are clichés a signal to question the stereotypes and underlying myths behind banal phrases. To provide a concise example, Ray Robertson's *Heroes* contains the oft-heard argument about Americans stealing and degrading the game. The protagonist, Bayle, recalls a conversation he had with his father, who is convinced that there was a conspiracy against Canadian teams: 'I wouldn't put it past those American bastards in New York who are calling the shots in the NHL these days ...'[18] Bayle refuses to believe this theory, rejecting it outright. Bayle's father goes overboard, but Bayle's response is also off the mark since, as hockey fans on both sides of the border have lamented, the current commissioner of the NHL is a New York lawyer with almost no hockey background. In a bar, or even on television, this slander about 'bastards in New York' would flit past without engendering a second thought; in Robertson's novel, the words so commonly heard are made strange through their literary context. Putting them on the printed page challenges the reader to see them as instances of anti-Americanism, hockey-based Canadian essentialism, and even paranoia. When we encounter such aversion in literature, there is less of a tendency to take it as the whole story. Where Roch Carrier argued, 'You can explain anything through hockey,' hockey literature often encourages questioning in place of pat answers.

Very often a naive narrator encourages us to scrutinize commonplace statements because, as is typical with structural irony, we know more than the narrator. In Pete McCormack's *Understanding Ken* (which is examined more thoroughly in the next chapter), the young narrator says,

After the game was over and the announcer said it was brought to us by Ford and Esso, the Hockey Night in Canada theme song came on. That song is twice as good as O Canada. It should be the national anthem.

We may have had similar thoughts ourselves about the admittedly catchy tune, but the fictional setting urges us to look further. McCormack links the melody, which is often referred to as Canada's 'second national anthem,' to corporate sponsorship. In light of this juxtaposition, we might consider priorities between the publicly funded CBC as a provider and supporter of Canadian culture and commodified hockey, between the historical importance and pomp of a national anthem and the theme song of *Hockey Night in Canada*. If the function of an anthem is to inspire the nation or rally the troops in the manner of 'Onward Christian Soldiers' or a battlefield melody on the bagpipes, McCormack's narrator has a legitimate point. Author Douglas Coupland, in his non-fictional *Souvenir of Canada*, expresses a similar idea regarding the proximity of 'O Canada' and hockey: the NHL is 'ugly and yet it's civil; and most tellingly, it's the one place where people still sing the national anthem.'[19]

After decades of neglect, popular and academic investigators have started to examine the connections between sport and nation. American writer Philip Roth plays with the cultural importance of the national pastime in *The Great American Novel*. The narrator, Word Smith, is a sportswriter who sets out to write the definitive novel of America. Naturally, the sportswriter believes such a novel must be about baseball. The novel is hilarious in its praise of baseball's alleged moral qualities and in its exaggerated views of the game's importance to America. For example, after a dying baseball team owner bequeaths the team to his morally relaxed wife, Angela Trust (no 'faithful angel'), by entrusting her with a baseball 'with a final effort of his patriarchal will,' her moral transformation is set in motion. Ten years later, the now virtuous owner recalls how her husband 'had died, leaving her holding the ball, and [how] the ball had been her salvation.' The power of this game is indeed enormous, which is why the loss of it would drive a stake through the nation's heart. At one point, Angela berates a player while informing him of an alleged Red Threat to cripple America by striking at the national game:

> ... now do you remember what it is that links in brotherhood millions upon millions of American men, makes kin of enemies, if only while the game is going on? *Baseball!* And that is how they propose to destroy America, young man, that is their evil and ingenious plan – *to destroy our national game!*

As with the Canadian fears of losing hockey, the fear in Roth is that without baseball there can be no America.[20] Roth's novel was a parody, but the claim that once the national sport is destroyed, the nation is also destroyed, has been uttered in earnest.

Roth's *Great American Novel* anticipates Canadian reviewers' stance towards hockey novels. Michael Bryson, praising Mark Anthony Jarman's *Salvage King, Ya!* for the *Danforth Review*, asks 'If it's the best hockey book ever written, does that make it The Great Canadian Novel?' This comment makes light of, even while acknowledging, the 'essential' link between hockey and Canada in the same way that Roth's novel overplays the moral and national importance of baseball in *The Great American Novel.* At the same time, it points to the fact that hockey was absent from Canadian literature for so long. Especially popular non-fiction abounds with saccharine accounts of the game's importance to Canada, as well as lengthy and poetical justifications of its mythic cultural status. In a column of 3 December 2006, the *Toronto Star's* Garth Woolsey calls this 'wide-eyed and ain't-it-wonderful Canadian gothic.' Such pronouncements invite us to believe that every Canadian plays hockey and that the game has no dark side. In the introduction to *Hockey Towns: Stories of Small Town Hockey in Canada,* Bill Boyd notes that he is not going to fall into this trap: 'I'm not interested in hockey as a metaphor for Canadian life or whether it's our wintry religion or a frozen chunk of our soul.'[21] Metaphors of hockey and Canada are not necessary because they have preceded Boyd's book; like that 60–metre hockey stick chosen as a symbol of Canada at Expo '86 in Vancouver, such metaphors and tropes of hockey's greatness loom large. Intellectual shorthand of a sort, they are common to most Canadians, and very few works of hockey fiction attempt to explain the game's importance. Explaining at length who Wayne Gretzky was or the prominence of Don Cherry's 'Coach's Corner' makes for tediously pedantic and unnatural prose.

Hockey as the Essence of Canada

If hockey is not literally natural, it is natural in the sense that few will question a Canadian's decision to play hockey. When parents push their children into the sport, there is no choice involved; they are simply born into the game. For Canadians, playing hockey is not a social or class statement in the way that golf or skiing is, even though the expenses are similar. Jeff Klein and Karl-Eric Reif's study *The Death of*

Hockey emphasizes a minor difference between growing up in Buffalo, and growing up a short car ride north of the border. Though the authors became avid hockey fans, there was a sense of discovery when they came to the game. If you are Canadian, 'you probably don't remember the first time you became aware of the game' because 'in Canada, the game is always there. It's in the family, it's in the culture, it's in the air.' Cecil Harris, meanwhile, describes growing up in a 'predominantly black neighborhood' in Brooklyn where 'devotion to hockey was a singular pleasure. There was nowhere for me to learn to play, nowhere to skate, no one to accompany me to a game, no one with whom I could talk hockey.' It is for this reason that hockey fiction as a whole makes the Canada-hockey connection in an understated manner. In Canadian hockey literature the assumptions are, for the most part, left unsaid. The writer need not explain the basis of 'a wintry religion' – it is understood to be what linguists and laypeople alike call common ground. The reader has to take it on faith and tradition.[22]

Ray Rains's *Hockey Night Down Under!* is perhaps the only English-language hockey novel from completely outside the tradition. The book, written in an Australian patois, is a 'fictionalized account of one team's attempt to win Australia's annual under-18 ice-hockey championship.' A picaresque tale of a ragtag group of unlikely athletes striving for minor sporting glory, the novel is fairly standard sports literature fare. Here the often very foreign idiom collides with the subject matter of hockey – so much so that the author (mercifully) includes a glossary to explain phrases like '*He skated down the ice flat tac* ["at full speed"]' and '*The team was home and hosed* ["an easy winner"].' In this novel, the linguistic hurdles defamiliarize the game even more so than ironical clichés in print. Rains dwells on the difficulties of playing hockey in sunnier climes, including the need to educate the locals about the sport. When a journalist finally covers the boys' hockey team, he presents hockey as a bloodsport, infuriating the narrator:

> Once again ice hockey had been portrayed as a game for goons who weren't the full quid [i.e., normal]. It made me as mad as a meat axe. It would only reinforce the average Ozzie's impression of ice hockey as World Wrestling on Skates.

Hockey is something exotic, unusual, entirely foreign, so that justifications, excuses, and cultural mediation are required for the book's primarily Australian audience.[23]

Canada is the constant benchmark for the narrator, with videotapes of professional games and equipment arriving like hockey aid packages from the Great White North. In one encounter, the narrator explains that his boys started skating at age seven. 'Too late!' is the feisty Canadian's reply, '[my boy] was on the ice at two years of age back in Medicine Hat.' The young Australians' careers were thus doomed from the start. In Australia, playing hockey at all is a bizarre recreation choice, and the only understandable reason for playing hockey Down Under is because of foreign proclivities: 'Most kids who play hockey here do so 'cos of a link to the game through their parents or 'cos they've seen some hockey somewhere, liked it an' thought they'd try it. But these kids [i.e., on the team] aren't even sure of the game's rules.' The foreignness of the game and the strangeness of playing hockey in such balmy surroundings are constantly underlined:

> Yer see, the problems associated with the playin' of ice hockey Down Under are almost too daunting to contemplate; an' for expatriate Canucks … the frustration of watchin' their national game played incessantly at a primitive level is often too much to koala [i.e., to bear].

Given the obstacles that hockey players in Australia face, including the proprietary airs of the uprooted Canadians and Czechs, the mere fielding of a team is a radical sporting decision. *Hockey Night Down Under!* is thus a literary antidote for works that naturalize hockey into something obvious and inevitable.[24]

Paul Quarrington's *King Leary* includes a compact example of the uncritical acceptance of hockey in Canada. Early in the novel, the elderly King Leary listens impatiently to an American professor discussing hockey's roots:

> And the lad from Minn. [i.e., Minnesota] starts talking about the *origins* of hockey. He went on and on about soccer and lacrosse, English foot soldiers playing *baggataway* with the Indians, some Scandinavian entertainment called *bandy*. I bit my tongue, but the truth of the matter is, I never knew that hockey originated. I figured it was just always there, like the moon.

The moniker 'lad from Minn.' is already condescending, and Leary believes geography gives rise to ignorance (though wintry Minnesota has a long tradition of hockey and is well acquainted with the cold). Leary betrays his us-and-them mentality, and for him the border demarcates an absolute division. This is a fine illustration of sport as short-hand for nation: Hockey is Canada's sporting story, America has something else. The irony is that Leary, for all the hockey he has played, has never thought about the origins of the game and therefore knows less about the origins of the Canadian myth of hockey than the 'lad from Minn.' Although hockey is the cornerstone of Leary's identity – he made his living at it, and he spends his days in the retirement home remembering and embellishing his on-ice exploits – his attitude towards the game is pre-cultural, as it is entirely unreflective.[25]

Steve Lundin's novel *When She's Gone* offers a more blatant, zestier example of King Leary's strict border mentality. The narrator, Mark, is a young, adult goalie whose physical and intellectual life revolves around hockey. He comments on exotic places like Anaheim acquiring NHL teams, while the Winnipeg Jets moved south, and concludes that this was 'the final humiliation of Canada's game, the theft of our myth nearly as horrendous as some Canadian blathering on about baseball.' Just as Leary believes any American should not discuss hockey, so should Canadians avoid discussing baseball. This absolutist concept of sporting nationalism is absurd because, especially in border regions, Canadians and Americans play and watch the same sports. 'America's game' is by no means beyond Canadians' conversational horizon. Nevertheless, and despite Canada's lengthy baseball tradition, the game is often seen as the 'Americanization' of Canada.[26]

Integration

We often claim, not always in jest, that a 'true' Canadian has a visceral, innate attachment to hockey and accompanying comprehension of the game. Bill Gaston, who has written a fair amount of hockey fiction, picks up on this in his non-fictional *Midnight Hockey: All about BEER, the BOYS, and the REAL CANADIAN GAME*. He recalls an unusual tryout for the single paid position on a hapless team from Toulon, France (the tryout took place during public skating hours). The other job candidate was a young man from Winnipeg, who happened to be in the region. Although Gaston was initially concerned about the competition, it turned out that Phil 'was such a bad skater that he would have easily been the worst player on the team, even on this *Ligue du Sud* team, which is saying something.' When later asked why he thought he had a chance, Phil replied, 'Well, I'm from Canada, eh?'[27] When it comes to hockey, a Canadian passport should suffice.

In hockey fiction, one can become Canadian even before acquiring a passport. Integration into the Canadian cultural landscape through the game is a common element in hockey fiction. Scott Young's adolescent novel *Scrubs on Skates* (originally published in 1952) includes one Bill Spunska, a Polish boy who takes to hockey. Unlike his parents, intellectuals who struggle in the new country, Bill's integration is smooth because he plays hockey. Bill adapts relatively easily to the game, and his peers are quick to accept him after he starts playing. This causes his mother to reflect on the relationship between sport and integration:

> I know that usually a family must live in a country one generation, or sometimes two or three, before the children are accepted for everything. But it seems to me that sport is different. It is what you are, not what you have been or what your parents have been ...

Bill is initially more an enthusiastic than talented player. When he finally sees ice time in a game, hockey becomes more than an integrative element; it is an elixir for Bill's mother, who had fallen ill. 'My mother is up today,' says Bill after learning that she followed his first ice time via radio: 'The first time in two months. The doctor said I should have got into the game before, it was better than his medicine!' The simple symbolism is in the ready reference to hockey, which functions not as a palliative escape but a source of energy and health for the immigrant mother.[28]

Although *Scrubs on Skates* is aimed at young readers, it has assumed its place in the thin hockey literature canon. The book is part of a trilogy for young people that also includes *Boy on Defence* and *A Boy at the Leafs' Camp* (there was actually a fourth book, *That Old Gang of Mine*, a saucy novel brimming with booze and sex and grown-up boys; it briefly appeared on a 2004 CBC list of recommended literature for young readers). First written fifty years ago, the books were updated slightly in 1985 in an apparent attempt to tone down their latent sexism and stereotyping. The formulaic rags-to-riches series of plots – clumsy Spunska moves from poor immigrant to potential professional player – has been criticized for being a simplistic allegory for (North) American-Dream-style capitalism. For example, Robert G. Hollands remarks,

> Bill Spunska symbolizes the immigrant making good in a system (whether it be hockey or capitalism) designed to produce a winner out of anyone who is hard-working, dedicated, and who, of course, possesses some natural talent.

Hollands's point about hockey being an incomplete marker or symbol
of integration into Canadian society is certainly valid, and such a simplified view of the world would be hard to stomach in quality Canadian
adult literature, where any hero worth his or her salt should ultimately
fail (as Margaret Atwood remarked in *Survival*). In *The Good Body*, Bill
Gaston mocks the simplistic Spunska narrative in a lowbrow literary
allusion:

> Bill Spunska, the clumsy immigrant, barely makes the team but scores the
> winning yadda with yadda left on the clock in the yadda yadda finals. Do
> you see the social comment? Do you see the team-as-microcosm thing?

Even readers unfamiliar with Young's trilogy will recognize the critique
of sports literature's brotherhood and unrealistic happy endings.
Because Young's trilogy has been read by generations of Canadians, the
reference will be readily identified as Gaston pokes fun at the superficial symbolism of integration and success that plagued sports literature
of the past.[29]

C.D. Minni's short story 'Details from the Canadian Mosaic' also
looks very briefly at the theme of integration through sport. An Italian
family moves to Canada in the 1950s, and the son Mario takes up the
New World sports of baseball and hockey. Because of an apparent belief
that Italians cannot excel at these sports, Mario's name is anglicized by
his peers:

> By the end of summer, he was Mario at home and Mike in the streets. It
> was Mike who pitched a five-hitter for the Giants, Mike who in August
> watched the salmon run upstream to spawn and Mike who returned to
> school in September. At Christmas he received his first pair of skates and
> toque on his head, planned to learn hockey. When he dreamed, it was of
> Rocket Richard or three-speed bikes ...[30]

The dual names are an apt symbol for identity in multicultural Canada,
as well as hockey's part in that split or layered identity. To Mario's ears,
as well as his friends', his Italian-sounding name is out of place in the
world of North American sports (even the baseball great Joe DiMaggio
began life as Giuseppe DiMaggio, Jr). In his desire for cultural integration, Mario does not seem overly concerned about giving up that part
of his identity. This transposing of 'Mario' into 'Mike' is a symbol of the
temporary jingoism that hockey fosters, as well as a reflection of the

many immigrants who decided to change their family names in the New World. For as long as the game continues, hockey unites many Canadians by providing a common focal point.

Though integration into Canadian society occurs more easily than elsewhere in the world, stories of smooth sporting oneness often ring hollow. They are, at best, representative – especially in light of the widely accepted idea of hockey as an escape from the rest of life. Literary critic Linda Hutcheon talks about Canadian writers' 'split sense of identity, both regional and national.' Geography and history, whether regional, national, or personal, feed this complexity, and it is not only 'where is here' that is important in the Canadian multicultural mosaic; 'where was there' also matters. In Dave Bidini's non-fiction hockey classic *Tropic of Hockey: My Search for the Game in Unlikely Places*, he explains 'the confusing issue of my Canadianness.' Bidini speaks about his own Italian heritage with reference to former star Phil Esposito, 'the most complex of all Canadian hockey players, and the most culturally significant, too.' Playing primarily in the 1970s, Esposito was a living symbol of a changing Canada, of a time when the options available to Canadians were no longer anglicization or cultural ghettoization. Although Canada has always been a nation of immigrants, Bidini claims that public cultural life in Canada was 'all British and Irish' until the flashy Esposito entered Canadians' homes and consciousness.[31]

Esposito was special not just because he was an excellent goal scorer or because he happened to have Italian roots. Esposito's voice made Canada stand up and take notice – by giving a stirring, impromptu live speech during the 1972 Summit Series against the Soviets. Team Canada had been soundly – and by now famously – defeated by the visiting Soviet team in Vancouver, and the Canadian fans had started booing the home team. After the game, Esposito gave an impassioned impromptu speech that was an alliterative masterpiece. He berated the fans for their lack of support: 'I'm disheartened, disillusioned, and disappointed' – and he promised an apology to all Canadians if the Soviet fans booed their team as the Canadian fans had. Bidini notes that, watching the game on television, he had expected a more subdued reaction to the booing:

> But Espo was no cake Loyalist. No: he looked and sounded different and, by seeing him every day on television and in the newspapers, you could tell that Canada's face was changing ... Afterwards, no one in Canada could deny that we Italians existed.

The 'we Italians' may sound parochial, but Bidini and Esposito are not trading away Canadianness in favour of the Old World identity of their forefathers. Because each is so firmly embedded in hockey culture, along with being born in Canada, their Canadianness may be 'confusing,' but it is never in question. Bidini presents a convincing argument: it was through hockey that multiculturalism entered the living rooms of the nation and became a mediated yet deeply felt reality. There have always been great hockey players with names that did not sound 'typically' Canadian, as in English. To refer once again to Morley Callaghan's 1943 essay 'The Game That Makes a Nation,' since names like 'Broda, Stanowski, Grosso' have long shown up on NHL payrolls and fan programs, Callaghan argues that the game 'does more for the racial [i.e., 'ethnic'] unity of this country' than any political efforts. Hockey is a key element of what might be called post-ethnic society. Bidini's analysis of Esposito is insightful because he points out that it was Esposito's *voice*, along with his skills, that made him famous – he was more than an Italian-looking name on a scoresheet.[32]

While some see multiculturalism as a challenge, Canada's main struggles have been geographical and political, with Quebec's post–Quiet Revolution attraction to sovereignty being most obvious. Michael McKinley's short story 'Next Year' takes the reader back to 1969, three years before Esposito's speech. The title refers to the Vancouver Canucks' 1970 arrival in the NHL, and the story is partly a satire on essentialist ideas of Canada and hockey. Cousin Dermot from Toronto visits the young narrator at Christmas in 'balmy' Vancouver and arrogantly proclaims: 'This isn't really Canada' because it's too warm. The satire stems from Dermot's reductive view of Canada. Later, Dermot the bully expounds on what is and is not Canada:

> Montreal isn't really Canada because of all those Frenchies, and Vancouver isn't really Canada because you can't skate outside, and there's no NHL team here anyway, so anyone with a brain can figure out that this leaves Toronto as your only real choice.

The chauvinistic tone has been heard before, but here McKinley renders it ridiculous by placing it in the mouth of a boorish simpleton. Dermot usefully spells out what lies unstated in the background of so much hockey culture in Canada: myths of winter and idolizing of the NHL (anti-Quebec sentiment exists too, but not to the same extent). 'Next Year' pits the cousins as foils: the arrogant, aggressive loudmouth from Toronto versus the milder younger cousin from Vancouver. Yet, for all their antagonism, the cousins are not very far apart in their views of hockey and Canada. The narrator himself is embarrassed by the lack of snow in his hometown and regrets that his own father preferred football to the national game. On the surface, this agreement between foes does little to undermine the fallacy that Canada equals hockey. The limited-ness of the cousins' viewpoint is mitigated by their obviously naive perspectives as they uncritically embrace the equation. Their lack of perspective reminds the reader that Canadianness cannot be reduced to an NHL hockey team or the English language.33

Eventually, Dermot has to stop beating up his cousin because a passing Elderly Gentleman joins the conversation. He happens to be Cyclone Taylor, a member of a 1915 Stanley Cup–winning team from Vancouver in the days before the NHL acquired a monopoly over the trophy. Learning that Vancouver once had possession of the magnificent Cup is deeply disturbing to Dermot; it upsets his world view and his theory about the heart and soul of Canada, which apparently resides in Toronto's Maple Leaf Gardens. Dermot also learns from Cyclone Taylor that Vancouver is to receive an NHL team the following year. The story that began with 'this isn't Canada' comes full circle with talk of a 'loyalty whose fabled torch had just been passed, backward to *that* year, and forward, forever, to the next.' The echoes of John McRae's 'In Flanders Fields' are obvious in this symbolic rebirth and continuity, and hockey fans might spot an NHL allusion of sorts. As McKinley has written elsewhere, these lines were somewhat callously posted in the Montreal Canadiens dressing room, 'though McRae was exhorting his fellow soldiers to kill more Germans, not the Toronto Maple Leafs.'34

Losing Hockey, Selling Hockey

Joining the game is portrayed as a sometimes rocky path to becoming more Canadian. The inverse, fears of losing part of Canada through loss of the game, is even more prevalent in hockey fiction. Canada's worries about hockey are twofold: the rest of the world has become too good at our game, and the professional game is being sold down the river. Though the complaint is often couched in general anti-American terms, the real discomfort is when sunny areas of the States that have little hockey tradition or experience of natural ice acquire NHL teams. This sense of insecurity became more acute when the Quebec Nordiques and the Winnipeg Jets left in the mid-1990s. The departure of the Jets has been well documented in fiction, but English fiction makes little or no mention of the Nordiques (perhaps because there is still an NHL team left in the province of Quebec).

Professional hockey actually began in the United States, though the players were almost all Canadians. The National Hockey League, like the National Basketball Association, is a misnomer – though less flamboyantly misnamed than Major League Baseball's (exclusively) North American *World* Series. North America is generally less interested in global sports like soccer, and until fairly recently there was no glory in defeating Argentina in basketball. For Canadian hockey players, Stanley Cup dreams are far more alluring than thoughts of Olympic gold. Part of the reason for this is that the NHL is the premier hockey league in the world, attracting the top prospects from around the world and paying them the most money; another, historical, reason is that professional players were once ruled ineligible for the main forums of high-level international competition. This is one of the reasons for the Soviet Union's great success in such competitions (often with teams of 'shamateurs' who enjoyed army sinecures while training at hockey full-time). Since our best never played against their best, there was no shame in losing to them.

This changed in 1972 when the 'Summit Series' was organized between Canada's best NHL players and the Soviet national team – the only international hockey tournament that appears regularly in Canadian fiction. For the first time many of the top Canadian players would measure themselves against the top Soviet players. Indicative of the NHL's dominance and control of Canadian hockey, only the 'right' professional players were eligible. Superstar Bobby Hull from the rival (and relatively short-lived) World Hockey Association was not allowed to suit up for Canada, despite Prime Minister Pierre Trudeau's best attempts. Canadians expected this eight-game series to be a laugher; Canada owned hockey, they would 'own' the series. Abusing a lowly opponent is hardly the material for national mythology, and before the series the general attitude was that this diplomatic circus would merely confirm Canada's hockey supremacy. In the event, the Soviets proved an awesome foe. Although Canada managed to win the series thanks to a last-minute Paul Henderson goal, the Soviets scored more goals in the series. To some, it was a classic case of 'winning ugly' and the on-ice nadir was surely when Bobby Clark intentionally slashed Valery Kharlamov, breaking his leg. Nevertheless, Canadians of a certain age remember where they were when 'Paul Henderson scored The Goal that beat the Soviets.'[35]

Frank Orr's 1982 novel *Puck Is a Four-Letter Word* injects grandeur-stifling honesty into a ribald account of how a team of semi-talented North American professionals beats a formidable Soviet squad:

We all know how we did it ... We used the dirtiest, sneakiest tricks that could be thought up. We used every gimmick ever invented and we probably couldn't win another game that way in a hundred years. Now, let's enjoy every stinking, goddam minute of it.

The Orr novel is not referring directly to the Summit Series, but the passage is useful for showing how the 1972 series was *not* interpreted by many Canadians. Hockey sociologist Michael Robidoux writes that although the Summit Series 'was a debacle, ... it is considered by many to be the greatest Canadian story ever told.' Canadians excel at irony, and given that the series morphed from cakewalk into potential trauma, it is fitting that this event was, through narration and re-narration, transformed into a tale of wonder. What could easily have become national sporting disaster was mythologized into a modern-day 'tale of the tribe' within a relatively short period of time. In *Hometown Heroes: On the Road with Canada's National Hockey Team,* Paul Quarrington notes the magnitude of the victory, adding a dash of destiny to the story:

If it only meant that we had won a hockey series, even the most exciting one ever, surely the memory would not have quite the force, the power. I think it's because it confirmed something in our hearts. We won because we were meant to win.

The tale of the series is now a common and widely accessible historical reference for all Canadians.[36]

There have been many passing references to Henderson's last-minute goal in hockey fiction and, along with Don Cherry, Bobby Orr, and Maurice Richard, it is one of the four standard hockey allusions. Richard Harrison's poem 'Russians' goes beyond referring to it simply as a big goal or important moment for Canada. He outlines the importance of a foil, opponent, or enemy for history:

We need them. They made the act of a single Canadian
Canada's act in '72, the shot so sweet it has replayed
a million times ...

'We need them' in the way that Ronald Reagan needed the Evil Empire against which America could compete and measure itself. Nothing binds a community better than an antagonistic Other. We identify with the Canadians on the ice, which is what Harrison clarifies in these lines: 'the act of a single Canadian' was taken over by an entire nation, objectified and whittled into a narrative that belongs to all of us. Harrison concedes that 'they played the better game and should have beaten' Canada. The series that led to the creation of this myth may have been a 'debacle,' but it was not an outright lie. In other words, though the Summit Series has been injected with symbolic import, it is one of those few times in life when the symbolic and the real collide because Canada competed both literally and figuratively against the Soviets in this Cold War on ice. The Series was thought to be of crucial importance at the time, not least because 'the Soviets openly declared that they played to prove the superiority of their socio-political system'; it has also subsequently gained one in the telling and proved a convenient point of departure for hockey literature because it meant so much to so many Canadians and also because it is an easily recognized allusion.[37]

Edo van Belkom's short story 'Hockey's Night in Canada' depends entirely on the reader's familiarity with the 1972 Summit Series. The title's suggestion that hockey had but a single 'night' in Canada negates the binding ritual of 'Hockey Night in Canada,' since without repetition there can be no ritual. The story considers the consequences a final Canadian loss in Moscow would have had. The fictional answer? We would have lost 'our' game to European players, and they would have gained a monopoly over North American professional leagues. Furthermore, the entire style of the game would have changed: those who 'played the better game' would be an occupying hockey power on Canadian territory. The story makes use of a standard cast of members for sports fiction, and it is structured like the typical tale of the rookie hoping to make a professional team. Kevin Wilson's physical attributes and skill seem adequate:

> He stood six feet tall, weighed in at just over two hundred pounds, and according to what had been written in a few of the Toronto papers, was just what the Leafs needed to help them make a serious run at Lord Stanley's Cup.

This is a typical introduction of the main sporting hero, of the type that focuses on the 'physical and biological' while neglecting the social. But van Belkom provides a variation on the trope, introducing the social and the historical as he undermines the rookie's chances. The job will go to another player, Smolnikov, 'a classic Russian hockey player, much smaller than Wilson ... an eggs-in-his-pocket, fancy-skating playmaker.' In a reversal of the Canadian way of playing hockey, the NHL now favours delicate and dainty skaters, shutting out the beefy, more physical types from NHL jobs (the stereotypes about precious European players and the idea of a 'right' way to play hockey remain intact).38

Wilson does not make the team because, as the coach explains, 'people want to see the Russians play, they think their style of hockey's more exciting, more entertaining.' The reason for the Canadian fans' sudden switch from a preference for rough, fight-filled hockey is provided:

> Maybe if Henderson hadn't hit the post in the dying seconds of that final game back in 1972, then maybe things would have been different. If he'd scored and we'd won the series, then maybe the Russians would have had to learn the game from us instead of the other way around. But no, he hit the post and they came back up the ice and scored ...

Sport deals in absolutes – a near-miss is still a miss – but here van Belkom takes it to extreme off-ice lengths. Losing the game by a single goal, it is argued, would have changed both hockey history and world history. In reality, losing that 1972 series would not have drastically altered Canada (or history), and the sense of 'loss' would likely have been a mere inkling of something not right in the hockey world. Hockey is too deeply entrenched in the Canadian psyche to be taken away by a single loss on the ice. As the coach breaking the news to Wilson explains, 'I'd love to stack the team with Canadian talent, play it tough, you know, real old-time hockey, but the owners want a team full of Russians.' At the conclusion of the story, Wilson is sent to Belarus, to the fictional Minsk Maple Leafs for finishing.39

The coach claims to be at the mercy of the owners. Most often the owners are American, and as the Canadian players head south, the concern with losing precious Canadian resources is as clear as in brain-drain commentaries or Free Trade critiques. It is understandable that much of Canada becomes proprietary about hockey: when foreign interests with no indigenous hockey tradition take control of the game, those who know the game best can become puppets. John Ralston Saul speaks sarcastically of hockey as a business and, referring to Wayne

Gretzky's trade, its spread to Hollywood: 'Hockey needed to be removed from Canada for its own good, so that it could grow through the freedom which would be produced by minimizing its peculiarities.' In the service of a broader argument against neo-liberalism, Saul – in an example of how we can 'explain anything' through hockey – overstates the Canadian hockey case. The 'good of the game' must somehow be Canadian. Of course, when hockey is a business there is no universal, disinterested 'good of the game.' Profit is always the guiding rudder and, as David Whitson points out, with great understatement, by the 1990s 'local hockey traditions were no longer sufficient to support NHL teams in Canadian provincial cities.'[40]

American interest has been with professional hockey from the start. In the early days of hockey, American teams from states bordering on Canada had no qualms about paying professionals. This meant that Canadian hockey talent departed to earn a living in leagues south of the border. As Eric Zweig writes in his novel *Hockey Night in the Dominion of Canada*, employing the language of violation and victimization, 'Professional leagues in the United States had been raiding the Canadian amateur ranks of their greatest players.'[41] Canada was left adhering to the cult of amateurism from the British 'public school' tradition, often with less skilled players. American interest and capital helped form the now revered NHL. Even in the period consistently referred to as the golden age, back when the overwhelming majority of the players hailed from Canada, two-thirds of the teams were American. There is therefore a further irony in the fear of losing our national symbol to the United States. On the one hand, it is merely a continuation of a trend that started with the advent of professional hockey – though now more than 80 per cent of NHL teams are based in the United States; on the other, it seems unnatural to have the American south take over the icy game.

In an article entitled 'Gretzky in Eighty-five,' Mordecai Richler asked Edmonton Oilers owner Peter Pocklington about rumours that he might be willing to trade Wayne Gretzky to the

nefarious Americans, say, Detroit or New York. Looking me in the eye, he [Pocklington] denied it adamantly. 'There's nothing to it,' he said. 'You can imagine what they would do to me here if I sold Wayne. It's almost a sacred trust.'

Canadians found little solace in Richler's prescience when Gretzky, still at the height of his hockey career, was traded to Los Angeles four years later. There was no obvious way to lessen the symbolic import, especially in the context of the then raging Free Trade debate. (The Pursuit of Happiness produced a redemption song: Gretzky was not sold or traded but left, 'to help bring hockey to the USA.' Gretzky was a hockey missionary spreading the word, not a human commodity.) Steven Galloway's adolescent novel *Finnie Walsh* remarks that the trading of Gretzky to Los Angeles 'was either the day the United States started to buy Canada ... or the day it completed the purchase.' Gretzky's trade is regarded as simony not only because the cash-strapped owner Pocklington received money for the 'sacred trust' but also because Gretzky seemed irreplaceable. But in the business world of professional hockey, this proved not to be the case. Since his trade, Gretzky has been evoked in hockey literature; the player has become a symbol or a living metaphor.[42]

Hockey provides a particularly Canadian wealth of symbols – so rich, in fact, that they are rarely explained or elaborated. Especially for non-Canadian readers, writing that states precisely what these symbols mean and what this history entails is helpful. Eric Zweig's historical novel *Hockey Night in the Dominion of Canada* painstakingly portrays the rise of professionalism in Canadian hockey. Zweig also interweaves the political issues of the pre–First World War period, and hockey players become mouthpieces for Canadian history. In one instance, player Newsy Lalonde explains to a less savvy teammate why some fans had been singing 'O Canada' (rather than 'God Save the King,' the official anthem at that time) before a hockey game:

> As I am sure you know, there are many French Canadians who do not share English Canada's strong ties to Britain. To them, the attachment of the English to England is like saying that Canada will never be more than a colony, and shows their failure to develop a true loyalty to Canada.

In this novel, hockey is the spoonful of sugar to help historical speech go down. When not explaining politics and history, the hockey players take time out to save Prime Minister Sir Wilfrid Laurier from an assassin's bullet. In Ottawa for a game, the players happen to be near the prime minister's residence when a would-be assassin takes aim. The teammates anticipate what might happen and work quickly to foil the anarchist-assassin's plot:

> With the strong bond of teamwork between them, formed through hundreds of hours of hockey, no more words were necessary.

Lester [Patrick] lunged at Laurier as the first shot was fired.
The Prime Minister collapsed to the ground.

It turns out that Laurier has not been shot. Everyone survives, and the order-loving hockey players rescue Canada, or at least its prime minister, from the throes of anarchy.[43] This obvious departure from history in the interest of a good hockey tale realistically shows the importance of hockey to Canada.

Robert Sedlack's 2004 novel *The Horn of a Lamb* also interweaves hockey and Canadian history, though the focus is more on contemporary events. The favourable reviews focused on the role that hockey plays in the book. For example, *Quill and Quire*, called this Prairie hockey book a 'quintessentially Canadian novel.' Ian Dennis, writing in *Canadian Literature*, disagrees with the more positive assessments. Among other things, he attacks the plot and the characters – including stock figures and patterns such as the 'young hockey talent, who is a lout until he learns true dedication and selflessness' – and concludes, '... this is not an adult novel, and should not be marketed as such.' The novel revolves around Fred Pickle, a former star for the Brandon Wheat Kings and a sure pick to play in the NHL. Playing after-hours shinny one night with some Wheat Kings teammates, Pickle is left critically injured after a less talented player drives him headfirst into the goal. Written off for dead, Pickle survives, albeit with extensive brain damage that makes his memory highly unreliable. He passes his existence on a Manitoba farm with his uncle, living only for his beloved NHL team and the outdoor rink that he builds each winter. (Perhaps a suggestion that such unyielding devotion to hockey is tantamount to intellectual limitations?) The NHL team clearly refers to Winnipeg and its now departed Jets.

After the team moves to the American sunbelt, Fred frantically rides his bicycle to their new home so that he can throw a pie in the face of the duplicitous owner. This robber baron is the outspoken American, Andrew Madison, who had once 'called Canada a socialist country. In another interview he had called Canada the fifty-first state. He had brought in a larger American flag to fly beside the now-smaller Canadian flag at the arena.' As the comical icing on the cake, Madison has a quotation from gangster Al Capone above his desk as a motivational aid.[44]

The counterpart to Andrew Madison, and the most quotable character in the novel, is an octogenarian firebrand socialist nicknamed

Badger. His favourite pastime is finding an audience for his anti-American rants. Speaking between periods at the hockey game to a small crowd of fans, this soapbox orator informs them:

> Today it's the hockey team [that is leaving]. Next week it's the airlines, the railroads. And then the trees and water. And a week after that we're walking around with American money jingling in our pockets, stuffing our faces with Big Macs and singing the 'Star Spangled Banner.'[45]

Stirring up the crowd, he asks them to define just what it is that makes one Canadian. The question merely confuses the crowd, and they offer tepid answers such as the monarchy, the then weak state of the Canadian dollar, and bilingualism (though none of them actually speaks French). Fred Pickle is about to answer but is interrupted by the start of the second period, when the smokers have to re-enter the arena and put aside questions of Canadian identity. The implied satirical point of this exodus is that hockey is the answer to what ails us.

Before hockey season begins, the Canadian flag hangs limply from the flagpole on the farm where Fred Pickle stays: 'the red and white fabric folded over, making it impossible to distinguish an image.' Come winter, it is replaced by a hockey flag on which

> two green hockey sticks stood guard on either side of the puck ... The blades were too fat and the shafts were too short but Fred didn't care. It wasn't the artwork that was important. It was the tingling in his belly that started as soon as he had hoisted it to the top. As if to share in his enthusiasm, a light breeze began to blow.

The pathetic fallacy here is as transparent as many of the hockey comments in the novel. Yet for all the playfully obvious symbolism and caricatures, Sedlack casts an ironic glance at hockey culture. There is, after all, gentle humour in the crowd's deserting an impassioned talk about national identity in order to watch a game (later Sedlack offers the unexpected answer to the question, and it is not hockey: Canada rejected revolution). As well, if Canada is reduced to hockey in this novel, the United States is reduced to 'Britney Spears and Chevron and *Baywatch*.' Few readers will overlook the fact that Pamela Anderson, *Baywatch*'s star, comes from British Columbia and placed fifty-first on the CBC Great Canadians poll. When Badger rants and rages against American imperialism, he does so as an American. He was born and educated there – the obvious suggestion is that being Canadian or American is a matter of values and behaviour, not birth. When Badger criticizes American hockey owners for only considering the profit motive, Fred responds, '... don't forget that Phil Esposito tried to sell the Sault Ste. Marie Greyhounds to some Americans.' Things are not quite as black and white as they may seem.[46]

Though *The Horn of a Lamb* is peopled with broken characters, those most involved in hockey fare worst. Fred Pickle continues to adore the game, even though he almost lost his life to it. Andrew Madison is an American cannibal capitalist, but he would be odious in any surroundings. Ryan, another rising star who may follow in Fred's footsteps by playing Junior hockey in Brandon, is incorrigibly arrogant and abusive towards Fred. In one scene, Ryan and some friends trap Fred for an alleged transgression and smear his testicles with heat rub before sodomizing him with a rake handle. Fred recalls such rituals from his playing days. Ryan 'didn't know any more whether a sadistic initiation ritual for rookies was appropriate for a grown man.'[47] This primarily comic novel criticizes aspects of hockey culture; on the whole, however, hockey is a panacea for Fred, just as it was for Bill Spunska's bed-ridden mother in *Scrubs on Skates*.

Steve Lundin's 2004 novel *When She's Gone*, like Sedlack's *Horn of a Lamb*, shows the horrible effects of losing the Winnipeg Jets. The novel also has similarities to Eric Zweig's *Hockey Night in the Dominion of Canada* in that Lundin weaves Canadian history around the game. He is, however, a far less literal interpreter of history and a far more creative inventor of tradition. The Foreword to *When She's Gone* retells the story of Louis Riel's rebellion before Manitoba joined the Dominion of Canada by adding echoes of the World Hockey Association's season-year battle with the NHL: '... it all came to a head when Louis Riel, left-wing for the Voyageurs, jumped leagues and signed with the Métis Traders ...' Lundin programmatically inserts hockey into many seminal moments in Canadian history, wildly stretching the official version of events: an increase in hockey ticket prices caused the 1919 Winnipeg General Strike; former New Democratic Party leader Ed Broadbent helps out in the CBC broadcast booth, commenting on a game that never happened involving ex–prime ministers Pierre Trudeau, Joe Clark, Brian Mulroney, and Jean Chrétien; and archaeologists are seen madly burrowing into the heart of Winnipeg in search of 'evidence of the first Native League.' Through such re-narration, Lundin makes hockey the guiding light of our history. Whereas

Zweig was apparently attempting to add hockey-tinted allure to Canadian history, Lundin adds value to the history by writing the game into history. Lundin goes beyond the usual statements about cultural symbolism and importance for Canada and says that the game is more than a metaphor. The minor metaphorical split between tenor and vehicle does not exist here, as Lundin opts for the copula: 'The game is a country.' The narrator later offers this false dichotomy: 'How can you moan about Canadian identity on the one hand while choking the life out of the myth of hockey with the other ...?' (implying that Badger's audience in Sedlack's *The Horn of a Lamb* was *right* to leave his lecture in order to watch the game). Without hockey culture, there is apparently no national culture.[48]

The historical hockey episodes are merely interludes in *When She's Gone*, a novel whose title refers at once to the departure of the Winnipeg Jets and the death of the narrator's mother. The main plot focuses on a young goaltender who 'steals' another fan's wife, has a child with the much older woman, and, injuries having ruined any chance of a career as an NHL goalie, wants to play professional hockey in Great Britain. Hockey is the ultimate unifier in this novel: the narrator first spots his dream-woman, and eventual wife, in the audience at a hockey game; later, when the ex-husband confronts the narrator, he quickly dispenses with the expected ('You've ruined my life'), before offering useful goaltending advice. For the cuckolded husband and hockey fan, there would apparently be less shame in losing his wife to a better goalie.[49]

In this very Canadian quest novel, the narrator and his brother fly to Scotland and embark on a canoe trip down to Cardiff, Wales, for the team try-out. In addition to symbolically colonizing the colonizers, the novel is less linear and far less formally conventional than most hockey fiction. Also, the tone of *When She's Gone* is utterly unapologetic in its love of the game and in its assertions of the game's importance to Canada. Whereas other novels mildly acknowledge that hockey is not all there is to Canada, Lundin speaks in strongly moral terms of the educational and edifying value of hockey. His writing is always passionate. Regarding the loss of the Winnipeg Jets and the subsequent building of a new hockey arena, Lundin's narrator rages, 'What was done was wrong. Just plain wrong. The new arena? You don't drop a pearl into a wasteland of decay ...'[50] This highly rhetorical tone is best for explaining the often irrational attachment of individuals and much of Canada to hockey. Stated as a matter of 'right' and 'wrong,' one can either agree or disagree.

When She's Gone's praise of the national sport, and competition in general, is open-handed. With its overemphasis on traditional, heroic masculinity, strength and power (including abundant references to sexual conquests and penis size, a minor motif in hockey writing), the novel is not solely a paean to the game. The values extolled in *When She's Gone* do not allow for whining, even about the loss of the beloved Winnipeg Jets. The narrator ridicules soccer players who exaggerate pain, and much prefers the grin-and-bear-it ethos of hockey culture. 'What's twenty-two stitches over the eye,'[51] he says, 'just get the sewing done before next period.' For him, competition builds character and is a cathartic outlet which helps young people to deal with the harsh realities of adulthood. The removal of games from physical education programs is a travesty because children no longer have an outlet for pent-up emotions. Hockey can be a vehicle for individual development and, in the logic of the novel, can also aid in the development of the nation as a whole, not least because a nation's future lies with its educational system and its youth.

In its firm pronouncement of how the game should be played, *When She's Gone* is never tempted by the Canadian specialty of victimology, present even in much of Canadian hockey writing. The advantage of being a victim is a moral one: the victim is not to blame. Mordecai Richler has sweepingly claimed that Canadians 'are all injustice collectors ... We not only remember old insults but cherish them.' Minority groups blame the majority culture; francophone Quebecers blame anglophones; and, especially when it comes to culture, English Canada blames the United States. As has been shown, many hockey works squarely blame American business interests for anything that is wrong with Canadian hockey, including the loss of 'Canada's game.' Against this, Lundin's novel begins with self-flagellation, noting that the decay of hockey is part of a wider corruption of sports in favour of profit:

> We sold our soul. No point in complaining, no point in blaming anyone else, not the Yanks, not anyone else. We've done it ourselves and if you were a Yank you'd be saying the same thing ... Being Canadian I'm thinking hockey ...

The active selling of the 'hockey soul' and assuming of responsibility is a refreshing change from simplistic claims that Canadians have been robbed.[52]

In *When She's Gone* a way to the better Canada exacts a full look at the worst of hockey culture. The narrator points out what he thinks are widespread misconceptions about hockey, including the NHL's dominant status as the essence of Canadian hockey. During the critical nostalgia-producing period of his childhood, he had been a fan of the World Hockey Association's Winnipeg Jets and their brand of fast, clean 'European-style' hockey. Though the Jets were one of the few teams to survive the WHA's demise and enter the NHL, most of their stars were sold, and fans thus lost a chance to see how this style of hockey would fare against the NHL's top teams. 'These days the NHL is more sacred than Canada itself,'[53] says the narrator; it is a holy cow that is necessarily positive, beyond reproach and criticism, and therefore a stifling object of devotion. As opposed to those critics, fictional or otherwise, who do not like hockey, the narrator's love of the game is beyond doubt, and he firmly believes that hockey is a cornerstone of individual and national character. It is for this reason that his criticism is so effective. Canada, as the keeper of the game, is also to blame for its degradation and loss.

The narrator's brother, Jack, fills *When She's Gone* with extempore rants about everything from nationalism to sexuality to theology. Early in the novel, we learn that 'sport and religion are the same thing. The contest between humans and nature. Life and death, quantum mechanics, the Big Bang, evolution.' The narrator is wary of Jack's eloquence and beliefs, noting his brother 'can go on and on like that' and asking himself whether it is 'bullshit or truth.'[54] This skepticism adds critical life to the shopworn claim that hockey is Canada's national religion because it takes us beyond either/or thinking. Lundin invites mythical thinking by leaving possibilities open as he wonders about Jack's argument. We may be inclined to reject the words because of their source, yet there is method, or a grain of possible truth, in them. Hockey is not religion, but there is no denying that it is understood as such by many Canadians (which renders its relative absence in hockey fiction somewhat puzzling). The game also functions as a nebulous source of inspiration and identity.

To conclude this chapter on the link between Canada and hockey, I turn again to David Adams Richards's *Hockey Dreams* and his particular understanding of the hockey-Canada connection. *Hockey Dreams* is far less subtle than Richards's fiction, and, as with *When She's Gone*, it is rage that fires much of the book. Richards prides himself on a traditionally masculine stance, hunting rifle and all, and does not shy away from patriotism. As many critics have emphasized, Richards is staunchly and unapologetically nationalistic, and his book, like many of his novels, freely attacks uppity academics. There are also, however, moments of tenderness and sentimentality that a lesser writer might turn purple. As well, *Hockey Dreams* offers a firm voice against the weak-kneed value systems so often scourged by Richards in his novels. In the Introduction, Richards recalls a stultifying conversation with colleagues when he was writer-in-residence at a Canadian university. When the intellectuals express a dislike for Wayne Gretzky – justifying it with 'Oh, he's just so Canadian' – Richards responds, 'You hate greatness or just Canadian greatness?' The anti-patriotism of 'just so Canadian' is an intellectually dubious position, and Richards hints that this academic Gretzky-bashing springs from a dislike of hockey's iconic status in Canada. Without argument to support it, the position is both bigoted and evasive (since there are plenty of rational arguments against hockey culture). By refusing to acknowledge greatness, the statement also indicates a wilful blindness.[55]

Throughout the non-fictional *Hockey Dreams*, Richards plays the straight-talking nationalist, stating directly what hockey fiction suppresses:

> We were and are all delusional spirits. The delusion is THIS. That perhaps HOCKEY – hockey can keep this country together. Hockey can save Canada – for we see to the bottom of our heart there is no Gretzky without Lemieux. Perhaps we are THAT delusional, and perhaps for one time when we really need it to – when we really want it to, a delusion can work for us instead of against us.

Doug Beardsley writes something very similar, arguing that the famous picture of Lemieux embracing Gretzky after a 1987 Canada Cup goal 'did more for the English-French relations in this country than a rinkful of Canadian politicians.' Each author clearly stretches the impact of hockey on Canada's political scene – as Richards's self-conscious admission of 'delusion' shows – and perhaps each was caught up in the euphoria of the time. The exaggerated argument in each case is that the anglophone Gretzky and the francophone Lemieux, and by analogy Quebec and *le reste du* Canada, necessarily belong together off the ice as well. More important here perhaps is the sense of political impotence, as a team of great players outperforms a bevy of past and present politicians in bringing Canadians together. Claiming that a mere game is the key to the future of a nation probably is delusional; but so is all mythic and visionary thinking, and the same charges of unreality are regularly levelled against bilingualism, multiculturalism, and, more recently, publicly funded health care, three other Canadian unity staples.[56]

Richards's bold vision departs from Canadian literature in another way. This nation-building rhetoric, while not absent from Canadian discourse, is hardly the dominant mode of telling our story. When Richards speaks of 'saving Canada,' he evokes the constant fear that Canada is about to be lost in some way. The benefit of hockey to Canada is that it provides a quick fix, proving that we exist in cultural terms and that there *is* a common element to this complicated country. Like all myths, it offers the benefit of an easy story and explanation; like all myths, it contains an aspect of falsehood; and like all myths, it allows for contradiction and a wide range of interpretation. In typical Canadian fashion, hockey literature is full of irony – a frank awareness that a mere game cannot offer the full picture of Canada – even while that shadow of loss, intrinsic to all nostalgia, hangs over so many novels and short stories.

Chapter Five

The Family Game

Jeff is being cut. Jeff keeps thinking, How am I going to tell my father.
Stuart McLean, 'Sports Injuries,' p. 146

Hockey fiction handles the family with everything from matter-of-fact-ness to romanticism to irony. This chapter focuses on the main literary variations on hockey and family, which usually means fathers and sons. It begins with a consideration of the standard tale of how hockey binds families, and moves on to hockey's singularity as a sport that demands the time and effort of the entire family. The subsequent section looks at parentless players who have been adopted by hockey culture. After that, the focus is primarily on the father-son dimension of hockey, including the ways that hockey both unites and divides families. Lastly, there is a brief search for the missing daughters in hockey fiction.

The Standard Tale

According to the tall tales, Canadians learn to skate even before language skills develop. We are purportedly born with a hockey stick in our hands. The narrator of Frank Paci's *Icelands* plainly states that learning to skate is 'the initiation rite of almost every boy in the country.' A toddler's progression from dry land to ice is a passage from one stage of social existence to another. Symbolically speaking, he grows into being Canadian (and, in the fiction discussed in this chapter, it is always a 'he'). Traditionally and typically, initiation rites are connected with religion, and since hockey is often called the 'national religion,' comparing a boy's first steps and tumbles on the ice to other sacred rituals is metaphorically apt. However, learning to skate differs from a bar mitzvah and the like because it occurs well before symbolic or biological maturity or manhood. It is more like baptism, with the crucial difference that the child is active, even in those cases where he has been pushed onto the ice by overzealous parents. Canadian boys often begin skating and playing hockey when childhood has barely begun, and Bruce Kidd and John Macfarlane therefore point out the 'revealing lie' of fathers who 'brag that their sons learn to skate before they walk.' Factual truth is no more important for personal memories than it is for collective mythologizing. The focus on 'sons' evokes the sexual division of initiation rites, in which societies dictate different ceremonial tasks for girls and boys on the symbolic road to adulthood. Many see hockey as a quintessentially masculine sport, but paternal boasting about their early skaters is not solely motivated by a desire to possess or create 'manly' toddlers. Rather, the passage is from generic child to truly 'Canadian kid.' The hockey passport is soon acquired when a child starts to play hockey and joins the Canadian family.[1]

Though hockey does not automatically make for better families, its bonding role cannot be ignored. Hockey writing abounds with vignettes of father and son – or father and daughter – living in harmony as their eyes follow a hockey puck. 'Saturday Evenings in the Church of Hockey Night in Canada,' Judith Fitzgerald's fictional glorification of the Detroit Red Wings, zeroes in on the communal and ritualistic aspects of the game. Once a week, the young female narrator's mother departs for the movies, and the two fatherless siblings listen to the CBC hockey broadcast. They 'flank Grandpa who presides over the proceedings with all the pomposity and pontificating punch he can muster' and puzzle over the mother's absence, wondering 'how anybody could skip our family congregations.' Despite the grandfather's incessant preaching and conviction that he alone can see into the light of things, that he alone possesses hockey 'truth,' he is a comically likeable character. Much of the humour in this story stems from seeing how an avid Leafs fan like the grandfather refuses to recognize the greatness of Gordie Howe and the Detroit Red Wings, the narrator's favourite team. This is a common motif – communal enjoyment of the game, including good-natured ribbing if they cheer for different teams, brings the family closer together (or, at least, allows for a détente). For as long as parent and child are on the ice, or watching the game, together, the prevailing mode of narration in hockey fiction is harmonic. Hockey represents shared, quality time.[2]

Hanford Woods's 'The Drubbing of Nesterenko' is an exception to the rule of familial harmony, and tension in the family adds an uneasiness to the overt violence on the ice. This story is appealing not least because it defies customary expectations of what a trip to the Montreal Forum should be. An elderly father takes his adult son (the narrator, who has a delinquent past) to an NHL game in hopes of lessening the tension in their obviously strained relationship:

> I do not know how my father and I wound up standing at the game together. We had never done so before. Since my arrest I had been nursing my grievances secretly.

There is an air of the accidental or coincidental here that undercuts the sense of tradition, and this is no schoolboy coming-of-age episode. The journey to and through the Montreal Forum, the climbing of the stairs, and the required standing for the duration of the game are physically taxing for the old man, and the narrator wonders why his father had exerted himself in this way. Since he fails to see the attempt at rapprochement, the game decays into intergenerational discord: 'We did not broach the subject of the game, for neither of us could be trusted not to use it as a weapon against the other.' Olive branches can also be used to harm. Even while rejecting his father at the hockey game, and allowing the fact that they cheer for opposing teams to further unsettle their relationship, the son achieves a moment of clarity. He realizes that 'our mutually inflicted wounds could only be healed face to face, not as we were, side by side.' Watching a game together, or even talking about hockey, can mean avoiding real dialogue, failing to address real problems. 'The Drubbing' expresses longing for the standard image of father and son enjoying the hockey game together, while showing that this time spent together is often superficial and shallow.[3] In this case, it is also too little, too late because the son has reached adulthood.

A particularly comic passage from Paul Quarrington's novel *Logan in Overtime* best illustrates the heartfelt harmony missing from Woods's story. Quarrington's mock play-by-play raises the question of what happens when the final buzzer goes:

> All the nice families clustered around the television sets. Father, mother, brother, sister and infant. Father smoking pipe! Mother nursing infant! Brother pretending to be Rocket Richard! Sister playing with doll! The television set is on. 'HOCKEY NIGHT IN CANADA.' Happiness! Content-

ment! The nuclear family, strong in the hinterland! The game begins. What-ho? HE SHOOTS! HE SCORES! Game over! Contentment vanished! Nuclear family disintegrating. Brother and sister turn to sex and drugs! Mother and father undergo painful divorce! Tragedy across our great nation!4

Quarrington travesties the well-known Canadian scenes, including traditional gender roles: mother nurses; sister nurtures the doll in preparation for adulthood. This all occurs while – and seemingly because – *Hockey Night in Canada* is blaring from the television set. That millions of Canadians enjoy playing and watching hockey is not to be converted to the belief that hockey is a cure-all. The family-nation-hockey triad is undermined through the phrase 'nuclear family, strong in the hinterland!' (for what is the hinterland of a family?). Through his comic hyperbole and utter ignoring of other societal factors that lead to premature sex, drugs, and divorce, Quarrington breaks a Canadian taboo by implying that a family held together by a mere hockey broadcast is a fragile unit. As well, the families may be gathered around the television sets, but they are engaged in different activities; as in Woods's story there is no face-to-face interaction around this new hearth. As soon as the individual game ends, the real world enters, and the family and the nation begin to collapse. There is a delightful irony as Quarrington moves from clichés about hockey's metaphorical importance to the suggestion that this single family not only represents but also *determines* the nation's well-being. A single divorce leads to national tragedy.

Quarrington's mock-hockey commentary stands out from the usual Canadian hockey nostalgia, and 'The Drubbing of Nesterenko' confirms that nostalgic background through its emphasis on missing harmony. Most non-fiction recalls hockey, especially professional hockey watched by the entire family on television or heard on the radio, in a positive or positively maudlin manner. Fiction shies away from happy families and depicts the game as a disruptive element in family life. That hockey can disrupt is understandable, since any activity that stirs the emotions is bound to upset some while it soothes others. As shall be shown, when hockey becomes an imperative, or when obsessing about the hockey player in the family means ignoring other children, it can seem as if hockey itself is to blame. Hockey fiction shows that familial harmony exists when parent and child share a physical space; generally, when parents watch their children from the stands, or when children escape their troubled home lives on their own to play hockey, the distance is both figurative and literal.

Hockey: The True Family Sport?

Hockey places singular sporting demands on the entire family. In examining sacrifices made for this sport, Tina Lincer First's sketch 'In the Penalty Box: Confessions of a Reluctant Hockey Mom' outlines her transformation from culture-vulture to puck-watcher. Recalling her earlier, more bookish, existence, she states, 'Once upon a time, I associated a puck with Shakespeare's mischievous "Midsummer" sprite and thought of a goal as something I wanted to achieve.' The sketch's title hints that not liking hockey should land one 'in the penalty box.' Later, the narrator notes in passing, 'I don't remember how my spouse responded to my hockey-hating confession, but five years later, we were divorced.' The paucity of information urges us to conclude that hockey itself led to the marriage break-up.[5]

Sometimes hockey can literally and directly break up a family, most obviously when professional or professional-track players are drafted or traded. In Scott Young's short story 'Player Deal,' a grizzled veteran learns that he has been traded and, though devastated, notes, 'A man ... like me can't go off in a corner and cry like a child cut from his high-school team.' When he calls home to tell his family the news, his young son does not recognize his voice: 'My daddy's not here ... My daddy plays defence for the Flyers ...' The scene concisely shows that parental absence is a fact of life for professional athletes. It also happens when young players leave their small hometowns to play on more competitive teams in (usually) larger towns, billeting with families found for them by their hockey team. Many will recall examples such as Guy Lafleur, who left cozy Thurso, Quebec, as a young teenager to play in Quebec City, or Wayne Gretzky, who left Brantford at age fourteen to play in Toronto. These players were exceptionally gifted, which is why their travels are common knowledge in Canada, yet their hockey stories are typical. For years, the professional path meant leaving home at a young age. As Mark Anthony Jarman's story 'The Scout's Lament' phrases it, these '*babies* really' find themselves motherless a 'million miles from home.' Pursuing a professional career also meant boarding with surrogate families at least for the length of the hockey season, and usually entailed minimal contact with one's own family.[6]

Even when the child hockey player does not move away from home, keeping a child in skates is a challenge. Ken Dryden and Roy MacGregor speak of a group of families that 'will never have a new car, will never take a southern vacation, will never get around to redecorating their home as long as the children are in hockey' – this even though no player on the team 'come[s] from a poor family, none from a family being held together by a single mother on a tight budget.' Since hockey is a game, and therefore materially unnecessary, many parents surely ask themselves whether there is a point to it all. New England author Jay Atkinson makes the extent of this investment clear in *Ice Time: A Tale of Fathers, Sons, and Hometown Heroes*:

> Alone among the major sports, [hockey] often requires the commitment of an entire family for an individual player to excel. The equipment and ice time are expensive, the hours at the rink are long and late, and it takes many years for a kid to master the elements of skating and team play.

Compounding these general requirements is the tremendous amount of travel required, at least for those in sparsely populated regions. For families not from Toronto or Winnipeg or Boston, this means that hours of driving for a game or practice are part of the daily routine.[7]

When the 'home' games are over an hour away, domesticity is a misnomer. Although children have been moving away from home to play hockey for decades, much hockey in Canada has given in to the bureaucratic organization typical of modern sport. This suffocating organization is partly the subject of Michael McKinley's insightful popular history *Putting a Roof on Winter: Hockey's Rise from Sport to Spectacle*, which follows hockey from outdoor rinks to what is sometimes an indoor circus. The times are long past when rural Canadian children learned and played most of their hockey on backyard ponds or rivers using catalogues or magazines for shin pads and stuffing their too-big skates with newspapers. All but gone are the days of local leagues on outdoor rinks (hence the ubiquitous longing for a simpler time). Today's North American NHL players have already been through a system of increasingly competitive and increasingly expensive leagues. Because of the expense involved, hockey is becoming limited to more affluent families – in contrast to games like basketball or soccer, whose finest players often honed their skills in unorganized, sometimes impoverished, environments (though this is changing, too, as sponsors

and teams seek out younger and younger talent).[8] Hockey may well
become a marker of economic class in the near future, if it is not
already so.

In the past, hockey was not overly expensive. Anyone able to scrape
together the money for a pair of skates and a stick could play shinny outdoors on natural ice. For the most part, NHL players emerged from
rural, often economically depressed, surroundings. Mordecai Richler
jokes revealingly about the influx of foreign players to 'Canada's game,'
recalling that 'once the [Montreal] Canadiens, as well as lesser teams
here, used to comb the northern bush and mining towns for raw talent.'
Hockey players were natural resources, and parents were absent or
superfluous appendages. Richler goes on to discuss the hockey players
that are more sophisticated, educated and, at least marginally, more cultured. These rubes from up north were often exploited financially even
when they starred for NHL teams; among the bright lights of the cities,
they were out of their element – much like their counterparts in American sports fiction, 'whose rural greenness,' writes Michael Oriard,
'must be modified' if they are to survive in the city. This is more than
the common suggestion that hockey has become corrupted and that
things were better in the old days. It is coupled with the myth that
hockey once enjoyed an organic link to the land, and that players were
previously happy just to play the game.[9]

If in the past hockey and hockey players were overly crude, it sometimes seems that money has refined the life out of the sport. There has
also been an increase in meddling parents and definitely an increase in
million-dollar contracts for what some consider mediocre players.
Another factor in the 'organic' career jump from natural ice near 'bush
and mining towns' to the big city is the agent, whose job it is to ensure
maximum dollars for NHL prospects. Many regard such professionals,
not as ones who help athletes get top dollar for their physical labour,
but as thieves who weasel their way into families, 'steal' gifted children,
and corrupt the game by making money off the backs of those young
men. Still worse, agents remind fans that hockey is a business, thus
destroying the illusion of pure play. In fiction, the agent is often
maligned as an odious, but 'important hockey type,'[10] and in both
Jarman's *Salvage King, Ya!* and MacGregor's *The Last Season*, the main
protagonist has been defrauded by his agent.

Roy MacGregor points out that many hockey parents regard agents
'as gods rather than devils,'

for it is the agent who will turn all the 6 a.m. practices, all the jumper cables, bad coffee and cold seats, all the money spent on equipment and summer hockey schools and out-of-town motels, all the anguish and jealousies, all the glass-pounding fury and fist-pumping cheering – he will turn all that and more into a career.[11]

MacGregor uses the future indicative to show that agents are revered as magical characters who, Rumpelstiltskin-like, can spin talent and effort into gold. More discomforting than agent idolatry is the statement that parents regard their hockey-playing child as an object that will yield financial returns, for which they are willing to sell their child into bondage. MacGregor is talking about parents of top-notch prospects with a definite chance of making a career out of hockey, and the collective parental attitude he discerns here is probably not representative of most hockey parents. Still, even parents whose children have no desire to become professionals must spend money on equipment, registration, and gasoline, while suffering early morning practices and bad arena coffee in order to pass on the joys of hockey.

Parentless Players

Much of the despair about the need for agents in the modern game, including complaints about rising costs and the generally perceived, though hard-to-prove, decline of the game, is really despair about the loss of the play spirit. The prevailing attitude among 'experienced' fans is that things were better in the old days, when professional players would have played for free, injured, and so on. This sense of decline is the background for Aaron Bushkowsky's 'Phantom of Great Slave Lake,' a lighthearted tale about an NHL scout who ventures to Canada's far north to track down a pure hockey talent. As Michael Kennedy writes in his introduction to the tale, 'The story of a star athlete, performer, or intellectual genius discovered in some isolated outpost by an agent or impresario is somewhat archetypical in fiction.' This is firmly within the romantic 'noble savage' tradition because the player is untainted by civilization and organized hockey. Bushkowsky's Phantom is apparently untainted by lineage too: 'half-Inuit, half-Canadian and half-Russian,' he is without parentage in the traditional sense. Players often talk about giving 150 per cent, and with his three halves, this mythic figure could literally do so. His abundant parentage also leans heavily on Canadian hockey stereotypes. The 'half-Inuit' evokes the traditional view that hockey is a natural link to the land (for who knows ice and snow better than the Inuit?); the 'half-Russian' suggests the Russians' reputed conditioning and skills, while the 'half-Canadian' stands for heart, devotion, and toughness. This hockey player is northern through and through, and he therefore has a 'natural' attraction to the game.[12]

The Phantom has developed his skills without parental intrusion or coaching. The reader learns that the fleet-footed hockey nomad is 'damned near impossible to spot. In the winter he stays out there and fishes. Skates from spot to spot.' Once the scout manages to track down the Phantom, he offers him a generously Faustian NHL contract. If readers of fiction are familiar with the backwater genius entering the big city, they are equally familiar with tales of lucre destroying these heroes. There is much to gain by signing a contract and moving to the city, but this story shows that there is more to lose. The Phantom refuses any contract: 'I live to play,' says the spectral genius, literally retreating from the scout and explaining, 'I do it for me. Me and this beautiful dream of a lake.' The phantom hockey player, who cannot be tempted indoors by wads of cash, is almost a Platonic ideal of the hockey player. He was and remains entirely free, accountable only to himself. There are no parents fawning over agents in this story; most cynically, against the modern backdrop of money-driven hockey, the clear suggestion is that such a talented embodiment of the play spirit cannot exist. He is, after all, ghostly.[13]

New Englander Peter LaSalle's short story 'Le Rocket Nègre' also includes a 'parentless' prodigy. The title refers to the other famous Rocket, whom all of Quebec and much of anglophone Canada claimed as their own. The fictional argument in LaSalle's tale is that this black player should have been adopted as an honorary family member the same way that Quebec folk hero Maurice Richard was. Tommy O'Brien's mother was from Port-au-Prince, while his 'only contact ... with his sailor father was the legacy of that Irish name.' His mother died soon after giving birth, and Tommy was sent to an orphanage to be raised. Like the Phantom of Great Slave Lake, Tommy plays his hockey on natural ice, far from any organized league:

Most years, the St. Lawrence was locked with ice by the middle of December. The boys who put in their long hours there never joined school or church teams. Yet they themselves seemed to know that, urchins or not, they were playing the best hockey of anybody their age in all of East Montreal – possibly in all of the city, where hockey was everything.

Tommy is the star among these hockey-playing urchins and is soon 'adopted' by a surrogate parent. At first it appears that the benevolent Mr Forsythe acts alone when he donates a large amount to Tommy's orphanage before whisking Tommy off to a New England school for further hockey training and education. In fact, Mr Forsythe had been scouting for, and bankrolled by, the Detroit Red Wings: Tommy's new father is a professional hockey team (a realistic note in the story, since in the past NHL teams often sponsored Junior teams, thereby gaining the rights to the players on these teams).[14]

LaSalle's story is unique in hockey literature because it depicts racism at length. He describes in detail how Tommy suffers verbal and even physical attacks from the spectators. In addition to the epithets 'nigger' and 'coon,' linguistically inventive racists in Hershey, Pennsylvania (of confectionery fame), chant 'THE ONLY CHOCOLATE IS … HERSHEY'S CHOCOLATE' whenever Tommy is on the ice. Elsewhere, fans throw food at him and regularly bloody him with other projectiles. Tommy's skin colour and lack of parentage give rise to other, more unusual theories among hockey fans, and 'there were whisperings of Tommy being a literal "Black Devil."' Long after he has disappeared from hockey there are 'claims for a while that Tommy O'Brien had never even played professional hockey, that there was only the *idea* of Tommy O'Brien' – that the existence of a black hockey player is as far-fetched as Bushkowsky's Phantom. Tommy existed only as a mirror of the rampant racism in the NHL in the era of the Original Six teams, an era in which Toronto Maple Leafs owner Conn Smythe allegedly stated, referring to a very talented black player who never played in the NHL, 'I'll give $10,000 to the man who can turn Herbie Carnegie white.'[15]

LaSalle's starting point is the traditional one of finding a diamond in the rough, but the story is not formulaic. 'Le Rocket Nègre' ends with neither the syrupy surmounting of, nor failure due to, racism. Although Tommy is a fabulous player, he never enjoys an NHL career. The narrator notes prejudice and lack of precedence in hockey, all but stating that Tommy's skin colour is what prevented him from playing at the highest level:

There had never been a black in all of professional hockey, and there was
a strangeness to the entire idea of it that appeared to frighten some
people, seeing that hockey was a game of the cold blue North, something
unnatural to begin with for anybody of tropical descent.

But LaSalle does not turn this story into a predictable cataloguing of
injustices. Even while citing examples of racial abuse against Tommy,
the author intuits that factors other than overt racism may have kept the
star from NHL stardom. Abused by fans on the minor league circuit,
Tommy does enjoy respect and 'considerable celebrity status' at home
in Montreal. He fully enjoys his status, including the parties, fast times,
and fast women that accompany celebrities, and he becomes a border-
line alcoholic even while at the height of his talents.[16]

Unlike Tommy's American patrons, the Detroit Red Wings, the Montreal Canadiens do give this star a chance. But Tommy does poorly at
tryouts. LaSalle, an American, adds the minor theme that Canada is
more open and tolerant than the United States. This is reflected by
how 'the Montreal Canadiens had been willing – even wanted eagerly
– to have Tommy O'Brien skate for them ...,' though this 'was a fact
known only to a few people. And none of them would ever say much
about it.' Though Canada, including hockey circles, has never been
free of racism, the *idea* of Canada as a more tolerant, less racist society
extends at least as far back as the Underground Railroad and remains
a contemporary trope in, for example, Michael Moore's films. It was
also in Montreal that Jackie Robinson first broke the 'colour barrier,'
when the Major League Brooklyn Dodgers assigned him to the Montreal Royals. In his autobiography, Willie O'Ree, the first Afro-Cana-
dian NHL player, notes, 'I never had any trouble with the Montreal
Canadiens or the Toronto Maple Leafs. Canada likes to think of itself
as a more tolerant society than the United States, and maybe it is,
though I have had my problems at home.' O'Ree provides the illustration of a bus trip north after a tryout for semi-professional baseball in
Georgia: 'I had to sit at the back of the bus ... As we drove farther
north, I moved farther up the bus. By the time we got to the Canadian
border, I was sitting up front.'[17]

In 'Le Rocket Nègre,' the scout Mr Forsythe continues to champion
his 'filial' cause, and in doing so he swivels the story's lens from one of
pure racism to lineage. The French-speaking orphan O'Brien is a
child of Montreal and should therefore be adopted by the city.
Forsythe remarks that 'it was time they gave a Negro a fair chance in

the game, ... time to take a stand and finally bring him home, where he belonged,' and, 'why didn't Montreal – the team, the entire city – come to its senses and do the necessary negotiating to acquire the rights to another one of their own ...?' Despite the impassioned words, it is possible that Forsythe is blinded by love for his discovered talent and the belief that O'Brien would be truly accepted as one of Quebec's 'own' on the Montreal Canadiens. After Tommy's hockey career winds down, he disappears, like the Phantom of Great Slave Lake. He is kept alive, however, as a sort of still-absent Prodigal Son, and there are constant rumours that he 'has been sighted, found after so many years.' The difference is that losing sight of the phantom players is watching a dream slip away; O'Brien's disappearance subtly depicts a wilful forgetting of an embarrassingly racist era in hockey culture.[18]

Fathers and Sons

In most hockey writing, references to fathers and sons are literal and do not refer to adoption by an agent, team, or province. Hockey is understood as the essence of familial tradition and continuity, a natural part of the country's broader traditions. In Rob Ritchie's *Orphans of Winter* (2006), an unusual sort of quest novel that connects hockey and various types of spiritual traditions, the narrator describes a professional scout's thoughts on making a career out of hockey: 'Why had he learned to play in the first place? He learned because his father had learned. He played – and now scouted – because that is what he does.'[19] Hockey runs in the family, and, like other family traditions such as working the family farm, continuing the legal profession, or taking over the family shop, hockey can be a tacit imperative. Ritchie's narrator does not even reflect on how he has ended up making his career out of hockey culture – it happened 'naturally,' without obvious and overt pressure from parents or agents.

When approached to write a book on the father-son-hockey triangle, Roy MacGregor initially hesitated because it seemed 'too obvious an observation to merit extra study.' Nevertheless, the prospect lingered; MacGregor was 'haunt[ed]' by his editor's letter, which mentioned

> rites of passage, family traditions – hockey is absolutely central and integral
> to the lives of boys and their dads, and much of what happens between
> them begins to unfold the very first time a young father leads his little one

out onto the ice. Hockey is the vehicle through that complex relationship, and it is also the expression of that relationship.

MacGregor was persuaded to begin what became *The Home Team: Fathers, Sons and Hockey* (which is part journalism, part study, part memoir). The study has the same starting point as Paci's fictional *Icelands*, in the sense that it considers the initiation rites and generational links that hockey provides between fathers and sons to be almost natural.[20]

Paci's novel begins with the father, Vince, watching a child learning to skate and recalling his own son's early skating practice, along with 'the basement games [that] had forged such a close bond between him and his son that they had become practically one person while playing.' The bond includes love of the game, love for a common object, and even a temporary loss of the father's individuality in play. As wonderful as Vince may feel about this submerging of selves, the child's perspective is neglected. This other perspective is indirectly voiced in Stuart McLean's short story 'Sports Injuries,' which includes a father's recollection of why a talented friend quit hockey: 'He said he couldn't stand it any more. Said it wasn't him out there skating. It was his dad. He had no sense of individuality.' The irony in that tale is that the father uses the anecdote to buttress his own sense of probity, and he follows up with a 'moral': 'That's why I don't tell you what to do unless you ask me' – the child's 'cue' to beseech his father for hockey advice.[21]

In Steven Shikaze's 'Hockey Dreams,' the author spins a father's reflections on three generations of hockey into a short story. There are three male characters, and the story as a whole digs into the often self-understood tradition of hockey through the generations. Grandfather, father, and son have hockey in common but there is no subsuming of the self in the game, and no corresponding becoming 'one person.' Even within hockey's lengthy shadow, each character remains an individual, which encourages the reader's reflection on the varying meanings of and attitudes towards the game. The narrative is focalized through the father as he watches his young son's house league game and considers the ways in which his son, his father, and he himself experience hockey.

The title 'Hockey Dreams' is an unmistakable reference to a specifically Canadian variation on a parent's yearning for the child's success: playing in the NHL, if only for one game. Thus, Shikaze's title anticipates yet another soupy tale of longing packed with wistful ruminations on the importance of the game to the country, rituals of growing up, spending quality time with dad, and so forth. Because the father is watching his son on the ice, the reference to dreams evokes the stereotypical 'hockey parent' who longs excessively for the son's success. This is itself a variation on the theme of parents pushing for their progeny's athletic or artistic progress through tennis lessons or endless piano practice.

Unlike sports, which are entirely about temporal and physical limitations, dreams are outside of the present, beyond the often cruel realities of time and space. Pleasant dreams can be a desire for fulfilment in the future, and, as hockey non-fiction consistently shows, they are just as often a nostalgic remembrance of things past. Shikaze's story has a timeless quality appropriate to its title, as the father considers the relatively unchanging surroundings of a local hockey arena. The father stands apart from the other, more jingoistic, parents 'with their cowbells, horns and other homemade noisemakers' and is both physically and figuratively away from 'their shrieks at the referee, the coach or the players.' In hockey-parent parlance, the omniscient narrator has placed the father in 'no man's land.' Thus, he does not belong to the crowd and is slightly excluded from the typical, mass hockey tradition.[22] He also possesses the critical and aesthetic distance that good judgment requires.

In spite of this difference, the arena conjures up memories of hockey past: 'The dim, soft arena light; the aroma of Zamboni fumes, sweat and coffee, this is an atmosphere that triggers such vivid memories of the father's own childhood that he doesn't know whether to smile or cry.' Of the five senses, the sense of smell most swiftly transports us to the past, here to the uniquely pungent odours of memory's hockey arenas. Hockey smells only like itself, and that particular stench remains as timeless as the essential, elemental form of the game. The odour leads the father down an ambivalent memory lane – 'he doesn't know whether to smile or cry' – reminding the reader that even hockey dreams may come in nightmarish forms. Broken dreams entail an unfulfilled potential; when the concrete dream is to make the NHL, the enormous investments mean an enormous opportunity cost and possibly the loss of the proverbially romantic carefree childhood. For anyone familiar with hockey culture, the mention of tears evokes the pain of getting cut from a team, riding the pines, and even perhaps the more literal pain of hockey injuries or the extremes of sexual abuse. As soon as the delight fades or as soon as one realizes the dream will not be achieved, melancholy's shrine becomes visible.[23]

The grandfather caused the father's hockey pain. The father had been a very skilled hockey player as a child, and the grandfather the eager coach. As the father watches his own son play house league hockey, it becomes obvious that the son lags behind his house league teammates and opponents. The boy appears 'oblivious' to his surroundings during the warm-up and is all but immobile during the actual game – 'his stick ... on the ice as if it was made of lead.' Despite the father's past as a potential NHLer, he has never revealed his abilities or spoken of his experiences with organized hockey. Whenever he is asked about his life as a hockey player, the father focuses on his leisurely recreational old-timer hockey, 'by saying that he plays after work on Fridays with his friends.'[24]

Hockey culture is filled with masses of fathers who trumpet their skills of yesteryear. These are the 'guys who sit in the ... bar bragging how they turned down NHL contracts ten years ago' in W.P. Kinsella's 'Truth,' or the diminutive father in Stuart McLean's 'Sports Injuries' who, 'if it wasn't for his knee he could have played in the NHL.' The father portrayed by McLean tells tales about two former NHLers with whom he had played, but these are always embellished accounts. In a brilliant emblem of how hockey discourse often bowdlerizes and reshapes the past, that father 'forgets' to mention that neither NHL career lasted very long, that the goaltender friend 'hadn't played hockey since' being embarrassed in his first game, and that the other turned into a 'drug addict.'[25]

In Shikaze's 'Hockey Dreams,' the father wants to protect his son from parts of hockey culture. He perpetuates the myth that non-competitive shinny or pick-up hockey is closer to the idealized spirit of the game, to 'real' hockey; the hockey he played as a youth does not seem to count. This is a unique hockey voice because it rejects the nostalgic trope of hockey being better in the 'good old days.' When the father withholds information from his son, he is also unusual in *not* staking a claim to the genuine game of the past. This minor subterfuge maintains the bond of hockey while exposing the harshness of the grandfather's immoderate attitude towards the game and his son. The grandfather/coach had tirelessly driven and put pressure on the father, with the result that hockey became a chore for the child, and, 'frustrated after years of trying to live up to his father's dreams,' he gave up hockey at thirteen. One of the reasons why the grandson is less able than the other players is that he started at the age of ten, precisely the age at which the father had stopped having fun on the ice. There is no submerging of the self here, but an affirmation of the independent individual as the intergenerational hockey story continues. It is as if the grandson's late start is an eradication of the father's painful memories of hockey. The youngest family member takes off from where the father had stopped.[26] The proper play conditions are encouraged because, as a late starter, he has little chance of making the NHL and thus plays only for the moment.

The reserved father sitting away from the other hockey parents and their noisemakers in Shikaze's 'Hockey Dreams' is a world apart from his counterpart in Michael Melski's *Hockey Mom, Hockey Dad* (2001). Melski's play focuses on two single parents, Teddy and Donna, who regularly come together as they watch their boys play hockey. Teddy, the grown man with a cuddly name, is a caricature of the hockey parent. He still wears the hockey jacket of his youth, as though his entire identity is anchored in his bygone playing days, and he desperately wants his son to succeed in hockey. The first step on that path towards the NHL requires that the son move from his house league team to 'rep,' the next level. House league, the level of the grandson in 'Hockey Dreams,' is the lowest level of organized hockey; all players of a single age and sex are allowed to play, there are no cuts or tryouts, and the general philosophy decrees that each child be given the same amount of ice time. After house league, hockey becomes labyrinthine in its teams and leagues. This knotty string of levels and rules of eligibility is governed by an overriding rule: for parents or children with any aspirations of making the NHL, the higher the skill level of a league, the better. The hockey rat race begins at a tender age, and, as Rob Beamish writes, the 'sweet, sweet temptress of success [draws players] deeper into the system.'[27]

Teddy has his sights on vicarious hockey glory. One day the son's team loses badly against another team when the 'rep' coach is at the game to scout prospective players from among these prepubescent children. Teddy sees this as a chance missed. When Teddy's fellow single hockey parent and love interest, Donna, offers the consoling cliché 'We'll have to get them [the other team] another day,' he replies, 'That's great. Except the rep coach isn't gonna be here another time. An we're not gonna get him to come here another time, cause we're last place.' The rep coach will not waste any more time with these players and therefore 'there's no next year. Next year starts today.'[28] This note about the future is not far from the plucky motivational posters reminding us that 'today is the first day of the rest of your life.' Teddy has bought into the proactive, competitive spirit, and uses the same type of clichéd language to express failure and negate the future. This is ironic because he does not live in the present: his jacket points to a hockey past, and his hopes for his son could only be realized in the future.

Teddy's overly competitive approach is not in accord with the league's recreational focus. Furthermore, his keening that 'there's no tomorrow' for an eight-year-old boy is farcically ominous because it suggests a life over before it has truly begun. In Canadian hockey terms, however, it is also true. Teddy's lust for success without the willingness of the child player, as well as his need to bask in his son's on-ice glory, make him a particularly odious hockey parent. Concerning the child, it is not impossible to enjoy hockey under watchful eyes, but playing under a hail of parental insults hardly invites pleasure. This behaviour provides a template against which Shikaze's story can be read. In 'Hockey Dreams' the three generations are rolled into a hockey tradition, but the attitudes and approaches to the game differ greatly. The grandfather, like Teddy in *Hockey Mom, Hockey Dad*, is depicted as a win-at-all-costs character who publicly berates and belittles the son he coaches; the father was obviously a skilled player, but 'the fun' had been drummed out of him by the overbearing grandfather. The youngest boy's hockey language is closer to the idealization of shinny discussed in chapter 2. Although he lacks skill, he skates after the puck 'with the enthusiasm of a puppy chasing after a tennis ball.' A clumsy, lolling young canine may be a coach's nightmare, but it is the epitome of enjoyment. Like those authors who praise the freedom of shinny, Shikaze offers two poles here: competitive hockey versus recreational varieties. Though 'competitive hockey' is a tautology because competition or *agon* is constitutive of all sports, in the less regimented and pressure-bound varieties of hockey there are no obvious material stakes.[29]

Shikaze's 'Hockey Dreams' concludes with the on-ice turning point typical of pulp sports fiction, when the underdog has the chance to snatch victory from the jaws of defeat. As the final seconds tick away on the clock, the son can break a 1–1 tie and win the game for his team:

> The puck bounces towards the son, who swats at it. He misses most of the puck but gets enough of it to knock it towards the net. The goalie smothers the puck and the final buzzer sounds. No overtime, no shootout. A tie.

Shikaze cleverly inverts the how-my-son-won-the-big-game story. The opportunity to win the game is there, but there is no soupy celebration of the goalie's save or rueful description of the son's shot. This runs counter to the usual language of sports, which always keeps Victory in view. Instead of 'fanning on it,' 'flubbing,' or 'failing,' the child neither misses nor gets the puck. The phrase 'He misses most of the puck but ...' takes on-ice possibilities beyond the success-failure binary. Even the opposing goalie, though not required to make a difficult save, is given his due when he 'smothers the puck.' The harmony of house league hockey seems complete; there will be no sudden-death 'overtime' or 'shootout,' and a tie is good enough for all.[30]

Many, probably most, parents are delighted just to watch their children play, and in spite of this rosy depiction of the missed shot, one might expect the boy to be disheartened. Whereas he had earlier seemed 'oblivious' to his surroundings during the warm-up, now he is blissfully unaware of the need to succeed, the general hockey ethos that even critical fiction does not doubt:

During the drive home, the son is glowing. Did you see my shot? I almost scored! We would have won the game! I saw it, the father replies. He, too, is glowing; his dream fulfilled.[31]

The excitement of 'would have won the game' and delight in 'almost' scoring is touchingly naive in a competitive sport. It is joy at something that did not transpire (though very different in tone from parental bragging about how they could have made the NHL if only they had not been injured, etc.). Grammatical modality expresses the boy's buoyancy of mood – and it is precisely this optimism, arising from the fecund inexperience of youth, that makes the 'Hockey Dreams' come true. The father's dream is a desire to see his son succeed in hockey. But here success is defined differently, and there is no need to measure it in wins and goals scored, or playing at the highest level. Hockey success means having fun playing a game and talking about it, face-to-face, afterwards. Significantly, the son in Melski's *Hockey Mom, Hockey Dad* has no lines, no voice, and the reader can only assume that he suffers under his father's yoke. Just as significantly, Shikaze's story ends with the more communicative bond of actual father-son conversation that continues after the game. In *Hockey Mom, Hockey Dad,* Teddy's sole communication with his son is yelling at him on the ice.

Family Bonding on the Ice

In hockey fiction, the family connection is most positively felt when family members share a physical space. This can mean watching a game with a parent, or playing with or against siblings. Although sports highlight inequality based on ability, they also provide settings where family members are equal before the rules, or where the younger generation can be superior to the father. Factors such as age and authority are less important when skill is the only thing that counts; and beating one's father or mother at a game is a crucial marker of development. In Richard Wagamese's novel *Keeper 'n Me* (1994), it is hockey that allows two estranged brothers to embrace each other. Narrated by Garnet Raven, the novel is a fictionalized autobiography about an Ojibway man who was taken from his family at a young age and placed in foster care. Though *Keeper 'n Me* does not take place entirely in hockey environs, and it is therefore not a 'hockey novel' per se, the game is crucial to Garnet's development. For this reason, the novel warrants lengthy examination in this study.

At the beginning of the novel, Garnet is sometimes comically in search of an identity as he drifts about in urban settings. When asked at a downtown Toronto bar what tribe he belongs to, Garnet's reply is an expression of emptiness: 'Don't know, really. Canadian Indian, I guess.'[32] Garnet does not know who he is because he was literally snatched from his grandmother's care at the age of three when a social worker (in a scene smacking of abduction) lured him into a car with a bar of chocolate. In the name of government-sponsored weaning, Garnet was taken to a strange territory, later bouncing from foster home to foster home, and then into jail for a minor drug charge of which he is innocent. While in jail, he receives a letter from family members who have finally managed to track him down. On his release from prison, Garnet returns to the White Dog Reserve, and to the family and traditions he was robbed of years before. The novel is told from the perspective of a changed, wiser Garnet who has been back on the Reserve for five years, and he looks back with humour and warmth on the naive, confused version of his younger self. Garnet is the typical autobiographical narrator who has gained in insight and looks back on a younger, more foolish self.

In this novel about rediscovering roots, hockey plays a key role in Garnet's reintegration into his own family and community. Though he is welcomed by most upon his return to the reserve, and eventually learns the language, traditions, and customs of his ancestors, his elder brother Jack remains aloof, and even harbours resentment for Garnet. He treats Garnet as he would a shifty guest, always observing him, but rarely engaging him in conversation. Even in the tight-knit community of the White Dog Reserve, Jack manages to avoid Garnet most of the time. It is not until the two meet on the ice that Garnet is able to overcome Jack's suspicion and the harmonic adult sibling relationship can begin. The tightly circumscribed ice rink necessitates confrontation or co-operation between the brothers.

It is easy to see how Jack could consider his own brother to be entirely different from the rest of his family and friends. Before moving to the pivotal on-ice scene of reacceptance, a few words on the entertaining extent of Garnet's estrangement are in order because they show the degree of hockey's importance to reintegration. A decidedly urban Garnet returns in style – by taxi and in an outfit to shame James Brown. Fashion is a key means of expressing one's identity, and Garnet clearly knows how to make a statement. He is wearing 'mirrored shades, a balloon-sleeve yellow silk shirt ..., lime green baggy pants with the little cuffs and ... platform shoes, all brown with silver spangles, and three gold chains around my neck.' The 'Indian world' of White Dog is understandably confused by this luminescence, and when the taxi driver cautiously notes that he bears little resemblance to the Raven family, Garnet barks, 'What? I ain't black enough ...?' The reference to colour is more than an easy pun on his last name. Away from his family for most of his life, Garnet feels most at home among other minority groups, and most of his friends were African-American or African-Canadian. This affinity reflects itself in his favourite style of music as well, and he fell 'in love with the blues' partly because 'us Indians have a lot in common with our black brothers and sisters when it comes to bein' blue about things.' He even suggests to the taxi driver that his fashion sense will win over the reserve, though this modish revolution is not to be.[33]

Garnet's way of dressing is an expression of that fact that he is more comfortable among the blues bars and their predominately black clientele than among family. On returning, he may have believed that his garish outfit and swagger strutted confidence, but in reality they represent a lack; they are an expression of confusion and distancing from the 'Indian world' of his birth. Before going back to that world, Garnet is something of a postmodern character who regularly chooses and discards ethnic identities in order to create and re-create himself. Recalling the entirely white foster home and school environment of his youth, he says unreflectively, 'I just figured I was a brown white guy.' For most of his childhood and youth, he never considered the issue of his heritage. Later on, he declared himself, among other things, a 'hopeless Hawaiian,' a 'Mexican/Apache boxer who'd quit fighting forever after killin' some guy in a bar fight in Taos,' and 'a half-Chinese guy' after taking a shining to the 1970s show *Kung Fu.* He sums up his situation on returning to his home:

> By the time I made it back here I was lost. At twenty-five years old I never figured on bein' no Indian. I didn't remember a thing about my earlier life and when I disappeared alone into the foster homes I disappeared completely from the Indian world.

Garnet's desperate instances of self-creation stem from the societal theft of his Indian self, and his many masquerades are an attempt to cover up the emptiness and loss of the world of his birth.[34]

When the taxi shuttles Garnet back to the reserve, it is to a world without the musical blues. There is, however, a hockey rink. Given hockey's widespread appeal to Canadians of all ethnicities, and the fact that all Canadians are familiar with the game, the hockey rink might be the one place where Garnet fits in easily. The sporting realm is an area that lets nations divided by politics, religion, and language come together and understand each other for the duration of the game by adhering to the same rules. At least Garnet has this space in common with the Indians who never left the reserve. Garnet's description of his playing style bodes well for fitting in on the White Dog Flyers' team:

> I played every winter in the pen for the farm team and I've always had pretty good wheels. I like passing more than scoring and I had a lotta pride in my play making and skating ability.

A good skater is always wanted; likewise a generous passer. What is more, Garnet is unlikely to cause rancour or pile up penalties through aggressive behaviour on the ice, since he is not a fighter. On hearing of Garnet's abilities, his brother Jack says, 'He's gonna get killed out there [playing] Indyun hockey ... Prob'ly spend mosta my time peelin' him offa the blueline.' Garnet may know the general sporting language, but, as the novel reveals, he doesn't speak the dialect of 'Indyun hockey.' Since Jack is the older brother, and remembers when Garnet was taken away from the family, he is clearly aware of Garnet's heritage. He slurringly suggests that Garnet has cast away this part of himself and thus properly belongs down south in the city. Jack's caustic comments, it is eventually revealed, spring from the pain of having seen his brother taken away by the authorities. This focus on the differences between styles of hockey – apparently even the hockey Garnet played in the penitentiary pales in roughness – contradicts the idea that hockey is always a social glue among players. Instead of allowing hockey to be the great Canadian connector, Jack sees hockey as a hedge.[35]

On learning that Jack practises by himself in the mornings, Garnet decides to join him. The two skate around on the same ice, initially limiting their conversation to insults about playing ability. They then pretend to ignore each other while sharing the same play space (like a feuding couple executing a smooth foxtrot). The insults continue, but the rapprochement between the brothers has begun – among teammates playful insults are often a sign of affection because, even when they are most apt, they are not to be taken at face value. The aggressive talk is male bravado minus the potentially harmful consequences of escalation. Reacting with violence to this 'trash-talking,' or even taking it too seriously, is taboo. When Garnet misses an empty net with a high slapshot, Jack criticizes his ability to shoot but provides his apparent enemy with a few helpful hints to improve his aim.

Before long they begin passing to each other, skating around in unison, trading the puck back and forth instead of words. From this wordlessness, the odd compliment emerges, and the siblings begin to compete more fervently; by playing with and simultaneously trying to outdo each other, they behave like ordinary brothers. The hockey rink provides a place for a dialogue of sorts to begin between family members too emotionally reserved or divided to risk conversation. Passing a puck back and forth is a form of communication, and seeking out a player, or refusing to pass to a player, sends a clear message. If the communication between brothers were to cease on the ice, if the hockey puck were their only means of contact, it would barely qualify as progress in their relationship. What hockey provides for the tongue-tied Jack is a forum for 'talking' with his brother. It is an utterly safe way of making contact, requiring little emotional investment and involving almost no clear content. At the same time, it is not a meaningless gesture, especially after the silence that had prevailed between them.

As the game between brothers continues, the distance between them literally decreases. From passing pucks, trading insults, and offering ten-

tative advice from across the ice, they move closer, nudging each other
off the puck until,

> finally, just as I was making my famous loop-de-loop at the blueline, he
> [Jack] reached out and bear-hugged me to the ice. The force made us slide
> into the corner with our arms wrapped around each other, sticks sprawled
> at the blueline and the puck forgotten. We were laughing real hard and
> almost choking from lack of breathing.

Jack finally admits his resentment for Garnet was a transferring of the
pain and hatred he felt when Garnet was kidnapped by the officials.
Hockey allows for a ceasefire and operates as peaceful communication
between hostile parties. In itself trivial, the game often dominates discourse, but it can also act as a 'conversational ramp ... that leads to
more elevated topics and sustained conversation.' Perhaps even more
importantly, it can join parties who might not speak at all.[36]

In *Keeper 'n Me*, Wagamese shows how hockey aids family unity.
Garnet and Jack are able to put their pain and ensuing feelings of
anger behind them, and carry their hockey friendship beyond the ice.
Wagamese writes that 'the Raven family really came together after'
Garnet began playing shinny; the magic of shinny helps them erase
the years that they were not together.[37] Because hockey as an institution is relatively stable, it is more likely to link families than other,
more fleeting and generation-bound markers of identity such as
Garnet's outrageous outfits, or even his blues music. When Jack Raven
regards his brother Garnet as a stranger, it is ironical in biological, yet
accurate in cultural, terms. Although Garnet is an Ojibway by birth, he
has not been able to live in the same way as the rest of his family on
the reserve. In a far more subtle, profound, and extended manner
than many works, *Keeper 'n Me* shows hockey as a path to healing and
reintegration.

Hockey as a Divider

Most fiction that deals with hockey as a path to cultural integration
focuses on new Canadians and their offspring. Because children usually
take to the customs and language of the new land more easily than their
parents, this gravitation to hockey is realistic. In Frank Paci's fiction,
hockey provides for uneasiness in the home. His young characters are
well aware of the ethnic background represented by their parents' gen-

eration, even as it erodes in the new country, and they sometimes use hockey as a means of rebellion against heritage.

Frank Paci is probably best known as a groundbreaking Italian-Canadian writer whose fiction, beginning in the 1970s, spoke for a community. Although he is slowly peeling off the ethnic writer label, much of his oeuvre focuses on family disharmony between children born in Canada and parents from the Old World. In his early novels *The Italians* and *Black Madonna*, the hockey rink was yet another forum for battles between second-generation children and their parents. Paci clearly depicts playing hockey as a means of becoming 'properly' Canadian and simultaneously moving further away from the parents' Italy. The 2006 CBC documentary *Hockey: A People's History* quotes Paci on sporting integration: to the children, born or at least raised in Canada, hockey was attractive because 'it made us different from our parents' and because it 'made us feel that we belonged in the new country.'[38]

This philosophy prevails in both *The Italians* and *Black Madonna*, each of which is set in the Italian-Canadian community of Sault Ste Marie (or its *nom de plume* 'Marionville'), and each of which focuses on intergenerational and intercultural tensions between family members. In *The Italians*, Paci exposes the many gaps between the generations in the Gaetano household. The parents and grandparents are far more comfortable in Italian, whereas the children speak English almost exclusively and even admonish their elders for their reluctance to do the same. For example, the daughter, Lorianna, bluntly reminds her father, 'We're in the new country. We speak English here,' indicating that an 'us' and 'them' binary exists in the household as well. At times, hockey appears as important as language in the new country. Hockey and other teams sports 'served as a melting pot for the Italian and Canadian kids' in small-town Ontario, and the Gaetano boy who did not participate in sports found it 'difficult to make friends with the Canadian kids, [and] the Italian kids taunted him.' While Lorianna focuses on the importance of speaking English, speaking English is not enough; it is hockey-obsessed Bill Gaetano who becomes the most 'Canadian' of the three siblings.[39]

Bill remembers his first skates with all the usual nostalgia and thoughts of freedom:

> He had come across them at the local Salvation Army second-hand store. Even though they were rusty and laceless and smelled of old stuffy clothes, he had looked upon them as magical shoes that would carry him wherever he wanted to go.[40]

Like Adelbert von Chamisso's Peter Schlemihl, who traded his shadow to the devil for a pair of seven-league boots, Bill can use these skates to travel the world. The sense of opportunity is as palpable as the reference to the 'magical shoes' is ominous. The skates will lead him away from Marionville and help him fulfil what he perceives to be his destiny. Hockey is what made Bill feel comfortable in Canada, where he was born, and thus Bill's decision to play hockey made him 'really Canadian.' Engaging in this initiation rite means becoming and being accepted as a Canadian, a need he feels most acutely: 'somewhat alien in a house filled with Italians,' he is 'at home on an ice surface.' Hockey also helps Bill develop as an individual and to garner the recognition and approval he does not receive at home. Because of his success on the ice, and in contrast to the experience of Aldo Gaetano, the older brother who entered the priesthood, Bill's 'school friends looked up to him, and his teachers, at least those who were fans of the game, treated him with deference. It seemed to make him less Italian.'[41] The latent desire to be 'less Italian' and the apparent benefits of losing this tag are unsettling in both *The Italians* and *Black Madonna*: gaining social acceptance means the deletion of his Italian heritage. This is an unfortunately limited choice because it ignores the possibility of layered identity. If maintaining one's cultural heritage for several generations in a new country is an uphill battle, striving to undo one's upbringing and erase one's ethnic roots is equally exaggerated.

Despite Bill's obvious social success, his father (Babbo) remains skeptical about the merits of the game. Bill both pleads with and patronizes his father:

> Babbo, this is Canada and hockey is king. I have a chance to play with teams that almost every boy in Canada would give his right arm to play on. Babbo, the Prime Minister cheers hockey players.

His father continues to view hockey as a game 'for children, ... and those who clap are children too, even the Prime Minister.'[42] Even when Bill is invited to attend a Chicago Black Hawks' training camp, his father remains suspicious, withholding praise and approval. 'Any other father in Canada would've been immensely proud, but not Alberto. He lived in another world.' Despite Lorianna and Bill's attempts to instruct their father about the ways of the New World, Babbo's stance is entirely understandable. He sees that Bill spends too much time and energy on hockey, neglecting his schooling. The shadow traded to obtain these 'magical shoes' is education.43

The scene and theme are repeated with minor variations in *Black Madonna*. In that novel, Joey has a chance to play Junior hockey. Although this is a great honour, he turns down the offer, partly because his incredulous father 'had looked hurt beyond measure,' asking in mock wonder, 'You want to leave home because of this?' Both fathers see hockey as a sporting child abductor that whisks their children further into the New World's strange and nebulous value system. Yet, despite these accusations, the father in *The Italians* is not living in a distant continent; he disapproves of hockey, not because it is a silly, juvenile undertaking, but because of the opportunity cost. As to hockey, Bill has a one-track mind, believing the game is his destiny and that he 'had to make the NHL [because] it was the only way he could prove his value to his father' (an unusual conclusion, since the father is clearly against the sport).44

Bill's father is also concerned about prejudice, and his concerns show that, far from existing in a cultural haze as to hockey's importance in Canada, he is well aware of the challenges for ethnic players in the hockey world. He says, quite rightly and in a rare instance of literary admission of the possibility of bigotry in the national game, 'I hear ... they don't give us a fair chance in these professional ranks.' What at first seemed a mere ruse to keep the son at home in Marionville later proves to have been an attempt to protect Bill. When Bill eschews his father's advice and eventually makes the NHL's Chicago Black Hawks, fears of prejudice are confirmed: 'The Chicago press had touted him as the "Red Shirt," at once alluding to the colour of the home uniforms and to the badge of Garibaldi.' The press may be American, but the Canadian team officials who control hockey in Chicago have similar attitudes.45

The Italians and, to a lesser extent *Black Madonna*, show that deeming hockey the essence of Canada and the entry ticket to Canadian culture is wide-eyed optimism. Bill's obsessive belief in sport as his destiny and his sole path to becoming truly Canadian (i.e., what he already is) is a variation on the athlete's bad faith – he is deluding himself by believing that sport is the only exit from his current social position. At the same time, Babbo's overprotective concern for his son and corresponding belittlement of a Canadian cultural icon is also misguided, not least because denying racism through the avoidance of hockey does not address the issue; rather, such silence would allow it to continue. Paci offers extreme views, neither one of which is reasonable.

Over-identifying with Hockey

The most unsettling literary example of a father pushing his son into hockey is surely Garasamo Maccagnone's 1998 story 'Goalie Boy,' which is a horrifying take on hockey writing's obsession with birth and regeneration as the Great Game is handed down. The story begins,

> I was Goalie Boy long before I was even born. My mother told me that my father used to talk to me from the earliest days of her pregnancy, always insisting to her that I was a boy, always ending his little pep talk by referring to me as 'Goalie Boy.'

The father, an American Korean War veteran, appears at the maternity ward with an infant-sized Detroit Red Wings uniform and will not pick up his child until they dress him in red. Life is to become a constant training camp for the child, and though his birth certificate name Stanley (as in 'Cup') might please even the most ardent hockey father, the father calls him only 'Goalie Boy.' The story effectively illustrates the straggled boundaries between autotelism and instrumental play. The father plays hockey with his boy and takes shot after shot on him, taunting him all the while. The narrator notes, 'I was just having fun' and 'I loved the feeling of stopping my father stone cold ... I would yell at him to give me his best.' The father, it transpires, was training the child, and later Goalie Boy realizes that his father was instilling a thirst for 'all-out war.' In a harshly accurate pun, the narrator notes: 'I was playing right into his hands, but I didn't know it.'[46]

Maccagnone portrays an aggressive father who is clearly trying to regain a lost youth and lost hockey glory through his son. This search of lost time is most clearly symbolized when Stanley catches his father having sex with a teenaged girl in the family car. The motives behind the father's craving for his son's on-ice success are typical: he had been a potential NHL prospect, until fate intervened. When Stanley asks why he never made the NHL, the enraged father yells, 'Do I look like a damn Canadian? I'm an American!' and adds, 'I got wounds to prove it!'[47] On first reading, the line is a cliché. The story, however, does not merely regard hockey as Canada's sole domain, or reproduce the commonly invoked militarism and aggression of the United States – psychology and historical context have given rise to the father's irrational behaviour. After shutting out the great NHL goaltender Roger Crozier as a young adult, the father had been drafted, not into the NHL, but into the US Army. Traumatized by the death of a friend in Korea, the hockey rink became his only place of comfort. For all his malignant characteristics as an overbearing hockey parent, Stanley's father clearly seeks not just to regain but somehow to undo the past by living through his son. Because he is trying to 'save' his past life by training a goalie, the story is darkened by a sense of desperation. The father is by no means a likeable figure, but Maccagnone's addition of personal and world history makes him easier to understand than those who merely wish to be parent to a star.

Canadianness is also a prominent theme in Pete McCormack's 1998 novel *Understanding Ken*, which is about a relative newcomer to Canada and his hockey-playing son. In this case, however, the immigrants are from England, and there are no real language difficulties for them in British Columbia. The boy narrator is fixated on making a name for himself in the NHL, but there are few references to proper names in the novel. Other players on his team are simply called 'our best player' or 'the big boy.' The title, meanwhile, suggests the intimacy or familiarity of *tutoiement* with Montreal Canadiens goalie Ken Dryden. Dryden was also a lawyer, though the young boy cannot identify with that part of his idol – like most fans, he sees Dryden's entire being in terms of the hockey player and has interest in the rest of the man's life only insofar as it affects his game. The narrator's parents are divorced, and he is shuttled between houses as they divide their time with him. Hockey is clearly a means of escape from the choppy waters of his home life. The distant world of professional hockey, because it has clear rules and is therefore more comprehensible, seems more real to the narrator than his own family and teammates and is therefore a safe haven. Although the boy is clearly too concerned with hockey and, especially, with the dream of playing professionally, his hockey-fanatic father does little to steer him away from this obsession. The boy's mother, also English, never manages to grasp the fundamentals or the attraction of the game. Each parent has a problematic relationship with hockey: one through over-identifying with the sport to the neglect of other spheres of life, and the other through indifference to what is so important to her son's sense of self and identity.

When the narrator finds out that Ken Dryden has left the team to article for a law firm, the foundations of his life are shaken. There is the typical sense of betrayal the fan feels when a player is traded to another team, or decides himself to go elsewhere, as well as dire concern for the future:

What's going to happen now?
How could Ken do this? Who would pick anything over hockey...? Sure, some kids at my school don't play, but they're total losers.

Quitting becomes a moral transgression because, in a country where only 'losers' avoid the game, choosing anything over hockey means letting down millions of fans. Dryden's personal decision upsets the narrator's world order, and later he causally links Dryden's 1973 decision to unfortunate subsequent events: 'Since Ken Dryden quit the Montreal Canadiens? Rex is dead. Hobey is dead. The [backyard] rink won't freeze. I missed the open net.' Dryden is to blame for the death of a dog and a boy (Hobey), as well as the typically mild Vancouver weather; and, in a stylistic trivialization of death, the statement culminates in a minor on-ice mishap.[48]

In a world where much is confusing, hockey provides tangible, steadfast rules that can be understood. Traditional arguments for sports as a means of personal development are that they teach the player to handle defeat, as well as the importance of teamwork, effort, and adherence to rules and conventions. The narrator's problem is that he tries to use hockey's specific rules as a path to understanding the world, and the tenuous link between the sports world and the benefits for the rest of life are thus displayed. In one scene, in trouble again for unruly behaviour in class, he literally attempts to elude the school principal's clutches. When caught, he cries out, 'Holding! Holding! ... It was a penalty, hundred percent.' To his mind there is no difference between the stable rules of hockey and the rules of the real world, and he establishes a relation of pure rather than metaphorical transference.[49]

Since his parents are divorced and acrimony reigns in the family, the boy is negatively aware of the importance of stability at home. He draws hasty conclusions about the links between parenthood, hockey, and an NHL career. 'It's good to have a dad,' he observes, because 'if you don't have one there's no way you can make pro. That's too bad but that's just the way it is.' Hockey is the only escape the boy knows, and he considers it a miraculous salve – though the reader sees clearly that hockey heals nothing in this novel. When tension rises in the household, the boy sighs, 'I wished my mom played street hockey. If she did we could take shots on each other and forget about everything.' He assumes that his own passion for hockey should suffice for everybody.[50]

Later in the novel, the narrator reaches a state of muddled clarity about the importance of family after realizing something about the best professional players: 'Their folks stay married no matter what.'[51] Again, the narrator's logic is faulty, as these players grew up in a time when divorce rates were lower, even if marriages were not always heavenly. More importantly, the effect of marital harmony on hockey ability is minimal (and perhaps even inverse if escaping hardship and strife through hockey is as common in real life as it is in fiction). The boy, like so many narrators in hockey fiction, has a skewed, limited viewpoint, but in *Understanding Ken* the limitations are traceable. Hockey fans are all too familiar with dynasties such as the Howe and Hull families, both of which produced two generations of fine NHL players. The Canadian popular focus on hockey parents is such that even Walter Gretzky, whose hockey credentials are limited to having spawned and trained superstar son Wayne, is a hockey hero of sorts. The narrator has ingested a strictly positive hockey story, and it has foreshortened his intellectual horizons.

The boy prefers living with his doctor father because 'it's all hockey. Hockey cards. Hockey magazines. Hockey games. Hockey practices. Hockey Night in Canada right after the Bugs Bunny/Roadrunner Hour.' As a doctor, the father has a responsibility to heal, yet he is no role model. With its focus on cut-throat competition, the father's credo is a mere extension of the worst aspects of the hockey rink – this in spite of the fact that his English upbringing might be expected to cultivate that nation's (former) ideals of sportsmanship. In *Icelands,* Frank Paci passes harsh, accurate judgment on this type of parent. The anger and need to see children succeed on the ice is fuelled by parents being 'unable to handle defeats. Because they saw hockey mirroring their own lives.' Rather than the chance of developing through sport, parents like Teddy in *Hockey Mom, Hockey Dad* see it as a public family failure. The father in *Understanding Ken* is a uniquely unpalatable hockey parent, one who goes against the grain by pushing his child to extremes without ever saying he wants him to play professionally. Most often, it is extrinsic rewards that feed an excessively competitive attitude, but here the father indoctrinates the child into a world where competition itself is the supreme value. It is tempting to psychologize and argue that the father's grief over a failed marriage stokes his rage; however, the focalized narrative does not mention this. All the reader learns is that sport is a poster-child for the valuing of competition in society, and in *Understanding Ken* everything else is secondary.[52]

The narrator's childish views and voice let the reader see immediately what is wrong with the situation. The boy's false conclusions manifest the worst possible mixing of hockey and family life. For example: 'After the game my dad was driving up the hill to his place and yelling at me. He yells at me but he loves me.' That the father, for all the verbal abuse, does indeed love the son makes his behaviour all the more disturbing. When the boy plays poorly, the father punishes him by demanding that he practise skating in full equipment at the local public skating rink. For a ten-year-old child, this is utterly shaming. The public rink is for hand-holding couples and the wee ones balancing themselves with chairs as they learn to skate, and making a child train there is like forcing the young violinist to scrape out scales at a busy intersection. Humiliated, the boy falsely concludes that he has to somehow produce his own rink in the backyard so that he can train in peace. Even the child's occasional praise for his father reveals a lack of insight. When a less skilled player is injured, the father provides medical aid. As the narrator proudly states, 'It doesn't matter to my dad. He saves them all, talent or not.' The boy's belief that the father might not help a poor skater arises from what he has been taught, through example. In the child's understanding of his father's mindset, in which competition, skill, and performance are the chief values, refusing aid to an injured player is actually an option.[53]

The boy's grandfather had died when the father was only four years old, and the son uses this as an excuse for his father, for why he had to 'settle' for being a doctor instead of a professional athlete. Whatever his motives, the father wants to help the child win. Somewhat predictably, he is among the belligerent parents who upbraid the referee as an immoral being. After a suspect call against his son, the father hollers out the hockey parent's mantra: 'You're teaching the kids to f—ing lie!' Swearing, it seems, is fine. This behaviour

> got him the penalty. He has to be the first parent in history to get a penalty from the stands. So there I was in the penalty box with my dad. Not that he was in the penalty box with me, but I had to serve my two minutes and his two minutes.

This is a travesty of the bond between father and son, of what Paci had described as becoming 'practically one person while playing.' The obvious difference is that here the father is not playing. In fiction the utopian element of hockey usually disappears when parents become kibitzing spectators who do not play alongside their children. When a teammate is injured and the boy's father rushes towards the ice to help out, the narrator unknowingly provides a study in parental contrasts: '[The boy's father] tripped. He went down worse than his son ...,' breaking his collarbone and thereby incurring the same injury as his son. One suffers along with his son; the narrator's father causes suffering.54

Stunted Parental Development

Hockey culture implies youthfulness and the childlike freedom of the play spirit, but it can also mean stunted development. In Richard B. Wright's *The Age of Longing*, for example, the local hockey talent Buddy Wheeler fails to grow up – in Jamie Fitzpatrick's words, he is 'is enfeebled by a lifetime of adolescence.' Wright's novel depicts the Depression-era small-town hockey surroundings as a Neverland 'world of play and irresponsibility' where grown men 'discussed the latest adventures of comic-strip figures.' Thus, there is little impetus for Buddy Wheeler to play the good father, work hard off the ice, or develop outside of hockey.55

When Buddy Wheeler's adult son returns to his hometown in that novel, a 'quarrelsome old man' recognizes him and says, 'You're Buddy Wheeler's boy, aren't you?' In this case, hockey anchors identity for the next generation too. The narrator reflects, 'When you are in your late fifties, it is something to be still called a boy ... People like myself are forever denied an adult identity.' Immediately slotting Howard Wheeler into a family tree is ironical because the late Buddy Wheeler had been estranged from his family for years. For some, notes the narrator, 'my father ceased to exist the moment he left town' and 'will forever be a quick small man on skates.' In reality, Buddy had died a poor alcoholic in a dingy Toronto hotel, far from the cheering crowds of home, and miles from the standard Canadian story of the hockey family. That tragic story has been rejected by the townspeople, who have chosen to retain memories of a hometown hero instead.56

In Bill Gaston's *The Good Body*, Bobby Bonaduce returns to New Brunswick, the starting point of his professional hockey career. Like Buddy Wheeler, Bobby has a child's name, and like Buddy, he is not entirely mature. When he left Fredericton at the age of twenty, he left his son Jason and his wife behind (assuming that they would soon join him later). His rights were initially owned by the star-studded Montreal Canadiens, and a trade to the less talented Torontó Maple Leafs seemed like a perfect chance to move up to the NHL. But the NHL was not to be, and his professional career was played out in the junior ranks of professional hockey – an itinerant life of low salaries and long bus rides punctuated by the occasional visit to his family in Fredericton.

When in town on those road trips, Bobby would play father by taking his son skating, and for a few years he remained convinced that this minimal time spent together was adequate for cultivating a familial bond. On one occasion, after leaving a now six-year-old Jason who has lost interest in his absent father, Bobby 'came away surprised at how naïve he'd been: The whole bus trip up he'd dreamed of what they'd do together, visions of skating on the river, himself showing off a little.' This is surely a painful realization, but Bobby is able to heal the wound through selective memory and careful narration on the team bus. He takes public pride in relating half the story, telling players on his various teams that he has a son: 'You understood it was the cheapest immortality any man had ever clung to. But there it was, a comfort.' Perhaps it is this penchant for always choosing the better story that leads Bobby back to New Brunswick after his professional career to enrol in a creative writing program – and to play hockey with his son on the university team.57

Bobby differs from the typical hockey parent. In a certain sense, he has made it as a hockey player: though never really tasting the NHL, he did manage to fashion a career out of the game he loves. On his return to Fredericton, he dreams of being playmaker to his son, and he describes these filial dreams in the hockey idiom: '... he'd send him in alone with a perfect bullet on the tape and Jace would score a fucking beauty ...' The dream does not quite work out according to plan, since Bobby, as a former professional, is ineligible for university hockey. He will have to settle for coaching Jason, which is already a one-step removal from being a teammate. By the time he is offered a coaching position, Bobby has realized that his son's love evaporated long ago. Nevertheless, the bond of hockey remains in Bobby's mind, and he retains visions of the magical uniting pass: 'Set a guy up, no matter how much he hates you he has to come and whack you on the ass' as a sign of gratitude. Bobby's situation differs from that of Garnet and Jack Raven in Wagamese *Keeper 'n Me*, whereas Garnet was taken away from his family, Bobby left on his own. Because of this, there is no possibility of melting away the years, and no touching on-ice embrace.58

Bobby is naive in some ways, but he is neither foolish nor stupid; his greatest difficulty is separating the hockey player from the parent. He approaches his son cautiously upon returning to Fredericton and first watches his now adult son from the anonymous stands during a team practice – almost like a scout hired to observe other young players with an objective eye. Any scout's job is to read each player's style, determining whether there are weaknesses that cannot be overcome, potential not yet realized or already played out, whether the player would fit into the new team's concept, and so on. Bobby also approaches his son's game like a text: 'Hard to read someone from the way he played hockey, but the young man out there on the ice seemed maybe kind of bland.' Bobby has no other option than to regard his son from afar. While scouts will eventually consider off-ice aspects of a player's life (university scouts, for instance, will be at least marginally or superficially interested in grades), and other parents observe their children because their dreams are wrapped up in them, Bonaduce's observing of Jason from the stands occurs because he has nothing else. He has neglected the child, now a man, for too long.[59]

When summoning up the courage to address Jason, Bobby says, 'Time to do the Gordie Howe thing' – referring self-ironically to what is perhaps Canada's most famous hockey family. Appropriately enough, Bobby and Jason's reunion takes place in the hockey arena. Their first adult words are exchanged in the dressing room; after Jason has seen his father on the ice, he asks, '… what the hell … was *that*? A cameo? What are you doing in town?' As the words are uttered in a mock-serious tone, their harshness is mitigated. Unaware of Bobby's hopeful plans of settling permanently in Fredericton, the son can only assume that this is yet another brief appearance from the father who occasionally took him skating. Bobby is tongue-tied by his son's directness. He realizes, 'he should speak, but found himself taking in the son's lanky body …' and concluding that with 'weight training, he'd make a decent power forward, bash the corners, crash the net …' The elliptical sentences reflect the disjointedness and confusion in Bobby's mind as he continues to regard his son merely as a hockey player.[60]

Bobby is an insightful individual, though not exactly sharp at applying his insights to his own life. For example, on the subject of fans, he wonders:

> How can you respect anyone who likes you and doesn't even know you? If people hate you for your skin or uniform colour, it's of course more painful than if they *love* you for the same reason, but the scenario is similarly stupid.

He fails to make the cognitive jump, and demands love from the son who no longer knows him. Bobby's fantasies of becoming the Howe family in miniature are shattered by Jason's straight-talking mother, Leah, a social worker to whom Bobby is still legally married. When

Bobby makes the analogy, Leah responds: 'Gordie Howe was totally different.' Bobby misunderstands her, believing it was a reference to Howe's on-ice greatness, and Leah has to clarify: '*No. Shit ...* He had the *right*. He was a goddamn *father*.' Only towards the end of the novel does Bobby come to clarity regarding his situation and the parenting shortcomings that led to it. When they play in a friendly intra-squad game together, Bobby assumes his aloof son is merely being coy (this just before the violent check described in chapter 3). Fittingly for a father who has spent his entire life enwrapped in hockey culture, he comes to clarity on the ice: '... the catchphrase he'd for two hours been breathing to himself, "we're both pretending I'm no one special," now transmuted to the thought *He's not pretending*.' The adult Jason, taciturn by nature, has no real voice in the novel. He is merely the object of many of the musings and conversations.[61]

Sibling Rivalry on the Ice

Wayne Johnston's *The Divine Ryans* scrutinizes the cult of masculinity in hockey by pitting brother and sister against each other. The 1988 novel takes place in the days of the pre-expansion NHL and is narrated by Draper Doyle, a hockey-obsessed ten-year-old of negligible talent. Hockey is the focus of Draper's life, and his family cannot understand his fixation. What the family does understand is the importance of hockey for settling disputes, as is shown when the entire Doyle family watches the 'Protestant' Toronto Maple Leafs play the 'Catholic' Montreal Canadiens. The Doyles become suddenly interested:

> It was a strange sight indeed, a roomful of people who otherwise never watched a hockey game, including Sister Louise and Father Seymour in their habits, acting as if their lives depended on the outcome.[62]

Clearly, this is not just a game, but a vehicle of proving religious supremacy. No matter that Toronto stars like Frank Mahovlich and Dave Keon attended the Catholic St Michael's College School in Toronto. The family milieu in which Draper lives is sometimes bizarre, but blessed with clear rules – and it was the breaking of a rule by Draper's father that set the novel in motion. A man of words who ran the local Catholic newspaper, he had been a tremendous hockey fan, if a reluctant husband. The novel begins shortly after the death of the father, who appears to Draper in recurring dreams, always holding a hockey puck. Draper suffers from a trauma of sorts, as his final, though suppressed, memory of his father was when he walked in on him having sex with a man at the newspaper office. The father committed suicide shortly after.

Because young Draper Doyle cannot fathom the father's homosexuality, he cannot articulate it (though it is clear enough to the reader). What Draper does examine at comical length is the battle of the sexes. This is tellingly and charmingly played out between Draper and his sister Mary on the ice. After spying on Mary and then publicly mocking her for her growth of pubic hair, Draper notes that 'this episode touched off a renewal of the sex versus age controversy.' More than simple sibling rivalry, this battle is a glib repetition of broader societal stereotypes, including his sister's partial acceptance of patriarchal views:

> My only comfort was that while she would always be older, I would always be a boy. Faced with the fact that most grown-ups of either sex agreed that boys were, as the saying went, 'better' than girls, Mary conceded inferiority in sex while trying to convince me that age was more important.

Draper would not listen to reason, and Mary often played hockey against him, usually winning, to prove that there was more to power than simply being male.[63]

When Draper goads her into playing one final game, the results are disastrous for his sense of masculinity, and irksome for puberty-stricken Mary. Under a barrage of sexual innuendos from the other players ('Got yer pads on, Mary?') – which elude the younger Draper ('You can see that she doesn't have any pads on') – Mary proves the better goalie. Her team wins, and when the siblings become physically entangled on the last play of the game, Mary literally casts off her male opponent:

> With a manoeuvre she might have been practising for years, she bounced me off her with one thrust of the pelvis. Then she got up and, without a word to anyone, left the rink. Holding her goalie stick on her shoulder, she went clomping up Fleming Street, her white skates making sparks on the pavement. I suspected that few goalies had ever marched so impressively to their retirement.

After rejecting the male aggressor with the timely pelvic thrust, Mary passes – as the hockey tradition of the time dictated – from hockey to womanhood, leaving the taunting teenagers behind. The defiant sparks made by her feminine 'white skates' add further humiliation to Draper's defeat. When his sister not only beats him at hockey but also proves physically stronger, Draper clearly feels like less of a man. Draper is surprisingly honest in his description of the incident, and his bigoted viewpoints on how each sex should behave. This world view, created to a great extent by his surroundings and upbringing, dictates that one who is less masculine is less valuable as a person. The irony of this loss is that it takes place within the space of modern sports, which has been understood as

> a social institution constructed by men, largely as a response to a crisis of gender relations in the late nineteenth and early twentieth centuries. The dominant structures and values of sport came to reflect the fears and needs of a threatened masculinity.

It is widely believed that males have an advantage in sports like hockey because of the emphasis on strength and speed. Draper, though still a boy, was able to choose the 'weapon,' had the history of gender relations in sports on his side, and still lost both the hockey battle and the skirmish when his sister 'bounced him off.' That Mary is the better player is not the source of laughs here. Rather, it is Draper's delusional eagerness that loses out to Mary's reluctant prowess as he receives his comeuppance.[64]

Literature of Absence

Gender issues, like racism, are rarely portrayed directly in hockey literature. If they do appear, it is usually as a peripheral element of the story. For example, in Michelle Berry's short story 'Henderson Has Scored for Canada!' a young farm girl decides to join her father in a trip to Toronto for a 1972 Summit Series game. When the matter is discussed at home, she recalls the immediate anti-hockey alliance struck between her mother and her younger sister:

> 'I hate hockey,' Mommy whispered and Maggie echoed, 'Me too,' just so she could be like Mommy, just so she could say something that made sense. Because she is a girl and Mommy is a girl and life moves like that, in circles. It's easy if it all makes sense.[65]

The diction and syntax reflect the mindset of a young child, and the simple message derived by the youngest daughter is that girls should not like hockey. As illustrative as this quotation may be, Berry's story is more about economic despair, marital infidelity, and the mania surrounding the 1972 Summit Series than gender divides in hockey. By attending the game with her father, the narrator 'sides' with him, much in the way that Diane Schoemperlen's young female narrator in 'Hockey Night in Canada' betrays her mother ever so slightly when she watches hockey with her father. These references are brief but enlightening as far as the predominantly male hockey story goes. In both cases, since there is no brother to watch with the father, the young girls appear to be surrogates.

There are very few fictional works that depict females who actually play hockey, and of these, even fewer – if any – focus on hockey as a family tradition. Marsha Mildon's 'Number 33' is the exception that proves, but also explains, the rule. The story is about a woman who begins playing hockey at the age of forty-nine, spouting the usual lines about a 'genetic Canadian imperative,' and her 'real life' being when she watched *Hockey Night in Canada*. When she finally starts to play herself, she concludes, 'I am one of "us": a hockey player, and therefore (I can't help feeling) a Canadian, fully-fledge at last.' Although a devotee of the game since the age of seven, she 'made it to 1994 without ever hearing of women's ice hockey.' The narrator tackles the question of this ignorance with Mark Twainian directness:

> The answer is: I have no idea. I can only assume that my [unwed] mother's determination that I should be an artiste simply anesthetized my awareness of women's hockey.

Mildon's story comes closest to stating why there were relatively few girls on the ice. It is partly attributable to the fact that most hockey fiction looks back to a time before women were given equal opportunities to play (if, indeed, that day has come). Mildon's story makes it clear that '*girr-ulls*, that horrible two syllable species to which I seemed to belong,' were not often seen on the ice during her 1950s childhood. That memory, coupled with the missing father, presents hockey as a father-son domain. Young women are ignored.[66]

Roy MacGregor, in *The Home Team: Fathers, Sons and Hockey*, repeats a revealing bon mot from the daughter in a well-known family of hockey stars: 'Unless your mind's like a hockey puck around here, nobody pays attention.' The daughter's existence has been marginalized by a mere game. In a similar manner, the narrator in Pete McCormack's *Under-*

standing Ken loves staying at his father's for the same reason his sister
despises it:

> When my sister visits my dad on the weekend she has to go to the rink with
> us all the time and watch me play hockey. I can't remember the last
> weekend my sister went to my dad's.

Particularly in competitive hockey circles, the daughter often slips from
memory. In fiction this attitude is best depicted in the behaviour of
Frank Paci's Vince in *Icelands*. Unlike his own parents, who had recoiled
from hockey, Vince enthusiastically provides his son with a chance to
enjoy the game. Vince's own father – like those of *The Italians* and *Black
Madonna* – had not supported him in his love for the game and had not
backed his attempts to become a professional player. But whereas his
father cared too little about the game, Vince cares too much and
focuses too much attention, not on Stevie the son, but on Stevie the
hockey player. In the words of Karen, the forgotten daughter, 'All he
thinks about is hockey. He hardly even notices me. It's like I'm invisible.
The invisible daughter.' When she confronts him later, Vince takes a
good look at her, reflects on how time flies, how his little girl has grown
up while he was away at the hockey arena, then says, 'We'll talk after the
game.' In the meantime, she should stick to her piano playing.[67]

Despite changes in recent years, female family members are most
welcome if they play supportive roles. Nancy Theberge, adding to Bruce
Kidd's comment that arenas are 'men's cultural centres,' describes
women's jobs in such a setting: '... they watch their brothers', sons' and
husbands' games, staff the concession stands and take tickets.' Lorna
Jackson writes in her non-fictional *Cold-Cocked: On Hockey* that 'when
women dare enter a debate about hockey, it is to be shut down and shut
up, ignored or derided, dismissed.' Jackson makes this observation in a
passage describing two loutish, under-informed male fans at a Vancouver Canucks game – one in which she belittles their meretricious knowledge of the game. Because Jackson's book contains far more detailed
analysis of individual games than most literary hockey books, her
comment is all the more revealing. She is not merely an appendage to
hockey culture who feigns interest. A complete insider in terms of
knowledge, she feels relegated by the very realm she so perceptively
observes in both strategic and cultural terms.[68]

Conclusion

Plenty of potential in that range of raw material, but plenty of danger as well.

Jamie Fitzpatrick, 'Logan, Buddy and Fred,' in *Hockey Write in Canada*, p. 74

This book has taken a thematic approach to hockey in Canadian litera-ture, adding literary criticism to the many cultural studies efforts that already exist. As was evident throughout, discussing hockey in literature without considering hockey as a general cultural phenomenon is not possible. The various focal points of the individual chapters – hockey as a symbol of Canada, a utopian play-world, a violent game, the crux of national identity, and a formidable family link – are all themes common to discussions of real, played hockey in Canada, and though few of the works examined here are programmatic, they are each informed by and add to general hockey discourse in Canada. The perspective of Roy MacGregor's *The Last Season* is hard to imagine without the raging debates over the role of fighting and violence in hockey; parts of Frank Paci's novels *Black Madonna* and *The Italians* depend on an understand-ing of the hockey as an aid to sporting integration into Canada; Mark Anthony Jarman's picaresque *Salvage King, Ya!* is far more entertaining and illuminating when read against a backdrop of idealist play concepts; and novels such as Steve Lundin's *When She's Gone* and Mordecai Richler's *Barney's Version* are surely far more enjoyable when read with an understanding of hockey nostalgia and the desire to escape the 'real world' in favour of the arena's comforts.

With the bumper crops of hockey fiction published within the past five years, one can no longer complain about a lack of hockey writing. Nevertheless, Don Gillmor's observation that hockey's mythical figures have not led to a 'mythic literature' remains valid. And this is a good thing, at least if mythic writing means feting the game and immortalizing its figures. Mordecai Richler cruelly claimed in 1985 that Wayne Gretzky, our greatest contemporary hockey icon, is 'nice, very nice, but incapable of genuine wit or irreverence.' Of course, if there is any truth to the Canadian congeniality, Gretzky is the right hero. In a later essay, Richler passed a harsher judgment, dubbing him 'one of the most boring men I ever met.' Whether or not Richler's estimation is warranted, and whether or not hockey fiction has mythologized him as it has Maurice Richard, Bobby Orr, and even Don Cherry, Gretzky remains a heroic figure.[1] Not arrogant, untainted by scandal, he is a model of pacifism and self-restraint, and cut from the stereotypical Canadian cloth.

Doug Beardsley argues that Canadians 'more easily worship mediocrity' and for that reason have failed to give Gretzky his due. Mark Anthony Jarman's *Salvage King, Ya!* sums up the sometimes ambivalent relationship to Gretzky, and in some ways reflects the general Canadian attitude towards heroes. Canadian fiction as a whole does not adhere to the standard American-style success tale, for which sports fiction is often a clear allegory of upward mobility. When Jarman's protagonist, Drinkwater, mentions having played for Los Angeles, he specifies, it was 'pre-Gretzky, pre-Cambrian,' a reference to the seismic changes Gretzky effected on the hockey world. Drinkwater also punctuates his narrative with often hilarious anti-Gretzky charges. Bland, bashful, and phoney, this created, literary Gretzky is mocked for everything from shyness, to sexual reticence, to trying to skimp on a cover charge at a club, to driving around Edmonton with fake licence plates. The clean-living *Wunderkind* is the polar opposite of Drinkwater, and – unlike in Richler's profiles of Gretzky – there is no journalistic claim to factual revelation or the truth about Gretzky. *Salvage King, Ya!* is, before all, a novel. In what is a fine literary work by any standards, Jarman makes the reader wonder if our heroes and mythical figures can be found within the hockey world. Neither the fictionalized Gretzky nor Drinkwater is a figure for off-ice emulation.[2]

Reading Hockey Abroad

I teach in Slovenia, where hockey is played, but not revered. There is a professional league here, but it is not the NHL, and the top Slovenian players, like the top Russian and Czech and Swedish players, long to

play on the other side of the Atlantic. One has even made it. The game
is not a given in Slovenia, but neither is it entirely foreign or 'unlikely'
in the sense of Dave Bidini's *Tropic of Hockey: My Search for the Game in
Unlikely Places*, Ray Rains's *Hockey Night Down Under!* or even the part of
Brooklyn, New York, described by Cecil Harris in his introduction to
Breaking the Ice: The Black Experience in Professional Hockey. In Slovenia it is
a matter of minor displacement rather than alienation.

Reading hockey fiction, or fiction that contains copious hockey references, can surely prove cryptic at times to the foreign reader, but the
division is not absolute: reams of German readers enjoyed Mordecai
Richler's *Wie Barney es sieht*, and many more Italians *La versione di Barney*,
despite its many Canadiens allusions. In a particularly cruel twist of fate,
especially given Maurice Richard's status in Quebec, the French translation of *Barney's Version* has 'la Fusée' in place of 'Le Rocket'[3] (adding
insult to lexical injury, the hockey player depicted on the cover appears
to be wearing a Detroit Red Wings uniform). These are small, but
crucial, details of cultural translation that would at best be a trifling
bother for those versed in hockey, and very few of the works examined
here would be unreadable for those unfamiliar with North American
hockey culture. Most would, however, be difficult: even those Canadians
who despise hockey will immediately recognize references to Paul Henderson's 1972 goal, Guy Lafleur's hair, or the entertaining persona of
Don Cherry. Adding footnotes to explain these larger-than-life Canadian characters would be redundant in Canada. For this reason, hockey
prose that stops along the way to explain heroes and events common to
all hockey fans often sounds like a sitcom's contrived telephone exposition, or as if the author is really trying to pitch his or her book to a
reading public in Alabama or Ireland. After an important playoff game,
nobody says, 'Did you watch game seven of the Stanley Cup finals, which
determined whether X or Y would be ...?' In Canada, even among
strangers, it would be enough to say, 'Did you see the game?' When a
group of people shares, or is assumed to share, a common ground, conversation is economical and elliptical. The best hockey writing is natural
in that it makes no concessions to outsiders to hockey culture, takes no
explanatory stops along the novelistic path.

In the Toronto house in which I grew up there is a side door that was
long ago painted shut. To my family and friends, it is obvious one does
not enter the house through that door. This self-understood fact might
be slightly perplexing to a visitor, showing that even 'the obvious' is relative. The situation with hockey literature is similar when hockey-igno-

rant foreign readers try to enter this house of Canadian fiction. Mordecai Richler points this out when he mentions an 'otherwise generous
review' of *Barney's Version* in which a British reviewer, Francis King,
'noting the sharpness of protagonist Barney Panofsky's intelligence and
the breadth of his culture,' did not find it credible that Barney might
also like hockey. King found Barney's 'cultural omniscience' highly
unlikely. In fact, intelligent, hockey-mad characters return Duddy
Kravitz–like throughout Richler's novels; it appears that the hockey side
of their personalities is entirely overlooked by Richler's British reading
public. Even the harshest Canadian reviews of the novel did not find
Barney's 'cultural omniscience' suspect. While Kerry McSweeney,
writing in *Canadian Literature*, found it incredible that decrepit Barney
executed a tap dance, he never doubted Barney's hockey knowledge
and passion. This minor difference in viewpoints reflects the varying
ways in which hockey literature is received outside the North American
context (as well as Europe's snobbier view of sports fans).[4]

Richler made the extravagant claim that hockey is our 'secret idiom,'
and that Canadians can use it to exclude 'sniffy foreigners' in the way
his parents could slip into Yiddish in public. In a comic scene in his
novel *St. Urbain's Horseman,* Richler shows a very practical use of the
hockey idiom. An English tax-hound sniffs about in Jake Hersh's
dubious books: 'I note a payment here of £1,000 advance to one Jean
Béliveau, script writer, of the Forum Apartments, St. Catherine St. W.,
Montreal ...' Given Béliveau's status, this act of putting one over on the
taxman is also a good test of who is Canadian. Hersh is playing with fire
by choosing such a prominent name; yet the joke also reveals how
poorly hockey travelled, especially in the days before globalized sports.
Richler reminds Canadians that this figure who is so important to Montreal means nothing to the rest of the world. As a Canadian writer who
lived and published in England for years, Richler was surely well aware
of this double perspective. Elsewhere, he writes,

> ... in 1985, NHL stars had to cope with a difficult paradox. Celebrated at
> home, they could, much to their chagrin, usually pass anonymously south
> of the forty-ninth parallel.

The Béliveau quotation exudes both intimacy and a sense of estrangement as it expresses this paradox.[5]

Teaching English literature in Slovenia has provided me with some-

times humbling insight into how alienating 'obvious' cultural references can be – humbling because I am forced to see that something so
important to Canada's culture means nothing to others.[6] A few years
ago, my class was to read and interpret Clark Blaise's 1974 short story
'I'm Dreaming of Rocket Richard.' The themes and motifs in the story
– including alcoholism, failure, growing pains, and the rich American
cousins – are hardly new to literature, yet the students were clearly
annoyed by what they deemed an inordinately difficult text. The direct
references to the Montreal Forum and to Maurice Richard were off-
putting. Blaise subtly explains the importance of the Forum and 'Le
Rocket' in his story, especially as filtered through the boy protagonist's
worldview, so that any attentive reader can dive into the tale. This is not
a work like Philip Roth's *The Great American Novel*, which cannot be read
sensibly without a rudimentary knowledge of baseball. Nevertheless, the
mere presence of hockey in Blaise's story was clearly a hurdle to that
initial aesthetic uptake that engagement with a work of art requires.
Compounding this is the lack of a cultural impetus regarding low or
popular culture. In contrast to references to biblical apocrypha or
Greek mythology, there is little sense of edification when one googles
'Don Cherry' or 'Maurice Richard.' An educated person is not
'required' to know these local heroes in a university setting.

There are surprisingly few works that will be limited only to Canadians or Canada-savvy readers. Keith Harrison's sketch 'World Hockey
Supremacy,' which takes the form of a hockey play-by-play commentary,
is a rare example. The author mixes the vocabulary of sports with literary events, including lines such as '… what about that surprise trade
which saw Mukherjee dealt for Shields, straight up?' and 'The ref had
absolutely no reason to call a penalty on Carrier for wearing the wrong
sweater.'[7] With its references to writers who left Canada for the United
States and vice versa, and allusions to Roch Carrier's 'The Hockey
Sweater,' it is safe to say that this sketch is impenetrable for anyone but
those select few familiar with hockey, Canadian literature, and Canadian literary gossip. The title of this piece indirectly points out that it is
literary provincialism of a witty sort. 'World Hockey Supremacy' is an
occasional work written for an 'expert' audience, and Harrison's goal is
obviously not to create lasting world literature. It thus raises questions
about writing for a limited audience, or limiting one's audience. Too
much hockey in a literary work can condemn it to the curiosity shop of
genre fiction.

Fruitful Allusions

Hockey references, like all allusions, can add depth and layers of meaning to fiction. Leonard Cohen's *Beautiful Losers* was first published in 1966, well before hockey fiction and references were usual. Cohen adds a hockey voice to Quebec's Quiet Revolution: 'Ten thousand voices that only knew how to cheer a rubber puck past a goalie's pads, [were] now singing: MERDE A LA REINE D'ANGLETERRE!'[8] This is a single line in a novel, but it alludes to an entire history of Quebec hockey adoration, including *les Canadiens* as a symbol of resistance against anglophone domination. Surrogate resistance on the ice cedes to more active – and violent – political awakening.

In Alistair MacLeod's 1999 novel *No Great Mischief*, a hockey metaphor aptly describes the tensions between a group of francophones and a Gaelic-speaking group from Cape Breton Island at an Ontario mining camp:

> We viewed them, as they did us, with a certain wariness; always on the lookout for the real or imagined slight or advantage; being like rival hockey teams, waiting for the right time to question stick measurements or illegal equipment; biding our time and keeping our eyes open.[9]

The comparison to a hockey game thickens this air of disdain. In this case, even the 'foreign' reader will understand the reference (though perhaps on a less intuitive level than one who has ever exploited, or seen exploited, an equipment rule). Comparing the possibility of real violence between these antagonistic groups to the litigious exploiting of marginal hockey rules implies that it is all a game and that, like all teams that agree to play together, these minority groups with a specific set of skills do have something in common. Although it is clear that the suspicions will culminate in physical abuse, the search for the 'right time to question stick measurements' suggests the presence of a controlling element, as if there were a referee. But the violence in this other masculine enclave of the mining camp is not very controlled. The reference to a hockey game heightens the seriousness in this passage by juxtaposing the trivial with the utterly serious.

Another example: in Alice Munro's story 'The Bear Came over the Mountain,' from her 2001 collection *Hateship, Friendship, Courtship, Loveship, Marriage*, a character drives down 'Black Hawks Lane' and notes, 'All the streets around were named for teams in the old National

Hockey League.'[10]As every hockey fan knows, for decades the National Hockey League consisted of just six teams, known and lionized as 'The Original Six.' Streets named after the teams of the pre-expansion NHL ooze stability and tradition, and evoke a soupy time when stars were rarely traded, money seemed less a part of the game, hockey life was sweet, and we knew not why. This street name is ironical because 'Black Hawks Lane' is in a subdivision where all the new houses once looked exactly the same. Munro's subtle hockey reference speaks volumes about how the past is packaged and marketed, and how hockey nostalgia is put to use. The choice of name is perfect in a story that takes place mostly in a rest home for people with dementia, and is therefore very much about people who are literally or figuratively trapped in the past.

As this book has shown, Canadian literature is not soft on hockey, neither in terms of volume, quality, or criticizing negative aspects of the game. There are passing references to hockey in works of Canadian literature from Cohen's *Beautiful Losers* (1966) to Kroetsch's *The Studhorse Man* (1969), with its epic list of 'sudden and glorious names,' as players past meet players present ('Mikita from the corner for the Black Hawks. A backhander by Laperriere. Kelly upended by Marshall. In for the puck goes Bobby Hull. Here is Delvecchio faking a shot ...'), to Carol Shields's small-town librarian in *Swann* (1990), who informs a group of academics about her 'very small budget. Last year it got cut twice, the hockey arena got a hike, but we got –'[11] This system of allusions is there to be exploited, employed, and shaped by all Canadian writers. In a country that – outside of Quebec – cannot clearly differentiate itself linguistically from the United States, hockey references often function like passages in dialect. As the short quotations from MacLeod and Munro show, most of the references will be vaguely understood by the non-Canadian reading public; Canadians will experience a crackling wit, perhaps irreverence, perhaps revulsion, but rarely apathy.

Notes

Introduction

1 Young and Robertson, *Face-Off*, 179.
2 Barthes, *Le Sport et les hommes*, 53. 'What is a national sport? It is a sport that springs forth from a nation's very material, from its soil and its climate. To play hockey is to restate, each time, that men have transformed immobile winter, the hardened earth, [and] a life suspended and that precisely out of all of this made a lively, vigorous and passionate sport' (my translation).
3 Hood, *Strength down Centre: The Jean Béliveau Story*, 102.
4 Gruneau and Whitson, *Hockey Night in Canada*, 4. The very titles of recently published academic studies indicate this broadening of the research territory: Robidoux, *Men at Play: A Working Understanding of Professional Hockey* (2001); Wong, *Lords of the Rinks: The Emergence of the National Hockey League, 1875–1936* (2005); Melançon, *Les yeux de Maurice Richard: Une histoire culturelle* (2006) (translated by Fred A. Reed in 2009); Whitson and Gruneau, eds, *Artificial Ice: Hockey, Culture and Commerce* (2006).
5 Woolf, 'American Fiction,' 118; Beardsley, *Country on Ice*, 36, 25f.
6 Bowering, 'Introduction,' 6; Fawcett, 'My Career with the Leafs,' 292.
7 Oriard, *Dreaming of Heroes*, 8. For a select bibliography of hockey writing (to 2003), see Michael Kennedy's *Words on Ice: A Collection of Hockey Prose*. David McNeil's extensive, searchable on-line bibliography is available at http://www.hip.english.dal.ca/.
8 For an analysis of the typical plot pattern in American sports fiction, see Evans, 'The All-American Boys,' 104–21. In 1988 Robert G. Hollands noted that Canadian sports novels follow the same patterns. Moreover, 'problems are not only resolved by the hero individually, but also by his

choosing a morally correct response (being honest, ethical, or hard-working)' (Hollands, 'English-Canadian Sports Novels and Cultural Production,' 220). There is no longer a focus on traditional morality in Canadian hockey fiction.

9 Ford, *The Sportswriter*, 362.

10 Jarman, *Salvage King, Ya!*, 108; Earle, 'Hockey as Canadian Popular Culture,' 326. Earle's investigation is much more nuanced than this isolated quotation implies.

11 Quarrington, 'Introduction,' 7.

12 Hollands, 'Canadian Sports Novels, Marxism and Cultural Production,' 358.

13 Whitson and Gruneau, 'Introduction,' 11. On sexual abuse, see Robinson, *Crossing the Line*. Less surprising, given the dominance of the male point of view in hockey culture, is the lack of fiction about female players.

1. Hockey as a Symbol of Nationhood

1 For the sake of simplicity and in keeping with everyday Canadian speech, 'nation' and 'state' are used synonymously in this study – with the occasional exception of references to Quebec.

2 Smythe and Young, *If You Can't Beat 'Em in the Alley*, 223.

3 Clark, 'Community of Communities,' 268.

4 Atwood, *Survival*, 65; Frye, *The Bush Garden*, 220; Sproxton, 'A Sunny Day in May – Newfoundland Time,' in *The Hockey Fan Came Riding*, 86.

5 McKinley, *Putting a Roof on Winter*, 244; Allen, *The Gift of the Game*, 31. McKinley's book is a critical history of the game, and here he is clearly mimicking ahistorical hockey talk. In the service of attacking hockey essentialism, academic critics often rob such statements of their context, or ignore the possibility of irony.

6 Dronyk, 'The Puck Artist,' 74.

7 Quoted in MacGregor, *The Home Team*, 42.

8 Richler, 'The Fall of the Montreal Canadiens,' 245; Woodcock, 'An Absence of Utopias,' 3.

9 MacGregor, e-mail message to author, 7 August 2008. On the lack of acceptance in literary circles, MacGregor continues: 'It speaks, I think, to the immaturity and insecurity of Canadian culture.' For an exhaustive discussion on sports in American fiction, see Oriard, *Sporting with the Gods*.

10 Gillmor, 'Hockey: The Great Literary Shutout,' 88.

11 Beardsley, *Country on Ice*, 61; Gowdey, 'Foreword,' ix ; Salutin, *Les Canadiens*, 11.

12 Bell, 'Hockey Night in Métabetchouan,' 35, 33.

13 Ignatieff, *Blood and Belonging: Journeys into the New Nationalism*, 177; Gzowski, *The Game of Our Lives*, 79.

14 Anderson, *Imagined Communities*, 5.

15 Saul, *Reflections of a Siamese Twin*, 81.

16 Guttmann, *Games and Empires*, 18; Cooper, 'Canadians Declare "It Isn't Cricket,"' 51; Robidoux, *Men at Play*, 221. Donald Guay examines the rise of hockey in Quebec as a cultural phenomenon. After emphasizing that a melting-pot approach to plurality results in a levelling of cultures that aids the dominant culture, he states, 'Le hockey, comme symbole d'identification nationale, est d'autant plus efficace qu'il fonctionne non seulement pour les Anglais d'origine, mais aussi pour les autres Anglo-Canadiens d'origine irlandaise ou écossaise et les Canadiens français qui, du moins dans le discours des nationalistes, tentent de s'identifier comme une société distincte' (Guay, *L'histoire du hockey au Québec*, 274) [Hockey, as a symbol of national identification, is all the more effective because it functions not only for (those of) English origins, but also for other Anglo-Canadians of Irish and Scottish origins and the French Canadians who, at least in nationalist discourse, attempt to identify themselves as a distinct society (my translation)].

17 Lundin, *When She's Gone*, 14.

18 Cameron, 'Theory and Criticism: Trends in Canadian Literature,' 127; Cohen, *Beautiful Losers*, 133; Hutcheon, 'The Canadian Postmodern: Fiction in English since 1960,' 21.

19 Atwood, *Survival*, 150.

20 Guttmann, *Games and Empires*, 183; Richler, 'Soul on Ice,' 203.

21 Guttmann, *Games and Empires*, 181. On the role of hockey in producing a very specific concept of the Quebec nation – namely, as an aid to 'the construction of a specifically heterosexual, homophobic and aggressive form of masculinity' – see Bélanger, 'The Last Game? Hockey and the Experience of Masculinity in Québec,' 294.

22 Callaghan, 'The Game That Makes a Nation,' 51.

23 Dryden and MacGregor, *Home Game: Hockey and Life in Canada*, 59.

24 Hobsbawm, *Nations and Nationalism since 1780*, 143.

25 Dowbiggin, *The Stick: A History, a Celebration, an Elegy*, 179, 180.

26 Dryden and MacGregor, *Home Game*, 9.

27 Kidd, *The Struggle for Canadian Sport*, 259; Gutteridge, *Bus-Ride*, 48. Don Reddick's novel *Dawson City Seven* explores the hockey-railroad-Canada triad in an era before mass media. The novel is a fictionalized depiction of the epic cross-Canada journey undertaken by the Dawson City Nuggets to challenge the Ottawa 'Silver Seven' for the 1905 Stanley Cup.

28 MacLennan, *Two Solitudes*, 319; Genosko, 'Hockey and Culture,' 140.
29 Dryden, *The Game*, 3.
30 Quarrington, 'Foreword,' 7; Bidini, *Tropic of Hockey*, xviii.
31 Zweig, *Hockey Night in the Dominion of Canada*, 69.
32 Quoted in Traill, *The Life of Sir John Franklin, R.N.*
33 Robinson, *Crossing the Line*, 1; Gruneau and Whitson, *Hockey Night in Canada*, 132.
34 Callaghan, 'The Game That Makes a Nation,' 51; Young, *Scrubs on Skates*, 27. Hockey is only *relatively* inclusive. As recently as 1988, Paul Quarrington wrote, 'I wager most of us still find it a strange sight; that is, a hockey uniform filled with a black man' (*Hometown Heroes*, 127). Mordecai Richler's reference to 'the goys of winter' in his essay 'Howe Incredible' plants hockey as a gentile sport (271). Marc Lavoie convincingly makes the less obvious claim that French Canadians are under-represented. See *Désavantage numérique: Les francophones dans la LNH*.
35 Orr, *Puck Is a Four-Letter Word*, 32.
36 Robidoux, 'Imagining a Canadian Identity through Sport,' 222.

2. The Hockey Dream: Hockey as Escape, Freedom, Utopia

1 Richards, *Hockey Dreams: Memories of a Man Who Couldn't Play*, 23.
2 Sanger, '5,6, Pickup Sticks,' 64.
3 Scanlan, *Grace under Fire: The State of Our Sweet and Savage Game*, 3.
4 Bidini, *Tropic of Hockey*, xix; Dryden, *The Game*, 73; Quarrington, *King Leary*, 72. To provide just one example of such competition: Pierre Létourneau's 1971 pop song 'Maurice Richard' provides an imaginary facing-off as he compares the then-young Bobby Orr to Le Rocket and notes that Orr is well behind Richard statistically. Moreover, the song's sugary refrain – 'Maurice Richard / C'est pour toi que je chante' – gives Richard the clear emotional edge.
5 Richler, 'The Fall of the Montreal Canadiens,' 244; Richler, *Barney's Version*, 121; Zweig, *Hockey Night in the Dominion of Canada*, 339. As Anouk Bélanger, points out, the Montreal Forum, though 'a commercial space,' was, more than any other such space in Canada, 'claimed symbolically over the years by "the people."' '*Les Canadiens*,' the Forum's most famous tenants, 'have acted to champion both Montreal's civic identity and Quebecois cultural identities for nearly a century' ('Sport Venues and the Spectacularization of Urban Spaces in North America: The Case of the Molson Centre in Montreal,' 391, 389).
6 Zweig, *Hockey Night in the Dominion of Canada*, 339.

7 Moore, 'Practical Nostalgia and the Critique of Commodification: On the "Death of Hockey" and the National Hockey League,' 311. In a more critical vein, Mary Louise Adams writes, 'Nostalgia is a powerful means of keeping us from imagining how Canada might be different' ('The Game of Whose Lives?' 82).

8 Kennedy, Preface, *Growing Up Hockey: The Life and Times of Everyone Who Ever Loved the Game;* Leacock, *Sunshine Sketches of a Little Town*, 1.

9 Gzowski, *The Game of Our Lives*, 82; Dryden, *The Game*, 55; Richards, *Hockey Dreams*, 68; Harlow, *The Saxophone Winter*, 45; Paci, *Icelands*, 50. Hans-Georg Gadamer postulates that play exists independently of the player: 'The player doesn't play the game … the game plays the player. Once you begin playing, you are taken over by the things that are serious within the game, regardless of how serious that same game is estimated to be in the eyes of the nonplaying world' (*Truth and Method*, 182).

10 Earle, 'The Stanley Cup and the Heroic Journey,' 100.

11 Lundin, *When She's Gone*, 23.

12 Gutteridge, *Bus-Ride*, 9.

13 Sutton-Smith, *The Ambiguity of Play*, 1; Fink, 'The Oasis of Happiness: Toward an Ontology of Play,' 19, 22.

14 Suits, *The Grasshopper: Games, Life, and Utopia*, 15.

15 Huizinga, Foreword, *Homo Ludens;* Ehrmann, '*Homo Ludens* Revisited,' 32.

16 Caillois, *Les jeux et les hommes*, 33, 50–68 ; McSorley, 'Of Time and Space and Hockey: An Imaginary Conversation,' 153. McSorley places these musings on hockey contingency in the mouth of Wayne Gretzky.

17 Oriard, *Dreaming of Heroes*, 20.

18 Suits, *The Grasshopper*, ix.

19 McLuhan, *Understanding Media*, 259; Lasch, 'The Corruption of Sports,' 24–30; Zweig, *Hockey Night in the Dominion of Canada*, 180.

20 Jarman, 'Righteous Speedboat,' 234, 233. Failure is a common theme in sports fiction. In Richard B. Wright's *The Age of Longing*, the narrator reflects on his father, who almost made it, rendering the special talent generic, dull: 'There have always been thousands of young men like Buddy Wheeler in small towns everywhere. Good? You bet! … That kid can't miss the major leagues, believe you me! Well, he can, and most likely will. Then he will have to settle for Plan B or C or D. Or no plan at all' (186).

21 Jarman, 'Righteous Speedboat,' 240.

22 Ibid., 242.

23 Ibid., 240, 241. Anti-Lindros ire was especially strong in Quebec, where his decision was widely understood as an anti-Quebec statement.

24 Stenson, 'Teeth,' 135.

25 Ibid., 130, 138.
26 MacGregor, *The Last Season*, 159.
27 Suits, 'Words on Play,' 19; MacGregor, *The Last Season*, 158.
28 Huizinga, *Homo Ludens*, 11.
29 Robidoux, *Men at Play*, 3; Sanger, '5,6, Pickup Sticks,' 65.
30 Beardsley, *Country on Ice*, 42; Zweig, *Hockey Night in the Dominion of Canada*, 109.
31 MacGregor, *The Home Team*, 147. Carrier's gruesome description: 'The fingers were closed and hard as a rock. There were black marks where their sticks had struck it' (*La Guerre, Yes Sir!* 26).
32 For a mordant critique of a culture that remains overwhelmingly male and overwhelmingly white, see Adams, 'The Game of Whose Lives? Gender, Race, and Entitlement in Canada's "National Game,"' 71–84. The title is a clear allusion to Peter Gzowski's *The Game of Our Lives*.
33 Beardsley, *Country on Ice*, 46.
34 Eichberg, 'The Societal Construction of Time and Space,' 153.
35 Novak, *The Joy of Sports*, 137.
36 Oriard, *Dreaming of Heroes*, 85; Sproxton, *The Hockey Fan Came Riding*, 104; Quarrington, *Hometown Heroes*, 33.
37 Richards, *Hockey Dreams*, 7. Other highly cultured or literate individuals describe 'their' sports with equal fire. Compare C.L.R. James on cricket in *Beyond a Boundary* (1963), Joyce Carol Oates's *On Boxing* (1995), Nick Hornby's soccer memoir *Fever Pitch* (1992), and Frederick Exley's masterful *A Fan's Notes* (though Exley's 1968 work is a novel, the drunken anti-hero is a football fanatic named Frederick Exley). None is the least contrite about embracing popular culture.
38 McGoldrick Goldberg, 'Growing Up with Hockey,' 199; Gzowski, *The Game of Our Lives*, 82. Recently published children's and adolescent fiction is far more gender-neutral than the literature in this study, as boys and girls play together. See the Brady Brady series for pre-teen readers by Mary Shaw and Chuck Temple; see also Roy MacGregor's Screech Owl series of hockey mystery novels written for adolescent readers. David Bouchard's *That's Hockey* cleverly twists the shinny tradition as he manipulates the typical reader's assumptions. Neither the players depicted nor the reader is aware that the narrator is a girl. The sex of the player is revealed at the conclusion, with the handing-down of the sweater to the next female generation.
39 Richards, *Hockey Dreams*, 24, 25.
40 Paci, *Icelands*, 134, 118f.

41 Paci, *Icelands,* 174, 62. On the typical individual protagonist, see Hollands, 'Masculinity and the Positive Hero in Canadian Sports Novels,' 73–84.

42 Paci, *Icelands,* 50; *Falla, Home Ice,* 13; Beardsley, *Country on Ice,* 52.

43 Suits, *The Grasshopper,* 30; Gzowski, *The Game of Our Lives,* 81. Norbert Elias and Eric Dunning highlight another aspect of maintaining tension in spectator sports: 'The game will be dull and boring' if the tension is too low. 'If the tension becomes too great, it can provide a lot of excitement for the spectators but it will also entail grave dangers for players and spectators alike. It passes from the mimetic to the non-mimetic sphere of serious crisis' (*Quest for Excitement,* 89).

44 Paci, *Icelands,* 50f; *Falla, Home Ice,* 65.

45 Carrier, 'The Hockey Sweater,' 15; Carrier, *Our Life with the Rocket,* 2. Clark Blaise's 'I'm Dreaming of Maurice Richard' focuses on the extent of such identification. The narrator's father has a massive tattoo of Maurice Richard – 'a kind of tribal marking' – and the narrator believes his American cousins might think that 'if I took off my shirt I'd have one too, only smaller' (35). This is a telling, concise observation on the slide from cultural decisions – choosing to get a gaudy tattoo – into perceptions of natural markers.

   Richard was adopted as the quintessential Quebec folk hero, a living emblem of what Quebec could achieve. Melançon's *Les yeux de Maurice Richard* considers how, two generations after his retirement, Richard has turned from folk hero to mythical figure in Quebec and in Canadian history as a whole. On the reception of hockey in Quebec and its changing meanings, see especially Harvey, 'Whose Sweater Is This?' 29–52. Harvey begins his article with an emblem of change: the fabled Red, White, and Blue is clearly no longer the hockey sweater of choice among Harvey's predominantly French-Canadian students.

46 *Falla, Home Ice,* 15. Michael Petrou's sketch 'Before the Spring' portrays hockey as an activity that belongs solely to childhood. A group of adults fly home for the funeral of a childhood friend who died at thirty, the 'victim of a bizarre stroke' (109). As a symbolic ode to the deceased and their lost childhood, the friends play hockey one last time. The final line is: 'They want to charge me extra to bring my hockey stick on the plane so I leave it leaning against a wall' (110). Petrou shows that hockey belongs to a different place, a different time in one's life.

47 Dryden, *The Game,* 56, 57.

48 Gzowski, *The Game of Our Lives,* 247; Caillois, *Les jeux et les hommes,* 56.

49 Dryden, *The Game,* 137.
50 Paci, *Icelands,* 51f. Eichberg, 'A Revolution of Body Culture? Traditional Games on the Way from Modernisation to "Postmodernity,"' 143.
51 Sproxton, *The Hockey Fan Came Riding,* 117.
52 Caillois, *Les jeux et les hommes,* 11. Guttmann, *From Ritual to Record,* 3.
53 Quarrington, *King Leary,* 34.
54 Cashmore, *Sports Culture: An A-Z Guide,* 299. W.P. Kinsella's short story 'Truth' concisely satirizes this viewpoint and its link with central power: 'I'm not sure what Sports Canada is, but I know they figure if they give us Indians enough hockey sticks ..., we forget our land claims, quit drinking too much, get good jobs so we can have the weekends off to play games' (154).
55 Quarrington, *King Leary,* 145.
56 Faulkner, 'An Innocent at Rinkside,' 48.
57 *Falla, Home Ice,* 95.
58 The poem is included in Michael Kennedy's *Going Top Shelf: An Anthology of Canadian Hockey Poetry,* 37.
59 Paci, *Black Madonna,* 57. The adoloscent narrator of Chris Fisher's 'Playing the Garden' has a similar dream: 'It's weird, but we never finish the season ... There's just miles to skate, goals to score, games to play forever' (174).
60 Paci, *Black Madonna,* 86f, 87.
61 McKinley, *Putting a Roof on Winter,* 12; Kennedy, 'I Am Hockey,' 22.
62 Quarrington, *Logan in Overtime,* 211.

3. Representations of Hockey Violence

1 Don DeLillo wrote *Amazons: An Intimate Memoir by the First Woman Ever to Play in the National Hockey League* under the pseudonym Cleo Birdwell.
2 Goyens and Turowetz, *Lions in Winter,* 60.
3 Some of these ideas are explored in Jason Blake, '"Just Part of the Game": Depictions of Violence in Hockey Prose.'
4 Eichberg, 'The Societal Construction of Time and Space,' 163; Messenger, *Sport and the Spirit of Play,* 5.
5 Saul, *Reflections of a Siamese Twin,* 144.
6 Smith, *Violence and Sport,* 3.
7 Messner, *Power at Play: Sports and the Problem of Masculinity,* 67.
8 Hughes-Fuller, 'The Good Old Game: Hockey, Nostalgia, Identity,' 230.
9 Bidini, 'Why I Love Wayne Bradley,' 38, 39. Michael Markus's macabre novel *East of Mourning* – about a coach who becomes so enamoured of a young hockey talent named Kyle Clark that he, like many a smitten lover,

refuses to see the boy's obvious faults – is rife with mixed sexual signals.
The coach befriends the child, tickles the boy, wrestles with him regularly,
and, even during love-making with the boy's mother, gazes (longingly?) at
Kyle's sweater. The friendship with Kyle continues through puberty, and
the narrator later spies on Kyle having sex. Even the coach's motives have
more to do with his own immaturity and vicarious hockey aspirations;
statements such as 'Are you in love with that [...] kid or what?' (42;
in literal reference to the child's abundance ice-time) are highly
ambiguous.

10 Gaston, *The Good Body*, 133. This relation to pain shows the constructed
nature of masculinity: although soccer players regularly feign pain and
injury in hopes of drawing a foul, that sport's manly image does not suffer
in Europe or South America.

11 Ibid., 118.

12 Burrs, 'My First Hockey Service,' 88, 89; Suits, *The Grasshopper*, 176.

13 Burrs, 'My First Hockey Service,' 89. The quotation is from Al Purdy's
1965 poem 'Hockey Players,' which is reprinted in Kennedy, *Words on Ice*,
25–6. For an excellent, brief overview of hockey poetry in Canada, see
Winger 'This Combination of Ballet and Murder.'

14 Richards, 'Hockey,' 92. David McGimpsey impudently asks, 'If Canadians
wholly adopt the less physical European style would they still be Canadians?' (McGimpsey, 'Rock 'em, Sock 'em, *Terre de Nos Aieux*,' 24).

15 Pronger, *The Arena of Masculinity*, 22, 177.

16 Sabo and Jansen, 'Prometheus Unbound: Constructions of Masculinity in
the Sports Media,' 211; Hood, Foreword, *Scoring: The Art of Hockey*. The
jockstrap and cup combination, which protects the male genitals, has a
decidedly female form; the jillstrap is quite phallic in shape. Shoulder
pads look like breasts, and hockey pants widen the hips. In terms of shape,
hockey equipment symbolically re-sexes.

17 MacGregor, *The Last Season*, 70. Much of *The Last Season* is like Scott
Young's *Face-Off* in that it is 'structured though a masculine ideology and
consciousness' and 'biased in the sense that we ... see the world through
the haze of ... masculine logic' (Hollands, 'Images of Women in Canadian
Sports Fiction,' 47). However, because MacGregor's novel includes fictional snippets from an extremely critical reporter's columns, Batterinski's
view is never offered as the only way to see the hockey world.

18 Oates, 'The Cruelest Sport,' 187.

19 Messner, *Power at Play*, 2; Birdwell, *Amazons*, 108; Etue and Williams, *The
Edge: Women Making Hockey History*, 38.

20 Kulisek, 'The Queen of Cottam Pond: A Memoir,' 40, 41.

21 Lenskyj, *Out of Bounds,* 139; Highway, *Dry Lips Oughta Move to Kapuskasing,* 120.

22 Liebling, *The Sweet Science,* 45.

23 Gruneau and Whitson, *Hockey Night in Canada,* 175; Oates, 'Rape and the Boxing Ring'; Weinstein, Smith, and Wiesenthal, 'Masculinity and Hockey Violence,' 834.

24 Lorenz, *On Aggression,* ix, 272.

25 Elias and Dunning, *Quest for Excitement,* 53; Gruneau and Whitson, *Hockey Night in Canada,* 177.

26 Plimpton, *Open Net,* 153; Gruneau and Whitson, *Hockey Night in Canada,* 177. Plimpton is a sympathetic, insightful outsider trying to come to terms with hockey culture; unburdened by widespread assumptions about hockey fighting and violence, he is well placed to examine the reasons behind this violence as he continues his tradition of embedding himself with professional athletes.

27 Plimpton, *Open Net,* 259; Dryden, *The Game,* 189.

28 MacLennan, 'Fury on Ice,' 8; Melançon, *Les yeux de Maurice Richard,* 22.

29 MacLennan, 'Fury on Ice,' 6, 9, 10; Jarman, 'A Nation Plays Chopsticks,' 47, 45.

30 Aristotle, *Poetics,* VI.2. For a short discussion of catharsis in sport, see Guttmann, 'Chariot Races, Tournaments and the Civilizing Process.'

31 Smythe and Young, *If You Can't Beat 'Em in the Alley,* 128, 258.

32 Vanderhaeghe quoted in Scanlan, *Grace under Fire,* 148; Richler, 'Writers and Sports,' 93. Perhaps because they are immune to the accusation of philistinism, literary writers often employ a base idiom when 'talking hockey.'

33 Saouter, '*Être Rugby*': *Jeux du masculin et du féminin,* 25.

34 Turner, 'Of Hipchecks, Highsticks, and Yellowjackets,' 21.

35 Bryant, 'Hakkanen's Move,' 169; Woods, 'The Drubbing of Nesterenko,' 247.

36 Schoemperlen, 'Hockey Night in Canada,' 85. A key difference between the cultivated theatre-goer and the sports fan is that bourgeois tradition dictates the former be disciplined, unbiased, and ever critical, while the fan's attitude is necessarily biased (Gebauer, *Poetik des Fußballs,* 50). For a thorough overview of fandom, see Wann et al., *Sport Fans: The Psychology and Social Impact of Spectators.*

37 Schoemperlen, 'Hockey Night in Canada,' 85; Wann et al., *Sports Fans,* 137. Rita's fandom represents a grotesque twisting of the colloquial term 'hockey widow'; whereas some women 'lose' their husbands to the television during hockey season, Rita's husband literally committed suicide.

38 Woods, 'The Drubbing of Nesterenko,' 247, 246.

39 Robidoux, *Men at Play*, 76.
40 Woods, 'The Drubbing of Nesterenko,' 247.
41 Ibid.
42 Ibid., 247, 247f.
43 Gaston, *The Good Body*, 129; Plimpton, *Open Net*, 257.
44 Bryant, *'Hakkanen's Move,'* 164, 167f. This eye to the future differentiates sport from real warfare. In sport, neither side has a real interest in destroying the rink, the puck, or the opponent, since that would mean the end of the game. See Theweleit, *Tor zur Welt: Fußball als Realitätsmodell*, 95. In overly competitive circles, injuring a key player is corrupt, but tempting, when winning becomes the only goal. Another crucial difference between sport and war is that, after a war, 'rule exists wholly as a result of victory; in sport, victory exists as a result of rule' (Fischer, 'Competitive Sport's Imitation of War,' 31).
45 Coady, *Saints of Big Harbour*, 37, 44, 49, 48. In the novel *Amazons*, the female narrator wryly describes escalation and the need to join in the violence: 'In hockey it is important to display solidarity, and in our win at Philly every single one of us had to go side-flopping over the top of that stupid plastic panel in order to rescue' a teammate (Birdwell, *Amazons*, 28).
46 Coady, *Saints of Big Harbour*, 63, 64, 49. Beer's role in hockey culture cannot be overestimated. It is in the title of two books discussed here – John B. Lee's anthology *That Sign of Perfection: From Bandy Legs to Beer Legs*, and Bill Gaston's *Midnight Hockey: All about BEER, the BOYS, and the REAL CANADIAN GAME* – and even Andrew Podnieks's family-oriented picture book *A Canadian Saturday Night: Hockey and the Culture of a Country* devotes a chapter to beer. Dave Bidini states baldly, '... hockey culture is as much about beer, sex, and violence as it is beauty, skill, and fearsome speed' (*The Best Game You Can Name*, 60).
47 Coady, *Saints of Big Harbour*, 151f.
48 Gaston, 'Your First Time,' 56. In Adrian Brijbassi's 2001 novel *50 Mission Cap* (named after The Tragically Hip song), about a junior hockey team in the Ottawa Valley, two young Russian players join the team. They confuse their Canadian teammates and opponents by fighting each other at centre ice: '... the perplexed officials were idle, probably aiming to remember what the rulebook said to do in such a case' (186). This violence is shockingly visceral because it does not serve strategy; nor is it a mere act for the fans, since the two players truly hate each other. Steven Galloway's *Finnie Walsh* provides a variation on this when a player rushes to aid his friend who plays on the opposing team: 'Even the referee and linesmen were momentarily stunned' (145) by this turn of events.
49 MacGregor, *The Last Season*, 185.

50 Ibid., 21, 20.

51 Ibid., 22.

52 Ibid., 21, 22; Vanderwerken, 'Gavin Grey, Felix Batterinski, and "Terminal Adolescent Syndrome,"' 46.

53 Jarman, *Salvage King, Ya!*, 130; MacGregor, *The Last Season*, 119.

54 Jarman, *Salvage King, Ya!*, 140, 68; Goyens and Turowetz. *Lions in Winter*, 276.

55 Jarman, *Salvage King, Ya!*, 73. As Drinkwater has rather more refined musical taste, the song 'I Think We're Alone Now' would be particularly bothersome to him.

56 Ibid., 153; Shilling, *The Body and Social Theory*, 37. The Soviet Union was often accused of producing automaton players out of raw human material spotted early and trained in a mechanical fashion. Jean-Pierre April's funny, fantastical story 'Le fantôme du Forum,' which first appeared in a science fiction anthology in 1983, contains a team of Guy Lafleur clones competing against 'les Robots russes' for the label of the best hockey team in history.

57 Dandyish Cherry seems a caricature of the traditional masculinity for which he stands – the very opposite of those who 'scrutinize their clothing' for traces of femininity (Etue and Williams, *The Edge*, 218). In *Cold-Cocked: On Hockey*, Lorna Jackson calls him a 'hockey gadfly who resembles a more toned Truman Capote' (126). Gary Genosko, while focusing on the 'diverse constituencies' and 'remarkable pluralism' of hockey, argues that Don Cherry simultaneously derides certain foreign players as 'sissies' – yet covertly addresses 'gay fans' ('Hockey and Culture,' 141).

58 Harrison, *Hero of the Play: 10th Anniversary Edition*, 50.

59 Lundin, *When She's Gone*, 141.

60 Robidoux, *Men at Play*, 75. Birk Sproxton's punning poem 'A Stitch in Time' argues that 'scars tell the story. Nicks and cuts scratched into flesh, worms buried and burrowing under the hide. My hide is an open book' (*The Hockey Fan Came Riding*, 59). Whereas the proverbial 'stitch in time' avoids problems completely, timely medical treatment merely limits damage.

61 Jarman, *Salvage King, Ya!*, 86. I owe the Drinkwater-Boileau parallel to an anonymous external reviewer.

62 Ibid.

63 MacGregor, *The Last Season*, 210.

64 Van Impe, *Philadelphia Flyers*, http://www.philadelphiaflyers.com/history/halloffame/vanimpe.asp (accessed 28 April 2007).

65 MacGregor, *The Last Season*, 213. In Bill Gaston's *The Good Body* there is

also a collusive wink. Bobby Bonaduce is in the penalty box after losing a fight to a player who 'would cut your face for no reason other than the colour of your jersey.' As Bonaduce, bleeding, contemplates the player's reckless style, their eyes meet and the crazy player gives him a 'quick wink,' as if all this bloodshed and violence were 'something like humour' and all for show (130).

66 MacGregor, *The Last Season*, 213, 214f, 215; Vanderwerken, 'Gavin Grey, Felix Batterinski, and "Terminal Adolescent Syndrome,"' 45. In Don Gutteridge's *Bus-Ride*, a hockey player comes to a similar realization regarding the fans' role: 'Were the spectators' cheers for him or for themselves? A self-congratulatory orgy reserved for ... the nameless faces in the blue jerseys?' (19).

67 MacGregor, *The Last Season*, 20.

68 Robertson, *Heroes*, 185.

69 Barthes, *Mythologies*, 21.

70 Woods, 'The Drubbing of Nesterenko,' 248f , 249.

71 Callaghan, *The Loved and the Lost*, 164. In this novel, Peggy Sanderson, a young white woman who moves in Montreal's black community, feels utterly alienated among the predominantly white audience of the hockey game (the sole hockey scene in the novel). In Young and Robertson's *Face-Off*, the narrator similarly describes escalation, including personal injury: 'The fight started when he cross-checked me after I hooked him. In that fight I lost two teeth: one artificial and one my own' (160).

72 Callaghan, *The Loved and the Lost*, 164; Falla, *Home Ice*, 13. In Falla's 2008 novel *Saved*, a conventional sports novel about an ageing NHLer's last chances at winning the Stanley Cup, the narrator argues (unconvincingly) that NHL violence is 'all part of an unwritten code we've known since we were kids playing on ponds and backyard rinks. Justice was built into our game, not tacked on by a rule book ...' (8).

73 Gaston, *The Good Body*, 55, 136.

74 Scanlan, *Grace under Fire*, 151; Frye, *The Great Code*, 37.

75 Peter Behrens's story 'Wives' relates an accidental shinny injury that results in the loss of an eye, and ends with a wife's plaintive reproach: 'They all keep their sticks low, those are the rules, those are the *rules!*' (199). Unwritten rules are morally, not just legally, binding.

76 Gaston, *The Good Body*, 20.

77 Ibid., 245; Fitzpatrick, 'Slash, Spear, Elbows Up: A Conversation with Bill Gaston,' 96.

78 Wiseman, 'Phone Calls Home (John Kordic d. 1992),' 45.

79 Gaston, *The Good Body*, 22, 23.

80 Ibid. In MacGregor's *The Last Season*, 'Poppa' Batterinski cannot see the point of suffering stitches for sport. Felix Batterinski is more 'Canadian' in his attitude: 'Every time I got a stitch he'd tell me it didn't pay to fight. Bullshit. Every stitch I took brought me one step closer to the NHL' (100).

81 Gaston, *The Good Body*, 134, 242, 154.

82 Safarik, 'The North Field Comets,' 74; Fischler, *The Ultimate Bad Boys*, 254. In Safarik's story there is no real sense of violence because the players take the zany coach's commands with a grain of salt; as well, there are no consequences to the on-ice aggression.

83 Harrison, *Hero of the Play*, 51.

84 Weinstein, Smith, and Wiesenthal, 'Masculinity and Hockey Violence,' 836; Robidoux, *Men at Play*, 75; Harrison, *Hero of the Play*, 51.

85 Daniels, 'Beyond the Ice,' 8.

86 Hood, 'The Pleasures of Hockey,' 54; Daniels, 'Beyond the Ice,' 11.

87 Paci, *Icelands*, 195, 196.

88 Jarman, *Salvage King, Ya!*, 178.

4. National Identity and Hockey

1 Wright, *Adultery*, 195; Jenkinson, 'Roy MacGregor: Profile'; Sproxton, *The Hockey Fan Came Riding*, 40. On popular media's aid in creating meaning and myth, especially as meanings change over time, see Melançon, 'Écrire Maurice Richard.' In Melançon's view, the Quebec press's constant assertion that Maurice Richard's eyes spoke for themselves is absurd because they indicated different qualities – from muteness to pure determination – in different periods.

2 Francis, *National Dreams*, 11, 167; Melançon, *Les yeux de Maurice Richard*, 180, 183.

3 Laba, 'Myths and Markets,' 343; Kennedy, 'Hockey as Metaphor in Selected Canadian Literature,' 81; 'The Virtual Hot Stove'; Kennedy, 'I Am Hockey,' 22.

4 On identity concerns and perceived Americanization of hockey, see Mason, '"Get the Puck Outta Here!" Media Transnationalism and Canadian Identity,' 140–67.

5 Schoemperlen, 'Hockey Night in Canada,' 86; Salutin, *Les Canadiens*, 132.

6 Ibid., 154; Posen, *A Goal-by-Goal Timeline*, 6; Melançon, 'Le Rocket chez les Anglais,' in *Les yeux de Maurice Richard*, 223–37. Elsewhere, Melançon points out an obsession with examining literature in nationalist terms in Quebec, and wonders whether we can continue to divide texts on Maurice

Richard (and, by extension, on hockey in general) into English *or* French. See 'Écrire Maurice Richard,' 2, 3. This divide is even sharper in anglophone studies. For example, Daniel Francis writes openly in a study of Canadian myths (including hockey as a binding element): 'Quebec is mentioned often in the pages which follow, but always as it is imagined by English Canadians, not as it is imagined by Quebeckers themselves' (*National Dreams*, 14).

7 Sutton-Smith, *The Ambiguity of Play*, 10; Jackson, *Cold-Cocked*, 9. On passivity versus involvement in televised sport, see Earle, 'Hockey as Canadian Popular Culture.' Earle argues that fans create meaning out of televised sport and are thus active observers.

8 Brennan, 'The National Longing for Form,' 172; Morrow, 'Paul Quarrington's Hockey Schtick,' 115.

9 Sproxton, *The Hockey Fan Came Riding*, 25. Concerning newly published children's books, and Maurice Richard and these books' role in 'rekindling parental nostalgia,' see Melançon, *Les yeux de Maurice Richard*, 100.

10 Oriard, *Dreaming of Heroes*, 212; Hughes-Fuller, 'The Good Old Game: Hockey, Nostalgia, Identity,' 159. Gunther Gebauer notes that history-rich Europe has are no monuments to soccer players; these are reserved for politicians and military commanders (*Poetik des Fußballs*, 124). Canada has no qualms about erecting public statues of New World heroes such as Wayne Gretzky (Edmonton), Maurice Richard (Gatineau and Montreal), and Gordie Howe (Saskatoon) – these statues concretely show how hockey players have been given a nation-building role.

11 Fulford, *Best Seat in the House*, 189.

12 Hood, *Strength down Centre*, 175.

13 Robidoux, 'Imagining a Canadian Identity through Sport,' 209; Richards, *Hockey Dreams*, 20.

14 Jarman, 'Love Is All around Us,' 21, 23, 24, 25.

15 Adams, 'The Game of Whose Lives?' 71; Kelly, 'A Puck in the Teeth,' 16. Bidini, 'Cortina.'

16 Beardsley, 'Introduction,' 9; Gruneau and Whitson, *Hockey Night in Canada*, 26.

17 Jacobs, 'Preface,' iii; Kennedy, 'Introduction,' 9, 10.

18 Robertson, *Heroes*, 169.

19 McCormack, *Understanding Ken*, 219; Coupland, *Souvenir of Canada*, 55.

20 Roth, *The Great American Novel*, 259, 261. Though the novel is a parody, Roth does not mock the game itself. Elsewhere he has praised it as 'America's great religion' and a model of integration and desegregation.

See Denis Scheck's interview of 14 September 2000 with Philip Roth, published in *Die Zeit*, 14 November 2001.

21 Bill Boyd, *Hockey Towns*, 3.

22 Klein and Reif, *The Death of Hockey*, 6. See also Harris, *Breaking the Ice*, 13. By emphasizing that they are *not* Canadian, the authors strengthen their attachment because theirs is not handed-down, forced love; they actively sought it out. For these fans, hockey is not a natural – as in self-understood – entertainment option.

23 Rains, *Hockey Night Down Under!* iv, 289, 290, 62.

24 Ibid., 15, 16, 14.

25 Quarrington, *King Leary*, 8. Andrew Holman notes, in an overview of American sports literature, that books published 'before 1919 are conspicuous in their depiction of ice hockey as a home-grown, indigenous *American* product' – as well as in their often clueless portrayals of the game. Perhaps because of the later 'massive commercial exportation of hockey to the U.S.,' American authors became more 'honest' after 1920. They began importing the socially unpolished Canadian rube as a stock figure into hockey fiction. That is, the rough-hewn Canadian functions as a nation-defining 'other,' or as a 'foil' for clean-living Frank Merriwell types (Holman, 'Frank Merriwell on Skates: Images of Canada in American Juvenile Sporting Fiction, 1890–1940').

26 Lundin, *When She's Gone*, 74; Villemure, 'Le baseball et ses success,' 77.

27 Gaston, *Midnight Hockey*, 160. Gaston retains and revels in much of hockey's masculinity but rejects rampant commercialism in favour of weekend warrior hockey.

28 Young, *Scrubs on Skates*, 190, 232.

29 Hollands, 'English-Canadian Sports Novels and Cultural Production,' 220; Gaston, *The Good Body*, 110. Bobby Bonaduce, the protagonist hockey player of *The Good Body*, can neither re-establish contact with his son nor fit in with his fellow graduate students. In this novel, the hockey player is excluded from the family or community.

30 Minni, 'Details from the Canadian Mosaic,' 56.

31 Hutcheon, 'The Canadian Postmodern,' 20; Bidini, *Tropic of Hockey*, 193.

32 Bidini, *Tropic of Hockey*, 196; Callaghan, 'The Game That Makes a Nation,' 51, 53. An audio clip of Esposito's speech is available on CBC's website. See 'Home fans boo, Espo lets them have it.' Other Canadians, perhaps the majority, interpret the speech solely as a moment of national reproach. For example, Andrew Podnieks says that 'Esposito's words struck the very core of the nation's relationship to hockey [and] forced all Canadians watching to feel shame for their negativity and lack of support,' but

he makes no mention of ethnicity (Podnieks, *A Canadian Saturday Night,* 39).

33 McKinley, 'Next Year,' 52.

34 Ibid., 60; McKinley, *Putting a Roof on Winter,* 167.

35 Francis, *National Dreams,* 168.

36 Orr, *Puck Is a Four-Letter Word,* 273; Robidoux, 'Imagining a Canadian Identity through Sport,' 221; Quarrington, *Hometown Heroes,* 205.

37 Harrison, *Hero of the Play,* 55; Jokisipilä, 'Waging the Cold War on Ice.' In 'A Child's ABC of Hockey,' poet Birk Sproxton defines a 'lie' as, first, 'any story about a hockey game,' and only then, 'the angle of the shaft of a stick' (in *The Hockey Fan Came Riding,* 73). By placing falsehoods ahead of the required equipment, Sproxton implies that the game itself is less important than telling tall hockey tales.

38 van Belkom, 'Hockey's Night in Canada,' 210; Hollands, 'English-Canadian Sports Novels and Cultural Production,' 219.

39 van Belkom, 'Hockey's Night in Canada,' 210, 216.

40 Saul, *Reflections of a Siamese Twin,* 479; Whitson, 'Hockey and Canadian Identities: From Frozen Rivers to Revenue Streams,' 297. On the economics of NHL hockey in places with little hockey tradition, see Bellamy and Shultz, 'Hockey Night in the United States? The NHL, Major League Sports, and the Evolving Television/Media Marketplace.' See also Mason, 'Expanding the Footprint? Questioning the NHL's Expansion and Relocation Strategy.'

41 Zweig, *Hockey Night in the Dominion of Canada,* 73.

42 Richler, 'Gretzky in Eighty-five,' 119; Berg, 'Gretzky Rocks'; Galloway, *Finnie Walsh,* 108. Steven Jackson places the trade in the context of the North American Free Trade debates that had been raging just before Gretzky left for Los Angeles, and argues convincingly that the *time* of the trade led to a veritable 'crisis of national identity' ('Gretzky, Crisis, and Canadian Identity in 1988,' 429). The two subsequent Gretzky trades in the mid-1990s, which could have brought him back to Canada, received far less media attention.

43 Zweig, *Hockey Night in the Dominion of Canada,* 207, 315f.

44 Dennis, Review of *The Horn of a Lamb,* 142; Sedlack, *The Horn of a Lamb,* 47.

45 Ibid., 87.

46 Ibid., 88, 21, 22, 53.

47 Ibid., 278. This, of course, is not a bonding ritual but sexual assault. Bonding rituals often have an 'an emphasis on nudity' in the name of 'group unity' (Robidoux, *Men at Play,* 221). While such rituals may strad-

dle the line between bonding and assault, this is unmotivated assault (though there is the paper-thin accusation than Fred had molested the perpetrator's sister); competitive hockey culture has provided the training for such attacks. In hockey fiction, such sadism is usually left out.

48 Lundin, *When She's Gone*, 7, 20, 103, 37, 73, 90.

49 Ibid., 110. In David Adams Richards's *The River of the Broken-Hearted*, a husband who finds himself in a similar position remarks incredulously, 'How could she go to a dance with anyone who shoots right?' (215). The real tragedy, it seems, is that his wife has absconded with a hockey deviant (since, in Canada, most people shoot left).

50 Lundin, *When She's Gone*, 39.

51 Ibid., 130.

52 Richler, 'Canadian Conundrums'; Lundin, *When She's Gone*, 9.

53 Ibid., 26.

54 Ibid., 10.

55 Richards, *Hockey Dreams*, 15. For an overview of Richards's parallels to Don Cherry, as well as the reception of his regards on hockey, see Hughes-Fuller, 'The Good Old Game: Hockey, Nostalgia, Identity,' 157–76.

56 Richards, *Hockey Dreams*, 234f; Beardsley, *Country on Ice*, 185. Graham Fraser, the current commissioner of official languages, has made a similar argument regarding crossing a linguistic divide through hockey. He emphasizes that 'hockey phenomenon Sidney Crosby [has] showed French-speaking television viewers' that he has become bilingual – 'a stark contrast with Eric Lindros' (Fraser, *Sorry I Don't Speak French*, 301).

5. The Family Game

1 Paci, *Icelands*, 213; Kidd and Macfarlane, *The Death of Hockey*, 4.

2 Fitzgerald, '*Saturday Evenings in the Church of Hockey Night in Canada*,' 72, 73. In a similar vein, American Jack Falla points out hockey's singular role in the sometimes stormy relationship he had with his father: '[We] had the usual problems that so often divided the World War II generation from the Woodstock and Vietnam generation. But we never had a problem or spoke an angry word in a hockey rink' (*Falla, Home Ice*, 83).

3 Woods, 'The Drubbing of Nesterenko,' 250, 252, 258. The Forum was closed in 1997, but Molson, the beer company that owned the Montreal Canadiens, strove to maintain the tradition, 'to produce for Montrealers a particular version of the past, invoking particular nostalgia, not only to legitimate their new arena project, but more importantly to convince the public to "let go" of the old one' (Bélanger, 'Sport Venues and the Spec-

tacularization of Urban Spaces in North America: The Case of the Molson Centre in Montreal,' 388).

4 Quarrington, *Logan in Overtime*, 131.
5 Lincer First, 'In the Penalty Box,' 57.
6 Young, 'Player Deal' 33, 34f; Jarman, 'The Scout's Lament,' 15.
7 Dryden and MacGregor, *Home Game*, 77, 59; Atkinson, *Ice Time*, 9.
8 In the style of the dime novel, where hard work is all that matters, struggling against poverty is sometimes depicted as a spur to athletic development. Robert Pitter, in an article otherwise focusing on hockey and the Canadian/North American context, refers to perceptions of basketball star Michael Jordan that have 'ignored his middle-class roots and the advantages that this gave him over working-class or poor blacks' ('Racialization and Hockey in Canada: From Personal Troubles to a Canadian Challenge,' 127).
9 Richler, 'The Fall of the Montreal Canadiens,' 244; Oriard, *Dreaming of Heroes*, 81.
10 Dopp, 'Win Orr Lose: Searching for the Good Canadian Kid in Canadian Hockey Fiction.'
11 MacGregor, *The Home Team*, 8.
12 Bushkowsky, 'The Phantom of Great Slave Lake,' 82.
13 Ibid., 88. Steve Lundin's *When She's Gone* includes a very similar tale. After a plane crash in northern Alberta, an agent happens upon a boy 'of the first nations, ... the greatest hockey player that ever lived' (164), playing hockey by himself. The agent manages to lead the boy to the city and 'a forty-year one billion dollar deal' (165), but eventually the player rejects the lucre and disappears.
14 LaSalle, 'Le Rocket Nègre,' 32f. The surrogate parent theme also arises in Rob Ritchie's novel *Orphans of Winter*, which includes an encounter between a hospitalized scout and a rambunctious player during visiting hours. The scout criticizes the goalie for trying to impress him during a game, only to be told, 'I WASN'T STARIN' UP INTO THE STANDS LOOKING FOR SOME GODDAMN FUCKING HOCKEY SCOUT!' (201). The young adult player has no delusions of 'making it' in hockey; rather, he had heard that his long-absent father might be in the stands. He was looking for a real father, not a substitute, and berates the scout for his arrogant assumption.
15 LaSalle, 'Le Rocket Nègre,' 44, 43 ; O'Ree and McKinley, *The Autobiography of Willie O'Ree*, 48. Smythe's biography is mum on whether he uttered any such racist statement against Carnegie. Cecil Harris writes that there is no proof – some 'regard the quote as apocryphal. Some regard the quote as

credible given Smythe's often grating personality and apparently bigoted remarks on other matters, yet they admit to having no concrete evidence' (*Breaking the Ice*, 48).

16 LaSalle, 'Le Rocket Nègre,' 42, 45.

17 Ibid., 49; O'Ree and McKinley, *The Autobiography of Willie O'Ree*, 71. Silence seems to be the Canadian way regarding racism in hockey. Robert Pitter notes a lack of scholarly, especially sociological, work on race in hockey, and adds, 'Few hockey institutions, certainly not the NHL, are willing to admit that racism is an issue in hockey' ('Racialization and Hockey in Canada,' 134).

18 LaSalle, 'Le Rocket Nègre,' 48, 54. While considering the meaning and constructions of masculinity, Anouk Bélanger critically examines the popular concept of hockey as a 'surrogate father' in Quebec (albeit in more modern times than those depicted in LaSalle's story). See Bélanger, 'The Last Game?' 298–303.

19 Ritchie, *Orphans of Winter*, 85.

20 MacGregor, *The Home Team*, 2f; Paci, *Icelands*, 7.

21 Paci, *Icelands*, 7; McLean, 'Sports Injuries,' 150, 151.

22 Shikaze, 'Hockey Dreams,' 202. Fred Stenson's 'Teeth' includes a comical instance of timelessness when a star NHL player daydreams on the bench. 'For a moment, I totally forgot where I was. All the hockey rinks and benches of my life merged into one and I didn't know whether I was twelve, eighteen or twenty-five – a bantam, a junior or an NHLer' (131). Even when lost in time, the hockey age categories remain intact.

23 Shikaze, 'Hockey Dreams,' 202f. Two exceptions to hockey fiction's silence on sexual abuse are Mark Anthony Jarman's 'The Scout's Lament' and *50 Mission Cap*, by Adrian Brijbassi. Jarman's narrator recalls a key minor hockey figure 'now in jail for molestation … Molesting eight or nine-year-old boys. Imagine what that did to their game, their love of the game' (19). Despite his disgust, the scout's primary concern seems to be for 'their game,' the boys' ability to play hockey. Brijbassi's novel culminates with the revelation and physical punishment of a coach who has a history of sexually abusing children. In neither work, however, is abuse the main focus.

24 Shikaze, 'Hockey Dreams,' 204, 203.

25 Kinsella, 'Truth,' 154; McLean, 'Sports Injuries,' 147, 155.

26 Shikaze, 'Hockey Dreams,' 204.

27 Beamish, 'Slipping the Surly Bonds of Earth: Discovering Hockey's Elusive Reality,' 31.

28 Melski, *Hockey Mom, Hockey Dad*, 67.

29 Shikaze, 'Hockey Dreams,' 204.

30 Ibid., 205.

31 Ibid.

32 Wagamese, *Keeper 'n Me*, 21.

33 Ibid., 31, 32, 14.

34 Ibid., 12, 15, 16, 12.

35 Ibid., 113, 104. W.P. Kinsella's short story 'Truth' suggests that native Canadians can play a different type of hockey altogether. A team of 'hung over' and untalented First Nations players wins a tournament in an unusual manner: 'Mad Etta, our four-hundred pound medicine lady,' blocks the net, before tiring of 'that little black biscuit [which] hurt like hell.' She sprinkles a magical substance over the goal-line, and 'it is like Etta bricked up the front of the goal with invisible bricks (155, 159). For a sociological viewpoint on First Nations hockey, see Robidoux, 'Historical Interpretations of First Nations Masculinity and Its Influence on Canada's Sport Heritage.'

36 Wagamese, *Keeper 'n Me*, 107; Falla, *Home Ice*, 83. This is obviously a very optimistic view of sports and communication. Both Edward Said and Umberto Eco have expressed an opposing view, arguing that sports talk replaces more important public discourse. Said feels that the 'American consciousness of sports ... is almost terrifying' because it is often coupled with a lack of 'awareness of what's going in the world' (Viswanathan, *Power, Politics, and Culture*, 206). Eco also speaks of replacement, arguing that sports 'chatter is the ersatz of political speech,' blinding the masses to more important topics ('Sports Chatter,' 163). Novelist Richard Ford adds weight to such accusations by placing them in the mouth of an insider. In *The Sportswriter*, a basketball team's general manager assails a reporter: '... do you *actually* realize how much adult conversation is spent on this fuckin business? Facts treated like they were opinions just for the simple purpose of talking about it longer? It's like romanticizing a goddamn rock by calling it a mountain range to me. People waste a helluva lot of time they could be putting to useful purposes' (256).

37 Wagamese, *Keeper 'n Me*, 109.

38 'Episode 6: The Golden Age,' in *Hockey: A People's History*.

39 Paci, *The Italians*, 16, 61.

40 Ibid., 39.

41 Ibid., 40.

42 Ibid. Affinity for hockey, of course, is not a mere matter of ethnicity or passport. In Richard B. Wright's *The Age of Longing*, the killjoy wife, Grace, belittles her husband's career aspirations: 'like sledding or skipping rope,'

hockey is something to grow out of. Her husband may be a potential NHLer, but in her view, 'sooner or later he will have to put aside such pastimes and get a job' (43, 77).

43 Paci, *The Italians*, 42.

44 Paci, *Black Madonna*, 17; Paci, *The Italians*, 49. Don Gutteridge's novel *Bus-Ride* provides a similar scenario. The protagonist, also a talented hockey player named Bill, realizes that 'hockey had been a way *in* – success, approval, local fame – and could now be a way *out*' of his small town. Like Paci's Bill, the young hero is revered by everyone but his father – 'Christ in Heaven, couldn't his father, his own flesh and blood, come to one game? Just one game. That's all he'd ask' (69). The father's avoidance of hockey accentuates the division precisely because everyone else adores Bill for what he can do on the ice.

45 Paci, *The Italians*, 47, 106. See Culbertson, 'The Paradox of Bad Faith and the Technological Attitude to the Sporting Body.' Culbertson argues that young athletes often lie to themselves by overlooking education as a way out of poverty or troubled surroundings.

46 Maccagnone, 'Goalie Boy,' 119, 123. Rudy Thauberger's essayistic story 'Goalie' is a perfect complement to Maccagnone's tale. 'To be a goalie,' he writes, 'is to be an adult too soon, to have too soon an intimate understanding of the inevitability of pain and failure' (213). Furthermore, since that position is the loneliest, even 'his mother can't help him' (216). The position lends itself to orphanhood.

47 Maccagnone, 'Goalie Boy,' 132.

48 McCormack, *Understanding Ken*, 16, 164. Of course, Dryden had a university education and was thus a rarity at the time. In an age before skyrocketing salaries, perhaps other NHL players would have done the same.

49 Ibid., 228.

50 Ibid., 228, 33, 94.

51 Ibid., 183.

52 Ibid., 32; Paci, *Icelands*, 63.

53 McCormack, *Understanding Ken*, 31, 87. Chris Fisher's 'Playing the Garden' ends with similar 'willing [for] the water to freeze' his backyard rink, 'the Garden.' After the older, more skilled brother quits hockey in favour of the arts at university, the younger brother tries to take his place: 'If blood is truly thicker than water, even the frozen kind, then the healing will have to start down at the Garden' (178).

54 McCormack, *Understanding Ken*, 84, 188.

55 Fitzpatrick, 'Logan, Buddy and Fred: The Hockey Player and the Canadian Novel,' 80; Wright, The Age of Longing, 101.

56 Ibid., 7, 114.
57 Gaston, *The Good Body*, 55, 58.
58 Ibid., 59, 167.
59 In Stuart McLean's 'Sports Injuries,' one father sits apart from the others: 'Sometimes visiting teams thought he was a scout' (151). The father in this story is obsessed with seeing his son succeed, so that the mistaken identity is accurate – his attitude towards the boy on the ice is closer to a scout's than to a father's (Gaston, *The Good Body*, 167).
60 Ibid., 168, 61.
61 Ibid., 137. In the desire for reflected glory, the hockey fan and the hockey parent are the same (Gaston, *The Good Body*, 123, 201).
62 Johnston, *The Divine Ryans*, 78.
63 Ibid., 105.
64 Ibid., 105, 107, 105; Messner, *Power at Play*, 16.
65 Berry, 'Henderson Has Scored for Canada!' 220.
66 Mildon, 'Number 33,' 205, 203, 209. *Amazons: An Intimate Memoir by the First Woman Ever to Play in the National Hockey League* is the most prominent exception; the narrator, Cleo Birdwell, plays for the New York Rangers, sleeps with many staff members, and tells team officials, 'Go swing *your* organs. I'm a hockey player,' when asked to pose semi-nude for an advertising campaign (85). Cara Hedley published *Twenty Miles*, the first hockey novel by a woman about women, in late 2007 (after this study was submitted for publication).
67 MacGregor, *The Home Team*, 169; McCormack, *Understanding Ken*, 28; Paci, *Icelands*, 32, 116. In *The Game of Our Lives*, Peter Gzowski glorifies hockey and hockey culture, but remains keenly aware of the cultural cost of the game: 'The sorrow is that there may also be Wayne Gretzkys of the piano or the paint brush who, because we expose our young to hockey so much more than to the arts, we will never know about' (191).
68 Theberge, 'Challenging the Gendered Space of Sport: Women's Ice Hockey and the Struggle for Legitimacy,' 292; Jackson, *Cold-Cocked*, 115.

Conclusion

1 Richler, 'Gretzky in Eighty-five,' 110; Richler, 'Writers and Sports,' 104.
2 Beardsley, *Country on Ice*, 109; Jarman, *Salvage King, Ya!* 173.
3 Melançon, *Les yeux de Maurice Richard*, 42.
4 Richler, 'Writers and Sports,' 93; McSweeney, review of *Barney's Version*. Francis King's review of *Barney's Version* was published in *The Spectator*, 4 October 1997.

5 Richler, 'Cheap Skates,' 142; Richler, *St. Urbain's Horseman*, 351; Richler, 'Gretzky in Eighty-five,' 115.
6 See Blake, 'Inviting Complexity: Teaching Hockey Where the Game Is "Ice Hockey,"' 4–12. The article discusses the fine line between dissecting the hockey myth and inadvertently reinforcing it by devoting attention to one of the few things every foreign student knows about Canada.
7 Harrison, 'World Hockey Supremacy,' 19.
8 Cohen, *Beautiful Losers*, 185. The novel as a whole presages Rick Salutin's play *Les Canadiens*, in which real political resistance replaces on-ice resistance. In a reversal of the typical role of hockey, in act 2 of *Les Canadiens*, players' and spectators' eyes are distracted from the action at the Forum as they follow a message board showing live results of the 1976 election that brought René Lévesque's Parti Québécois to power.
9 MacLeod, *No Great Mischief*, 158.
10 Munro, 'The Bear Came over the Mountain,' 310. Sarah Polley's film adaptation, *Away from Her*, adds several more hockey references, including a former play-by-play commentator who wanders the rest home describing all he sees in a monotonous staccato.
11 Kroetsch, *The Studhorse Man*, 122. Shields, *Swann*, 259.

Bibliography

Adams, Mary Louise. 'The Game of Whose Lives? Gender, Race, and Entitlement in Canada's "National Game."' In *Artificial Ice: Hockey, Culture and Commerce*. Ed. David Whitson and Richard Gruneau, 71–84. Peterborough, ON: Broadview Press, 2006.

Allen, Tom. *The Gift of the Game: A Father, a Son, and the Wisdom of Hockey*. Toronto: Doubleday, 2005.

Anderson, Benedict. *Imagined Communities: Reflections on the Origin and Spread of Nationalism*. Rev. edn. London and New York: Verso, 1995.

April, Jean-Pierre. 'Le fantôme du Forum.' In *Chocs baroques*, 161–84. Montreal: Bibliothèque québécoise, 1991.

Aristotle. *The Basic Works of Aristotle*. Ed. R. McKeon. New York: Modern Library, 1957.

Atkinson, Jay. *Ice Time: A Tale of Fathers, Sons, and Hometown Heroes*. New York: Three Rivers Press, 2001.

Atwood, Margaret. *Survival: A Thematic Guide to Canadian Literature*. Toronto: Anansi, 1972.

Barthes, Roland. *Mythologies*. Trans. Annette Lavers. London: Granada. 1972.

– *Le sport et les hommes*. Montreal: Les Presses de l'Université de Montréal, 2004.

Beamish, Rob. 'Slipping the Surly Bonds of Earth: Discovering Hockey's Elusive Reality.' *Queen's Quarterly* 113 (Spring 2006): 21–35.

Beardsley, Doug. *Country on Ice*. Winlaw, BC: Polestar Press, 1987.

– 'Introduction.' In *Our Game: An All-Star Collection of Hockey Fiction*. Ed. Doug Beardsley, 9–12. Victoria, BC: Polestar, 1997.

Behrens, Peter, 'Wives.' In *Our Game: An All-Star Collection of Hockey Fiction*. Ed. Doug Beardsley, 194–9. Victoria, BC: Polestar, 1997.

Bélanger, Anouk. 'The Last Game? Hockey and the Experience of Masculinity in Québec.' In *Sport and Gender in Canada*. Ed. Kevin Young and Philip White, 293–309. Don Mills, ON: Oxford University Press, 1999.

– 'Sport Venues and the Spectacularization of Urban Spaces in North America: The Case of the Molson Centre in Montreal.' *International Review for the Sociology of Sport* 35, no. 3 (2000): 378–97..

Bell, Don. 'Hockey Night in Métabetchouan.' In *Ice: New Writing on Hockey*. Ed. Dale Jacobs, 33–47. Edmonton: Spotted Cow Press, 1999.

Bellamy, Robert, and Kelly Shultz, 'Hockey Night in the United States? The NHL, Major League Sports, and the Evolving Television/Media Marketplace.' In *Artificial Ice: Hockey, Culture and Commerce*. Ed. David Whitson and Richard Gruneau, 163–80. Peterborough, ON: Broadview Press, 2006.

Berg, Moe. 'Gretzky Rocks.' Thornhill, ON, Iron Music, 1995.

Berry, Michelle. 'Henderson Has Scored for Canada!' In *Story of a Nation: Defining Moments in Our History*, by Margaret Atwood et al., 218–39. Scarborough, ON: Doubleday, 2001.

Bidini, Dave. *Tropic of Hockey: My Search for the Game in Unlikely Places*. Toronto: McClelland & Stewart, 2000.

– *The Best Game You Can Name*. Toronto: McClelland & Stewart, 2005.

– 'Cortina.' In *The Five Hole Stories*, 73–106. Edmonton: Brindle & Glass, 2006.

– 'Why I Love Wayne Bradley.' In *The Five Hole Stories*, 33–9. Edmonton: Brindle & Glass, 2006.

Birdwell, Cleo [Don DeLillo?]. *Amazons: An Intimate Memoir by the First Woman Ever to Play in the National Hockey League*. Toronto: Lester & Orpen Dennys, 1980.

Blaise, Clark. 'I'm Dreaming of Rocket Richard.' In *Our Game: An All-Star Collection of Hockey Fiction*. Ed. Doug Beardsley, 30–7. Victoria, BC: Polestar, 1997.

Blake, Jason. 'From Fact to Fiction: An Introduction to the Mythology of Ice Hockey in Canadian Life and Literature.' *ELOPE* 1, no. 1 (2004): 81–94.

– 'Inviting Complexity: Teaching Hockey Where the Game Is "Ice Hockey."' In *Canada: Text and Territory*. Ed. Maire Aine Ni Mhainnin and Elizabeth Tilley, 4–12. Newcastle, UK: Cambridge Scholars Publishing, 2008.

– '"Just Part of the Game": Depictions of Violence in Hockey Prose.' In *Canada's Game? Critical Essays on Ice Hockey and Identity*. Ed. Andrew C. Holman, 65–80. Montreal and Kingston: McGill-Queen's University Press, 2009.

Bouchard, David. *That's Hockey*. Victoria: Orca Book Publishers, 2004.

Bowering, George. 'Introduction.' In *Great Canadian Sports Stories*. Ed. G. Bowering, 6–8. Canada: Oberon Press, 1979.

Boyd, Bill. *Hockey Towns: Stories of Small Town Hockey in Canada.* Toronto: Random House, 1998.

Brennan, Timothy. 'The National Longing for Form.' In *The Post-colonial Studies Reader.* Ed. Bill Ashcroft, Gareth Griffith, and Helen Tiffin, 170–5. London and New York: Routledge, 1995.

Brijbassi, Adrian. *50 Mission Cap.* Victoria: Trafford Publishing, 2001.

Bryant, Justin. 'Hakkanen's Move.' In *Ice: New Writing on Hockey.* Ed. Dale Jacobs, 164–71. Edmonton: Spotted Cow Press, 1999.

Bryson, Michael. Review of *Salvage King, Ya!* by Mark Anthony Jarman. *Danforth Review* (1998). http://www.danforthreview.com/reviews/fiction/jarman.html.

Burrs, Mick [Steven Michael Berzensky]. 'My First Hockey Service.' In *That Sign of Perfection: From Bandy Legs to Beer Legs – Poems and Stories on the Game of Hockey.* Ed. John B. Lee, 88–9. Windsor, ON: Black Moss Press, 1995.

Bushkowsky, Aaron. 'Phantom of Great Slave Lake.' In *Words on Ice.* Ed. Michael Kennedy, 81–9. Toronto: Key Porter, 2003.

Caillois, Roger. *Les jeux et les hommes: Le masque et le vertige.* Paris: Gallimard, 1967.

Callaghan, Morley. *The Loved and the Lost.* Toronto: Macmillan, 1973.

– 'The Game That Makes a Nation.' In *Riding on the Roar of the Crowd: A Hockey Anthology.* Ed. David Gowdey, 50–2. Toronto: Macmillan, 1989.

Cameron, Barry. 'Theory and Criticism: Trends in Canadian Literature.' In *Literary History of Canada: Canadian Literature in English.* 2nd edn. Vol. 4. Ed. W.H. New, 108–32. Toronto: University of Toronto Press, 1990.

Carnegie, Herb. *A Fly in a Pail of Milk: The Herb Carnegie Story.* New York: Mosaic Press, 1997.

Carrier, Roch. 'The Hockey Sweater.' Trans. Sheila Fischman. In *Our Game: An All-Star Collection of Hockey Fiction.* Ed. Doug Beardsley, 15–17. Victoria, BC: Polestar, 1997.

– *Our Life with the Rocket: The Maurice Richard Story.* Trans. Sheila Fischman. Toronto: Penguin, 2001.

– *La Guerre, Yes Sir!* Trans. Sheila Fischman. Toronto: Anansi, 2004.

Cashmore, Ernest, ed. *Sports Culture: An A-Z Guide.* London and New York: Routledge, 2000.

Clark, Joe. 'Community of Communities.' In *Who Speaks for Canada? Words That Shape a Country.* Ed. Desmond Morton and Morton Weinfeld, 267–9. Toronto: McClelland & Stewart, 1998.

Coady, Lynn. *Saints of Big Harbour.* Scarborough, ON: Doubleday, 2002.

Cohen, Leonard. *Beautiful Losers.* New York: Vintage, 1993.

Cooper, David. 'Canadians Declare "It Isn't Cricket": A Century of Rejection of

the Imperial Game, 1860–1960.' *Journal of Sport History* 26, no.1 (Spring
1999): 51–81.

Coupland, Douglas. *Souvenir of Canada*. Vancouver: Douglas & McIntyre, 2004.

Culbertson, Leon. 'The Paradox of Bad Faith and the Technological Attitude
to the Sporting Body.' In *Philosophy of Sport and Other Essays*. Ed. Dušan
Macura and Milan Hosta, 193–208. Ljubljana: Eleventh Academy, 2004.

Daniels, Calvin. 'Beyond the Ice.' In *Skating the Edge*, 7–14. Saskatoon: Thistle-
down Press, 2001.

Dennis, Ian. Review of *The Horn of a Lamb*, by Robert Sedlack. *Canadian Literature* 188 (Spring 2006): 141–2.

Dopp, Jamie. 'Win Orr Lose: Searching for the Good Canadian Kid in Canadian Hockey Fiction.' Paper presented at 'Canada's Game? Critical Perspectives on Ice Hockey and Identity,' Plymouth, MA, 2005.

Dowbiggin, Bruce. *The Stick: A History, a Celebration, an Elegy*. Toronto: Macfarlane, Walter and Ross, 2001.

Dronyk, Levi. 'The Puck Artist.' In *Our Game: An All-Star Collection of Hockey
Fiction*. Ed. Doug Beardsley, 61–75. Victoria, BC: Polestar, 1997.

Dryden, Ken. *The Game*. 3rd edn. Toronto: McClelland & Stewart, 1999.

Dryden, Ken, and Roy MacGregor. *Home Game: Hockey and Life in Canada*. Rev.
edn. Toronto: McClelland & Stewart, 1994.

Earle, Neil. 'Hockey as Canadian Popular Culture: Team Canada 1972, Television and the Canadian Identity.' In *Slippery Pastimes: Reading the Popular in
Canadian Culture*. Ed. Joan Nicks and Jeannette Sloniowski, 321–43. Waterloo, ON: Wilfrid Laurier University Press, 2002.

– 'The Stanley Cup and the Heroic Journey: Wayne Gretzky and the Carl Jung
Face Off in the Time of Heroes.' In *Putting It on Ice, Volume One: Hockey and
Cultural Identities*. Ed. Colin Howell, 99–104. Halifax: Gorsebrook Research
Institute, 2002.

Eco, Umberto. 'Sports Chatter.' In *Travels in Hyperreality*, 159–65. Trans.
William Weaver. London: Picador, 1985.

'Ed Van Impe.' *Philadelphia Flyers*. http://www.philadelphiaflyers.com/history/
halloffame/vanimpe.asp (accessed 28 April 2007).

Ehrmann, Jacques. '*Homo Ludens* Revisited.' Trans. Cathy Lewis and Phil Lewis.
Yale French Studies 41 (1968): 31–57.

Eichberg, Henning. 'A Revolution of Body Culture? Traditional Games on the
Way from Modernisation to "Postmodernity."' In *Body Cultures: Essays on
Sport, Space and Identity*. Ed. John Bale, Chris Philo, and Susan Brownell,
128–48. London and New York: Routledge, 1998.

– 'The Societal Construction of Time and Space as Sociology's Way Home to
Philosophy.' In *Body Cultures: Essays on Sport, Space and Identity*. Ed. John

Bale, Chris Philo, and Susan Brownell, 149–64. London and New York: Routledge, 1998.

Elias, Norbert, and Eric Dunning. *Quest for Excitement: Sport and Leisure in the Civilizing Process*. Oxford: Blackwell, 1986.

'Episode 6: The Golden Age.' In *Hockey: A People's History*. DVD. Dir. Robert Macaskill. Warner Home Video / CBC Home Video, 2006.

Etue, Elizabeth, and Megan K. Williams. *The Edge: Women Making Hockey History*. Toronto: Second Story Press, 1996.

Evans, Walter. 'The All-American Boys: A Study of Boys' Sports Fiction.' *Journal of Popular Culture* 6, no. 1 (Summer 1972): 104–21.

Exley, Frederick. *A Fan's Notes*. New York: Vintage, 1988.

Falla, Jack. *Home Ice: Reflections on Backyard Rinks and Frozen Ponds*. Toronto: McClelland & Stewart, 2000.

– *Saved*. New York: Thomas Dunne Books, 2008.

Faulkner, William. 'An Innocent at Rinkside.' In *Essays, Speeches and Public Letters*. Ed. J.B. Meriwether, 48–51. London: Chatto & Windus.

Fawcett, Brian. 'My Career with the Leafs.' In *Riding on the Roar of the Crowd: A Hockey Anthology*. Ed. David Gowdey, 278–92. Toronto: Macmillan, 1989.

Fink, Eugen. 'The Oasis of Happiness: Toward an Ontology of Play.' Trans. Ute Saine and Thomas Saine. *Yale French Studies* 41 (1968): 19–29.

Fischer, Norman. 'Competitive Sport's Imitation of War: Imaging the Completeness of Virtue.' *Journal of the Philosophy of Sport* 29 (2002): 16–37.

Fischler, Stan. *The Ultimate Bad Boys*. Toronto: Warwick Publishing, 1999.

Fisher, Chris. 'Playing the Garden.' In *Show Me a Hero: Great Contemporary Stories about Sports*. Ed. Jeanne Schinto, 170–8. New York: Persea Books, 1995.

Fitzgerald, Judith. 'Saturday Evenings in the Church of Hockey Night in Canada.' In *Original Six: True Stories from Hockey's Classic Era*. Ed. Paul Quarrington, 62–85. Toronto: Reed Books, 1996.

Fitzpatrick, Jamie. 'Joining the Hockey Conversation.' In *Hockey Write in Canada*. Special issue of *New Quarterly* 94 (Spring 2005): 11–16.

– 'Logan, Buddy and Fred: The Hockey Player and the Canadian Novel.' In *Hockey Write in Canada*. Special issue of *New Quarterly* 94 (Spring 2005): 73–81.

– 'Slash, Spear, Elbows Up: A Conversation with Bill Gaston.' In *Hockey Write in Canada*. Special issue of *New Quarterly* 94 (Spring 2005): 95–8.

Ford, Richard. *The Sportswriter*. London: Vintage, 2003.

Francis, Daniel. *National Dreams: Myth, Memory, and Canadian History*. Vancouver: Arsenal Pulp Press, 1997.

Fraser, Graham. *Sorry I Don't Speak French: Confronting the Canadian Crisis That Won't Go Away*. Toronto: Douglas Gibson, 2006.

Frye, Northrop. *The Bush Garden: Essays on the Canadian Imagination.* Toronto: Anansi, 1971.
– *The Great Code: The Bible and Literature.* New York: Harvest/HBJ, 1981.
Fulford, Robert. *Best Seat in the House: Memoirs of a Lucky Man.* Toronto: Collins, 1988.
Gadamer, Hans-Georg. *Truth and Method.* Trans. Joel Weinsheimer and Donald G. Marshall. London and New York: Continuum, 2004.
Galloway, Steven. *Finnie Walsh.* Vancouver: Raincoast Fiction, 2000.
Gaston, Bill. 'Your First Time.' In *Sex Is Red,* 53–64. Dunvegan, ON: Cormorant Books, 1998.
– *The Good Body.* Dunvegan, ON: Cormorant Books, 2000.
– *Midnight Hockey: All about BEER, the BOYS, and the REAL CANADIAN GAME.* Scarborough, ON: Doubleday, 2006.
Gebauer, Gunther. *Poetik des Fußballs.* Frankfurt am Main: Campus Verlag, 2006.
Genosko, Gary. 'Hockey and Culture.' In *PopCan: Popular Culture in Canada.* Ed. Lynne Van Luven and Priscilla L. Walton, 140–50. Scarborough, ON: Prentice-Hall, 1999.
Gillmor, Don. 'Hockey: The Great Literary Shutout.' *The Walrus,* February 2005, 88–93.
Gowdey, David. 'Foreword.' In *Riding on the Roar of the Crowd: A Hockey Anthology.* Ed. David Gowdey, ix-xi. Toronto: Macmillan, 1989.
Goyens, Chrys, and Allan Turowetz. *Lions in Winter.* Toronto: Penguin, 1987.
Gruneau, Richard, and David Whitson. *Hockey Night in Canada: Sport, Identities and Cultural Politics.* Toronto: Garamond Press, 1993.
Guay, Donald. *L'histoire du hockey au Québec: Origine et développement d'un phénomène culturel.* Chicoutimi, QC: Les Editions JCL, 1990.
Gutteridge, Don. *Bus-Ride.* Canada: Nairn, 1974.
Guttmann, Allen. *From Ritual to Record: The Nature of Modern Sports.* New York: Columbia University Press, 1978.
– 'Chariot Races, Tournaments and the Civilizing Process.' In *Sport and Leisure in the Civilizing Process: Critique and Counter-Critique.* Ed. Eric Dunning and Chris Rojek, 137–60. London: Macmillan, 1992.
– *Games and Empires: Modern Sports and Cultural Imperialism.* New York: Columbia University Press, 1994.
Gzowski, Peter. *The Game of Our Lives.* Toronto: McClelland & Stewart, 1981.
Harlow, Robert. *The Saxophone Winter.* Toronto and Vancouver: Douglas & McIntyre, 1988.
Harris, Cecil. *Breaking the Ice: The Black Experience in Professional Hockey.* Toronto: Insomniac Press, 2003.

Harrison, Keith. 'World Hockey Supremacy.' In *Textual Studies in Canada* 12 (1998): 19–23.

Harrison, Richard. *Hero of the Play: 10th Anniversary Edition.* Toronto: Wolsak & Wynn, 2004.

Harvey, Jean. 'Whose Sweater Is This? The Changing Meanings of Hockey in Quebec.' In *Artificial Ice: Hockey, Culture and Commerce.* Ed. David Whitson and Richard Gruneau, 29–52. Peterborough, ON: Broadview Press, 2006.

Hedley, Cara. *Twenty Miles.* Toronto: Coach House, 2008.

Highway, Tomson. *Dry Lips Oughta Move to Kapuskasing.* Saskatoon: Fifth House, 1989.

Hobsbawm, Eric J. *Nations and Nationalism since 1780: Programme, Myth, Reality.* Cambridge: Cambridge University Press, 1990.

– 'Mass-Producing Traditions: Europe, 1870–1914.' In *The Invention of Tradition.* Ed. Eric Hobsbawm and Terence Ranger, 263–308. Cambridge: Cambridge University Press, 1997.

Hollands, Robert G. 'Canadian Sports Novels, Marxism and Cultural Production.' In *Proceedings: Sporting Fictions.* Ed. Michael Green and Charles Jenkins, 344–73. Birmingham: Centre for Contemporary Cultural Studies, 1982.

– 'Images of Women in Canadian Sports Fiction.' In *Sport and the Sociological Imagination.* Ed. Nancy Theberge and Peter Donnelly, 40–56. Fort Worth: TCU Press, 1982.

– 'Masculinity and the Positive Hero in Canadian Sports Novels.' *Arete* 4, no. 1 (Fall 1986): 73–84.

– 'English-Canadian Sports Novels and Cultural Production.' In *Not Just a Game: Essays in Canadian Sport Sociology.* Ed. Jean Harvey and Hart Cantelon, 213–26. Ottawa: University of Ottawa Press, 1988.

Holman, Andrew C. 'Frank Merriwell on Skates: Images of Canada in American Juvenile Sporting Fiction, 1890–1940.' Paper presented at the 13th Biennial Conference of the Association for Canadian Studies in Ireland, Galway, Ireland, 27–9 April 2006.

'Home fans boo, Espo lets them have it.' Canadian Broadcasting Corporation. Broadcast, 11 September 1972. http://archives.cbc.ca/IDC-1–41–318–646 /sports/summit_series/clip3

Hood, Hugh. *Strength down Centre: The Jean Béliveau Story.* Scarborough, ON: Prentice-Hall, 1970.

– 'The Pleasures of Hockey.' In *The Governor's Bridge Is Closed,* 49–57. Ottawa: Oberon, 1973.

– *Scoring: The Art of Hockey.* [Illus. S. Segal.] Ottawa: Oberon, 1979.

– 'The Sportive Centre of Saint Vincent de Paul.' In *Our Game: An All-Star Col-*

lection of Hockey Fiction. Ed. Doug Beardsley, 117–29. Victoria, BC: Polestar, 1997.

Hornby, Nick. *Fever Pitch.* London: Penguin, 2000.

Hughes-Fuller, Patricia. 'The Good Old Game: Hockey, Nostalgia, Identity.' PhD diss., University of Alberta, 2002.

Huizinga, Johan. *Homo Ludens: A Study of the Play-Element in Culture.* Boston: Beacon Press, 1950.

Hutcheon, Linda. 'The Canadian Postmodern: Fiction in English since 1960.' In *Studies on Canadian Literature: Introductory and Critical Essays.* Ed. Arnold E. Davidson, 18–33. New York: Modern Language Association of America, 1990.

Ignatieff, Michael. *Blood and Belonging: Journeys into the New Nationalism.* New York: Farar, Straus and Giroux, 1993.

Jackson, Lorna. *Cold-Cocked: On Hockey.* Emeryville, ON: Biblioasis, 2007.

Jackson, Steven. 'Gretzky, Crisis, and Canadian Identity in 1988: Rearticulating the Americanization of Culture Debate.' *Sociology of Sport Journal* 11, no. 4 (December 1994): 428–46.

Jacobs, Dale. 'Preface.' In *Ice: New Writing on Hockey.* Ed. Dale Jacobs, iii–v. Edmonton: Spotted Cow Press, 1999.

James, C.L.R. *Beyond a Boundary.* London: Serpent's Tail, 2000.

Jarman, Mark Anthony. 'Righteous Speedboat.' In *Our Game: An All-Star Collection of Hockey Fiction.* Ed. Doug Beardsley, 233–43. Victoria, BC: Polestar, 1997.

– *Salvage King, Ya! A Herky-Jerky Picaresque.* Vancouver: Anvil Press, 1997.

– 'Love Is All around Us.' In *19 Knives,* 21–5. Don Mills, ON: Anansi, 2000.

– 'The Scout's Lament.' In *19 Knives,* 13–19. Don Mills, ON: Anansi, 2000.

– 'A Nation Plays Chopsticks.' *New Quarterly* 94 (Spring 2005): 40–9. Reprinted in *My White Planet,* 125–47. Toronto: Thomas Allen Publishers, 2008.

Jenkinson, D. 'Roy MacGregor: Profile.' *Canadian Review of Materials.* 1998. http://www.umanitoba.ca/cm/profiles/mcgregor.html.

Johnston, Wayne. *The Divine Ryans.* Toronto: Vintage, 1990.

Jokisipilä, Markku. 'Waging the Cold War on Ice: International Ice Hockey Tournaments as Arenas of Ideological Confrontation between East and West.' Paper presented at 'Canada's Game? Critical Perspectives on Ice Hockey and Identity,' Plymouth, MA, 2005.

Kelly, M. T. 'A Puck in the Teeth.' In *That Sign of Perfection: From Bandy Legs to Beer Legs – Poems and Stories on the Game of Hockey.* Ed. John B. Lee, 14–20. Windsor, ON: Black Moss Press, 1995.

Kennedy, Brian. *Growing Up Hockey: The Life and Times of Everyone Who Ever Loved the Game.* Canada: Folklore Publishing, 2007.

Kennedy, Michael. 'Hockey as Metaphor in Selected Canadian Literature.' In *Textual Studies in Canada* 12 (1998): 81–94.

– 'Introduction.' In *Words on Ice: A Collection of Hockey Prose.* Ed. Michael Kennedy, 9–10. Toronto: Key Porter, 2003.

– 'I Am Hockey.' In *Going Top Shelf: An Anthology of Canadian Hockey Poetry.* Ed. Michael Kennedy, 19–22. Surrey, BC: Heritage House, 2005.

Kidd, Bruce. *The Struggle for Canadian Sport.* Toronto: University of Toronto Press, 1996.

Kidd, Bruce, and John Macfarlane. *The Death of Hockey.* Toronto: New Press, 1972.

Kinsella, W.P. 'Truth.' In *Our Game: An All-Star Collection of Hockey Fiction.* Ed. Doug Beardsley, 153–60. Victoria, BC: Polestar, 1997.

Klein, Jeff, and Karl-Eric Reif. *The Death of Hockey: Or How a Bunch of Guys with Too Much Money and Too Little Sense Are Killing the Greatest Game on Earth.* Toronto: Macmillan, 1998.

Knight, Stephen. Review of *The Horn of a Lamb,* by Robert Sedlack. *Quill and Quire,* February 2004. http://www.quillandquire.com/reviews/review.cfm?review_id=3726

Kroetsch. Robert. *The Studhorse Man.* Markham, ON: PaperJacks, 1977.

Kulisek, Lisa. 'The Queen of Cottam Pond: A Memoir.' In *That Sign of Perfection: From Bandy Legs to Beer Legs – Poems and Stories on the Game of Hockey.* Ed. John B. Lee, 40–1. Windsor, ON: Black Moss Press, 1995.

Laba, Martin. 'Myths and Markets: Hockey as Popular Culture in Canada.' In *Seeing Ourselves: Media Power and Policy in Canada.* Ed. Helen Holmes and David Taras, 334–44. Toronto: Harcourt Brace Jovanovich Canada, 1992.

LaSalle, Peter. 'Le Rocket Nègre.' In *Hockey sur Glace,* 29–57. New York: Breakaway Books, 1996.

Lasch, Christopher. 'The Corruption of Sports.' *New York Review of Books.* 28 April 1977, 24–30. Available on-line at: http://www.nybooks.com/articles/8525.

Lavoie, Marc. *Désavantage numérique: Les francophones dans la LNH.* Hull: Vents d'ouest, 1998.

Leacock, Stephen. *Sunshine Sketches of a Little Town.* Toronto: McClelland & Stewart, 1987.

Lee, John B., ed. *That Sign of Perfection: From Bandy Legs to Beer Legs – Poems and Stories on the Game of Hockey.* Windsor, ON: Black Moss Press, 1995.

Lenskyj, Helen. *Out of Bounds.* Toronto: Women's Press, 1986.

Liebling, A.J. *The Sweet Science*. New York: North Point Press, 2004.

Lincer First, Tina. 'In the Penalty Box: Confessions of a Reluctant Hockey Mom.' In *Ice: New Writing on Hockey*. Ed. Dale Jacobs, 141–50. Edmonton: Spotted Cow Press, 1999.

Lorenz, Konrad. *On Aggression*. Trans. Marjorie Kerr Wilson. London and New York: Routledge, 2002.

Lundin, Steve. *When She's Gone*. Winnipeg: Great Plains Publications, 2004.

Maccagnone, Garasamo. 'Goalie Boy.' *Aethlon: The Journal of Sport Literature* 11, no.1 (1998): 119–37.

MacClancy, Jeremy. 'Sport, Identity and Ethnicity.' In *Sport, Identity and Ethnicity*, Ed. Jeremy MacClancy et al., 1–12. Oxford: Berg Publishers, 1996.

MacGregor, Roy. *The Last Season*. Toronto: Penguin, 1995.

– *The Home Team: Fathers, Sons and Hockey*. Toronto: Penguin Canada, 2002.

MacLennan, Hugh. *Two Solitudes*. Toronto: Macmillan, 1945.

– 'Fury on Ice.' In *Riding on the Roar of the Crowd: A Hockey Anthology*. Ed. David Gowdey, 4–16. Toronto: Macmillan, 1989.

MacLeod, Alistair. *No Great Mischief*. London: Vintage, 2001.

Markus, Michael. *East of Mourning*. Victoria: Trafford Publishing, 2001.

Mason, Daniel S. '"Get the Puck Outta Here!" Media Transnationalism and Canadian Identity.' *Journal of Sport and Social Issues* 26, no. 2 (2002): 140–67.

– 'Expanding the Footprint? Questioning the NHL's Expansion and Relocation Strategy.' In *Artificial Ice: Hockey, Culture and Commerce*. Ed. David Whitson and Richard Gruneau, 181–200. Peterborough, ON: Broadview Press, 2006.

McCormack, Pete. *Understanding Ken*. Vancouver: Douglas & McIntyre, 1998.

McGimpsey, David. 'Rock 'em, Sock 'em, *Terre de Nos Aieux* : Legends of Hockey, Canadian Nationalism and Television Violence.' *Aethlon: The Journal of Sport Literature* 14, no. 2 (1997): 21–33.

McGoldrick Goldberg, P. 'Growing Up with Hockey.' In *Ice: New Writing on Hockey*. Ed. Dale Jacobs, 198–200. Edmonton: Spotted Cow Press, 1999.

McKinley, Michael. 'Next Year.' In *Our Game: An All-Star Collection of Hockey Fiction*. Ed. Doug Beardsley, 52–60. Victoria, BC: Polestar, 1997.

– *Putting a Roof on Winter: Hockey's Rise from Sport to Spectacle*. Vancouver: Greystone, 2000.

McLean, Stuart. 'Sports Injuries.' In *Stories from the Vinyl Café*, 143–63. Toronto: Penguin, 1995.

McLuhan, Marshall. *Understanding Media: The Extensions of Man*. London and New York: Routledge, 2001.

McSorley, Tom. 'Of Time and Space and Hockey: An Imaginary Conversation.' In *Pop Can: Popular Culture in Canada*. Ed. M. Van Luven and P.L. Walton, 151–6. Scarborough, ON: Prentice-Hall, 1999.

McSweeney, Kerry. Review of *Barney's Version*, by Mordecai Richler. *Canadian Literature* 159 (1998): 188–90.

Melançon, Benoît. 'Écrire Maurice Richard: Culture savante, culture populaire, culture sportive.' *Globe: Revue internationale d'études québécoises* 9(2) (2006): 1–27.

– *Les yeux de Maurice Richard: Une histoire culturelle*. Montreal : Fides, 2006.

– *The Rocket: A Cultural History of Maurice Richard*. Trans. Fred A. Reed. Toronto: Greystone Books, 2009.

Melski, Max. *Hockey Mom, Hockey Dad*. Wreck Cove, NS: Breton Books, 2001.

Messenger, Christian. *Sport and the Spirit of Play in Contemporary American Fiction*. New York: Columbia University Press, 1981.

Messner, Michael. *Power at Play: Sports and the Problem of Masculinity*. Boston: Beacon Press, 1992.

Mildon, Marsha. 'Number 33.' In *Our Game: An All-Star Collection of Hockey Fiction*. Ed. Doug Beardsley, 200–9. Victoria, BC: Polestar, 1997.

Minni, C.D. 'Details from the Canadian Mosaic.' In *Anthology of Canadian-Italian Writing*. Ed. Joe Pivato, 54–60. Toronto: Guernica, 1999.

Moore, Philip. 'Practical Nostalgia and the Critique of Commodification: On the "Death of Hockey" and the National Hockey League.' *Australian Journal of Anthropology* 13, no. 3 (December 2002): 309–32.

Morrow, Don. 'Paul Quarrington's Hockey Schtick: A Literary Analysis.' In *Putting It on Ice, Volume One: Hockey and Cultural Identities*. Ed. Colin Howell, 111–18. Halifax: Gorsebrook Research Institute, 2002.

Munro, Alice. 'The Bear Came over the Mountain.' In *Hateship, Friendship, Courtship, Loveship, Marriage*, 279–336. Toronto: Penguin 2001.

New, W.H., ed. *Literary History of Canada: Canadian Literature in English*. 2nd edn. Vol. 4. Toronto: University of Toronto Press, 1990.

Novak, Michael. *The Joy of Sports: Endzones, Bases, Baskets, Balls, and the Consecration of the American Spirit*. Rev. edn. Lanham, MD: Madison, 1994.

Oates, Joyce Carol. 'Rape and the Boxing Ring.' *Newsweek*, 24 February 1992. Available on-line at http://jco.usfca.edu/boxing/rape.html.

– 'The Cruelest Sport.' In *On Boxing*, 185–201. New York: Harper Perennial, 1995.

O'Ree, Willie, and Michael McKinley. *The Autobiography of Willie O'Ree*. Toronto: Somerville House Publishing, 2000.

Oriard, Michael. *Dreaming of Heroes: American Sports Fiction, 1868–1980*. Chicago: Nelson-Hall, 1982.

– *Sporting with the Gods: The Rhetoric of Play and Game in American Culture.* Cambridge: Cambridge University Press, 1991.

Orr, Frank. *Puck Is a Four-Letter Word.* Toronto: Methuen, 1984.

Paci, Frank. *The Italians.* Ottawa: Oberon Press, 1978.

– *Black Madonna.* Ottawa: Oberon Press, 1982.

– Frank. *Icelands.* Ottawa: Oberon Press, 1999.

Petrou, Michael. 'Before the Spring.' In *Putting It on Ice, Volume One: Hockey and Cultural Identities.* Ed. Colin Howell, 109–10. Halifax: Gorsebrook Research Institute, 2002.

Pitter, Robert. 'Racialization and Hockey in Canada: From Personal Troubles to a Canadian Challenge.' In *Artificial Ice: Hockey, Culture and Commerce.* Ed. David Whitson and Richard Gruneau, 123–39. Peterborough, ON: Broadview Press, 2006.

Plimpton, George. *Open Net.* New York: W.W. Norton, 1985.

Podnieks, Andrew. *A Canadian Saturday Night: Hockey and the Culture of a Country.* Vancouver: Greystone Books, 2006.

Posen, Sheldon. *626 by 9: A Goal-by-Goal Timeline of Maurice 'The Rocket' Richard's Scoring Career in Pictures, Stats, and Stories.* Gatineau, QC: Canadian Museum of Civilization, 2004.

Pronger, Brian. *The Arena of Masculinity: Sports, Homosexuality, and the Meaning of Sex.* New York: St Martin's Press, 1990.

Purdy, Al. 'Hockey Players.' In *Going Top Shelf: An Anthology of Canadian Hockey Poetry.* Ed. Michael Kennedy, 25–6. Surrey, BC: Heritage House, 2005.

Quarrington, Paul. *King Leary.* Toronto: Doubleday, 1987.

– *Hometown Heroes: On the Road with Canada's National Hockey Team.* Toronto: Collins, 1988.

– *Logan in Overtime.* Toronto: Doubleday, 1990.

– 'Introduction.' In *Original Six: True Stories from Hockey's Classic Era.* Ed. Paul Quarrington, 5–9. Toronto: Reed Books, 1996.

Rains, Ray. *Hockey Night Down Under!* Rostrevor, South Australia: R & R Downunder, 1991.

Reddick, Don. *Dawson City Seven.* Fredericton: Goose Lane, 1993.

Richards, David Adams. 'Hockey.' In *A Lad from Brantford and Other Essays.* 86–93. Fredericton: Broken Jaw Press, 1994.

– *Hockey Dreams: Memories of a Man Who Couldn't Play.* Toronto: Anchor, 2001.

– *River of the Broken-Hearted.* Toronto: Anchor, 2004.

Richler, Mordecai. *St. Urbain's Horseman.* Toronto: McClelland & Stewart, 1985.

– 'Howe Incredible.' In *Riding on the Roar of the Crowd: A Hockey Anthology.* Ed. David Gowdey, 264–77. Toronto: Macmillan, 1989.

- *Barney's Version.* Toronto: Knopf, 1997.
- 'Canadian Conundrums.' Lecture, University of Waterloo, Waterloo, ON, 23 March 1999. http://economics.uwaterloo.ca/needhdata/richler.html.
- 'Cheap Skates.' In *Dispatches from the Sporting Life,* 141–7. Toronto: Knopf, 2002.
- 'The Fall of the Montreal Canadiens.' In *Dispatches from the Sporting Life,* 241–74. Toronto: Knopf, 2002.
- 'Gretzky in Eighty-five.' In *Dispatches from the Sporting Life,* 105–19. Toronto: Knopf, 2002.
- 'Soul on Ice.' In *Dispatches from the Sporting Life,* 203–9. Toronto: Knopf, 2002.
- 'Writers and Sports.' In *Dispatches from the Sporting Life,* 93–104. Toronto: Knopf, 2002.
Ritchie, Rob. *Orphans of Winter.* Hamilton, ON: Seraphim Editions, 2006.
Roberts, Charles G.D. 'The Skater.' In *Going Top Shelf: An Anthology of Canadian Hockey Poetry.* Ed. Michael Kennedy, 37. Surrey, BC: Heritage House, 2005.
Robertson, Ray. *Heroes.* Toronto: Dundurn Press, 2000.
Robidoux, Michael. 'Artificial Emasculation and the Maintenance of a Masculine Identity in Professional Hockey.' *Canadian Folklore Canadien* 19, no. 1 (1997): 69–87.
- *Men at Play: A Working Understanding of Professional Hockey.* Montreal and Kingston: McGill-Queen's University Press, 2001.
- 'Imagining a Canadian Identity through Sport: A Historical Interpretation of Lacrosse and Hockey.' *Journal of American Folklore* 115, no. 456 (Spring 2002): 209–36.
- 'From the Sweat Lodge to the Hockey Rink: Saturday Night Ice Hockey in the Esketemc First Nation.' Paper presented at 'First Nations, First Thoughts,' Centre of Canadian Studies, University of Edinburgh, 5–6 May 2005.
- 'Historical Interpretations of First Nations Masculinity and Its Influence on Canada's Sport Heritage.' *International Journal of the History of Sport* 23, no.2 (2006): 267–84.
Robinson, Laura. *Crossing the Line: Violence and Sexual Assault in Canada's National Sport.* Toronto: McClelland & Stewart Inc, 1998.
Roth, Philip. *The Great American Novel.* Harmondsworth, England: Penguin, 1986.
Sabo, Don, and Sue Curry Jansen. 'Prometheus Unbound: Constructions of Masculinity in the Sports Media.' In *MediaSport.* Ed. Lawrence Wenner, 202–27. London: Routledge, 1998.
Safarik, Allan. 'The North Field Comets.' In *That Sign of Perfection: From Bandy*

Legs to Beer Legs: Poems and Stories on the Game of Hockey. Ed. John B. Lee, 70–85. Windsor, ON: Black Moss Press, 1995.

Salutin, Rick. *Les Canadiens.* Vancouver: Talonbooks, 1977.

Sanger, Daniel. '5,6, Pickup Sticks.' *The Walrus,* December/January 2007, 62–7.

Saouter, Anne. '*Être Rugby*': *Jeux du masculin et du féminin.* Paris: Éditions de la Maison des sciences de l'homme, 2001.

Saul, John Ralston. *Reflections of a Siamese Twin: Canada at the End of the Twentieth Century.* Toronto: Viking, 1997.

Scanlan, Lawrence. *Grace under Fire: The State of Our Sweet and Savage Game.* Toronto: Penguin Canada, 2002.

Scheck, Denis. 'Bleib nicht, wo du bist!' Interview with Philip Roth. *Die Zeit,* 14 November 2001.

Schoemperlen, Diane. 'Hockey Night in Canada.' In *Our Game: An All-Star Collection of Hockey Fiction.* Ed. Doug Beardsley, 84–93. Victoria, BC: Polestar, 1997.

Scott, F.R. 'The Canadian Authors Meet.' In *An Anthology of Canadian Literature in English.* Vol. I. Ed. Russel Brown and Donna Bennet, 348. Toronto: Oxford University Press, 1982.

Sedlack, Robert. *The Horn of a Lamb.* Toronto: Anchor Canada, 2004.

Shields, Carol. *Swann.* London: Fourth Estate, 2000.

Shikaze, Steven. 'Hockey Dreams.' In *Ice: New Writing on Hockey.* Ed. Dale Jacobs, 202–5. Edmonton: Spotted Cow Press, 1999.

Shilling, Chris. *The Body and Social Theory.* London: Sage Publications, 1994.

Smith, Michael. *Violence and Sport.* Toronto: Butterworths, 1983.

Smythe, Conn, and Scott Young. *If You Can't Beat 'Em in the Alley.* Markham, ON: PaperJacks, 1982.

Society of North American Hockey Historians and Researchers. 'False Gods and Profits.' http://www.sonahhr.com/sonahhr/index.cfm?fuseaction= home. History &chapter=8.

Sproxton, Birk. *The Hockey Fan Came Riding.* Red Deer, AB: Red Deer College Press, 1990.

Stenson, Fred. 'Teeth.' In *Our Game: An All-Star Collection of Hockey Fiction.* Ed. Doug Beardsley, 130–9. Victoria, BC: Polestar, 1997.

Suits, Bernard. *The Grasshopper: Games, Life, and Utopia.* Toronto: University of Toronto Press, 1978.

– 'Words on Play.' In *Philosophic Inquiry in Sport.* Ed. W.J. Morgan and K.V. Meier, 17–27. Champaign, IL: Human Kinetics, 1988.

Sutton-Smith, Brian. *The Ambiguity of Play.* Cambridge: Harvard University Press, 1997.

Thauberger, Rudy. 'Goalie.' In *Our Game: An All-Star Collection of Hockey Fiction.* Ed. Doug Beardsley, 213–17. Victoria, BC: Polestar, 1997.

Theberge, Nancy. 'Challenging the Gendered Space of Sport: Women's Ice Hockey and the Struggle for Legitimacy.' In *Gender and Sport: A Reader.* Ed. Sheila Scraton and Anne Flintoff, 292–9. London and New York: Routledge, 2002.

Theweleit, Klaus. *Tor zur Welt: Fußball Als Realitätsmodell.* Cologne: Kiepenheuer & Witsch, 2004.

Traill, Henry Duff. *The Life of Sir John Franklin, R.N.* London: John Murray, 1896. Available on-line at http://www.canadiana.org/ECO/PageView?id.

Turner, Brian. 'Of Hipchecks, Highsticks, and Yellowjackets.' In *Ice: New Writing on Hockey.* Ed. Dale Jacobs, 15–26. Edmonton: Spotted Cow Press, 1999.

van Belkom, Edo. 'Hockey's Night in Canada.' In *Words on Ice: A Collection of Hockey Prose.* Ed. Michael Kennedy, 209–17. Toronto: Key Porter, 2003.

Vanderwerken, David L. 'Gavin Grey, Felix Batterinski, and "Terminal Adolescent Syndrome."' *Aethlon: The Journal of Sport Literature* 11, no. 1 (1993): 43–8.

Villemure, Marie-Claude. 'Le baseball et ses succès: Une unité canadienne virtuelle.' In *Virtual Canada / Le Canada virtuel.* Ed. Marie-Claude Villemure, 75–82. Baia Mare, Romania: Editure Universitatii de Nord, 2006.

'The Virtual Hot Stove.' In *Hockey: A People's History.* http://www.cbc.ca/hockeyhistory/virtualhotstove/topic02/04.html

Viswanathan, Gauri. *Power, Politics, and Culture: Interviews with Edward W. Said.* New York: Pantheon Books, 2001.

Wagamese, Richard. *Keeper 'n Me.* Toronto: Doubleday, 1994.

Wann, Daniel L., et al. *Sport Fans: The Psychology and Social Impact of Spectators.* New York: Routledge, 2001.

Weinstein, Marc D., Michael D. Smith, and David L. Wiesenthal, 'Masculinity and Hockey Violence.' *Sex Roles: A Journal of Research* 11–12 (1995): 831–7.

Wenner, Lawrence, ed. *MediaSport.* London: Routledge, 1998.

Whitson, David. 'Hockey and Canadian Identities: From Frozen Rivers to Revenue Streams.' In *Passion for Identity: Canadian Studies for the Twenty-first Century.* 4th edn. Ed. David Taras and Beverly Rasporich, 297–318. Toronto: Nelson College Indigenous, 2001.

Whitson, David, and Richard Gruneau. 'Introduction.' In *Artificial Ice: Hockey, Culture and Commerce.* Ed. David Whitson and Richard Gruneau, 1–25. Peterborough, ON: Broadview Press, 2006.

Winger, Rob. 'This Combination of Ballet and Murder: Some Thoughts on Hockey Poetry in Canada.' *Arc Poetry Magazine* 53 (Winter 2004).

http://www.arcpoetry.ca/logentries/reviews/000136_this_combination_of_
ballet_and_murder.php.

Wiseman, Christopher. 'Phone Calls Home (John Kordic d. 1992).' In *Textual Studies in Canada* 12 (1998): 45–7.

Wong, John Chi-Kit. *Lords of the Rinks: The Emergence of the National Hockey League, 1875–1936*. Toronto: University of Toronto Press, 2005.

Woodcock, George. 'An Absence of Utopias.' *Canadian Literature* 42 (1969): 3–5.

Woods, Hanford. 'The Drubbing of Nesterenko.' In *Our Game: An All-Star Collection of Hockey Fiction*. Ed. Doug Beardsley, 244–59. Victoria, BC: Polestar, 1997.

Woolf, Virginia. 'American Fiction.' In *Collected Essays*. Vol. 2. Ed. Leonard Woolf, 111–21. London: Chatto & Windus, 1972.

Wright, Richard B. *The Age of Longing*. Toronto: HarperCollins, 1995.

– *Adultery*. Toronto: Harper Perennial, 2004.

Young, Scott and George Robertson. *Face-Off*. Toronto: Macmillan, 1971.

Young, Scott. *That Old Gang of Mine*. Don Mills, ON: Fitzhenry & Whiteside, 1982.

– *Scrubs on Skates*. Toronto: McClelland & Stewart, 1985.

– *A Boy at the Leafs' Camp*. Toronto: McClelland & Stewart, 1989.

– 'Player Deal.' In *Seven Parts of a Ball Team and Other Sports Stories*, 31–57. Toronto: HarperCollins, 1990.

– *Boy on Defence*. Toronto: McClelland & Stewart, 1993.

Zweig, Eric. *Hockey Night in the Dominion of Canada*. Toronto: Lester Publishing, 1992.

Index